Date Due

St. Paul of the Cross

St. Paul of the Cross

FOUNDER OF THE PASSIONISTS

by Charles Alméras

TRANSLATED BY

M. ANGELINE BOUCHARD

HANOVER HOUSE

A Division of Doubleday & Company, Inc.

Garden City, New York

1960

Nihil Obstat: Gall Higgins, O.F.M. Cap.
Censor Librorum

Imprimatur: ✠ Francis Cardinal Spellman
Archbishop of New York,
August 9, 1960

The nihil obstat and imprimatur are official declara-
tions that a book or pamphlet is free of doctrinal or
moral error. No implication is contained therein that
those who have granted the nihil obstat and imprimatur agree with the contents, opinions, or statements
expressed.

ACKNOWLEDGMENTS

It is a special pleasure to thank the French Passionist Fathers, two of whom at least are very close to us, for having entrusted this beneficial work to our hands, and to thank the Italian retreats which so graciously received us when we went in search of traces of St. Paul of the Cross.

The welcome we received at Monte Argentario was grace and light!

CONTENTS

PREFACE

LETTER TO A PASSIONIST

FATHER, I am indebted to you for a discovery. Forgive me for being so ignorant. For when you came to see me, I must confess in all humility that your Order was not much more than a name to me. At most I knew that the Passionists had been founded in the 18th century by a contemporary and compatriot of St. Alphonsus Liguori. That was the sum of it. But I was ignorant of the life, the work, and the thought of St. Paul of the Cross. Thanks to you, thanks to Father Alméras' beautiful book, thanks to Abbé Combes' penetrating introduction, I have discovered an admirable figure. Once again I marvel at the inexhaustible barn where the Church stores the harvests of souls born of her.

I shall leave to others to tell in the following pages, much better than I could, the greatness, the heroism, and the wisdom of your Founder. During the period known as "the century of enlightenment," when the fundamental intellectual and moral crisis was in preparation that was to set in motion a process whose effects we do not yet fully know nor have yet fully endured, St. Paul of the Cross, like St. Alphonsus Liguori, and like St. Louis Mary de Montfort a short while before them, appears to have been invested with the significance of a witness. He was the incarnation of the Christian denial, the Catholic denial of certain errors and certain compromises.

Paul's time, just as our own does still more emphatically, refused the Cross and sought means of evacuating it. In the dialectics of triumphant rationalism there remained less and less room for what Paul the Apostle had definitively called "the folly of the Cross." What is the use of preaching Jesus crucified, what sense does it make in a world where material facts seem to force themselves each day more compellingly on men's minds, in a world where for almost two hundred years a subversion has been going on which Péguy defined to perfection when he spoke of "money be-

9

come master in God's place"? Money alone? No. But everything that can be seen, touched, experienced, everything that can convince humanity that it has nothing to hope for from horizons beyond those of this life, and that it must seek its one and only future within itself.

St. Paul of the Cross spoke no differently. Throughout his life he had his eyes fixed on a scene that we cannot bear to look at and that would, if we thought about it, take away even our desire to live. It is the spectacle of a man who is God, and infinite charity, and the overflowing of mercy, hanging on the wood of a gibbet and bleeding eternally from five wounds. It is said that when your Founder evoked the Passion of Jesus he would suddenly stop speaking, and silent tears welled from his eyes. How often did not the prophetic words of the great Isaias come from his lips: "Surely he hath borne our infirmities and carried our sorrows." Yes, this Saint, whose mission and message you want to prolong, spent his life issuing this call to the Cross.

You are right, Father. Your Saint has meaning for us here and now, and his words are not vain. Our times are indeed crucified. Everywhere blood flows, has flowed, or will flow again in the very near future. But our times do not know, or rather no longer know, the meaning of their suffering. Nor do they know that they make up, whether they want to or not, what is lacking to the Passion of Christ. The blood that dyes the earth in our century — a century smitten with its own enlightenment, the nameless misery that bears down on so many men and women in this "civilized" epoch, the hunger and thirst that torture half of the human race today, all this is assumed by the charity of Christ in the sacrifice of Calvary and is mysteriously associated in the work of the Redemption.

This is the meaning of your apostolate, and a most necessary one it is. Courage, my dear Father! May generous souls join forces with you! May your missions teach this unique and uniquely necessary truth as powerfully as possible, the truth that your Founder repeated untiringly. It is simply this: that all the experience and all the hope of Christians depend upon the blood shed by a God-made-man. In closing, I reread the profound words that Edith Stein wrote before collaborating by her own offering in the divine holocaust which was for her, as it is for us, the only chance: "It is not human achievements that can help us, but only the Passion of Christ. I want to participate in it."

DANIEL-ROPS
Eau Vive, January 5, 1957

INTRODUCTION

Nothing is more persistent than a legend. Nothing is more fatal to an exact knowledge of the saints than the impressions produced by a few biographical scraps bloated with arbitrary interpretations. Who can flatter himself that he knows St. Paul of the Cross? And yet who can speak of St. Paul of the Cross without eliciting veritable shudders of terror, without unleashing a sort of spiritual panic at the thought of the uncouth ascete of Monte Argentario or Vetralla, the fierce missionary who preached only death and passion, the pitiable barefoot man who terrorized the crowds by conjuring up the tortures of hell or by having himself scourged until the blood flowed?

The admirable Founder of the Passionists has perhaps been the victim of certain of his biographers. It is customary to pass rather harsh judgment on these historians of former times. It would be more just, to my mind, to incriminate an overly active imagination and a lack of balance on the part of misinformed readers. For after all, St. Vincent Strambi, in his *Life of Blessed Paul of the Cross* (which appeared in Rome in 1786 and was published in French in 1861), gave more than a scrupulous account of all that related to the mortifications of his Father. He did not forget to emphasize other still more important aspects of a singularly profound and complex spiritual physiognomy. To quote him, "His maxim was that meekness heals all wounds, and that harshness, instead of healing one, creates ten."[1]

This gives us something to think about with regard to snap judgments.[2] But the very competence of the men who introduced Paul of the Cross to France is perhaps another reason why he is still so unpopular in that country. The paradox is not as stark as might at first glance appear.

While St. Paul of the Cross is highly esteemed by connoisseurs, he remains unknown or dreaded by the great majority. Father Charles Alméras deserves our warmest thanks for bringing remedy to such an abnormal situation and for the technical effort and literary talent he has devoted to the preparation of this sorely needed biography. The more we learn about the subject, its various aspects and unique difficulties, the less we hesitate to praise the merits of a work so well written and making such felicitous use of the most reliable and patiently gathered documents. Indeed, this work needs no recommendation.

When I finally yielded to my dear Father André Marie de la Croix's entreaties and agreed to write an introduction to this biography, which I was one of the first to read, it was in the hope of encouraging many to read it. My intention is less to point out the great benefit to be derived from reading it than to stress a trait of St. Paul of the Cross which made a profound impression on me, and to underline the deep kinship between the greatest saint of modern times (St. Thérèse of the Child Jesus) and a saint who may be looked upon by too many superficial readers as no longer belonging to our era.

When Father Alméras reaches Chapter XIX of his biography, at what he calls "the human summit of the life of Paul of the Cross," he pauses. From this culminating point he casts a penetrating glance over the ground he has already covered. And fully aware of what such a vantage point permits him to do, he writes: "The time has come to interrupt our account for a moment to try to grasp the driving force behind his remarkable spiritual ascent. While a complete exposition of Paul's spirituality would require a volume in itself, we shall try to set forth briefly the dominant idea that governed his life."[3]

The title of this central chapter suffices to explain this dominant idea: "God's Will Be Done." This pause, this inquiry, this discovery do the greatest possible honor to the biographer. They give his work a spiritual dimension that the mere narration of events could never have attained. They allow him to penetrate into the heart of Paul of the Cross, into the marrow of his doctrine, into the essence of his message. This chapter is a summit too.

Humility is always fruitful. Humbly Father Alméras has turned to the master who first studied this fundamental question. He finds his inspiration expressly in the article by Father Viller (cf. p. 262). By this very fact he invites his reader to join him in looking up this source. I take the liberty of adding my invitation to his, since his chapter is necessarily much shorter than Father Viller's ample monograph and cannot reproduce all the texts that give it its richness. Father Alméras does make a valuable suggestion of his own, however. Father Viller named only St. Francis de Sales among the probable spiritual teachers of St. Paul of the Cross in the doctrine and practice of abandonment. With all requisite prudence, Father Alméras proposes Tauler as well. This opens up a fruitful trail that ought to be followed to the end.[4] But it is not the essential. For it really does not matter so much whether Paul of the Cross owes this or that notion to this or that doctor.[5] What does matter in the highest degree is the very special efficacy of this dominant idea in St. Paul of the Cross. And this efficacy is prodigious.

To a great many Christians the formula "God's Will be done" seems quite commonplace. When it is not emptied of all meaning, it too often expresses a desire that is the exact opposite of the formula itself. The lips say: *"Fiat voluntas tua,"* but the heart asks: *"Fiat voluntas mea."* Because of this aspiration of self-love, even when the instinctive contradiction is almost completely eliminated, the Will of God is most often conceived as a foreign and implacable power to which one must submit because one cannot do otherwise. But it is looked upon as a power to which one submits without loving it. Since it remains outside the vital movement of the soul, heterogeneous to the living forms of devotion, it weighs on the spiritual life, constraining but not quickening it.

To do the Will of God would thus consist in adopting an extrinsic rule that can thwart, upset to its very depths — indeed, annul — the spontaneity of the soul. It is somewhat as if in the creation or execution of a symphony an exterior influence suddenly compelled a modification of its tonality, rhythm, or structure, or even reduced the orchestra to silence.

That is exactly the opposite of what happened in the soul of St. Paul of the Cross. The more aware we become of this contrast which is at the root of the human problem, the more we become

15

convinced that this Saint is a creator of genius; we also discover the essence of his genius and the scope of his creation. For him, *fiat voluntas tua* is the theme that begets the entire symphony, because it is inseparable from the most spontaneous upsurge of the soul and its very religion. And this identification is integrally realized because this vital theme has its origin at the point of conjunction between the sinful soul that was created for God, and the love of the Father Who comes toward the soul to save it: namely, the Passion and the Cross.

Staying as close as possible to these texts, Father Viller was able to write: "Why does St. Paul of the Cross push abandonment to such lengths? What has contributed to give such depth and extension to his doctrine of the Will of God? The answer is to be found only in his teachings on the Passion of Christ and on the suffering of the Christian as a participation in His Passion. 1) They have furnished abandonment a favorable climate in which to develop freely. 2) The reasons why our sufferings make us like Christ in His Passion perpetually strengthens abandonment."[6]

Father Alméras in his turn expresses the essence of the doctrine in these terms: "The Passion of Jesus! This was the food of his soul, the constant subject of his meditations, the raison d'être of his foundations, and the explanation for the fruitfulness of his apostolate. . . . But, above all, the Passion is the explanation of the spirituality of St. Paul of the Cross: *it is the center toward which everything converges, and from which everything flows.*"[7] Nothing could be truer, nor could it be said with greater clarity and power. But if this is so, we must be permitted to make a step farther in the same direction.

Starting from this central and supremely mystical notion of the Will of God, and from the immediate, vital, and ineluctable bond that exists between the Will of God, the Passion of Christ, the Christian's suffering, and the salvation of souls, St. Paul of the Cross, with singular mastery, formulated a spiritual synthesis. When compared to his synthesis, one finds that other lives and other doctrines often lack one or the other of its integrating elements or show a lack of balance. St. Paul of the Cross has done more and he has done better. Impelled by the dynamism of this perfect synthesis, he founded — in a church that was already well developed and rich in spiritual families adapted to her various needs — a new Order whose reason for being and whose program actually coincide with this synthesis. It is this combination of circumstances that compels our admiration.

The genius of man never rises higher than when he succeeds in deciphering the supreme laws of the universal order and in governing his life by these principles. Could a spiritual genius go beyond the ultimate expression of infinite wisdom and love? The foundation of the Passionists was a return to Calvary in order to relive the essential drama. To be more exact, it made the drama of Calvary live again among us. It restored to the bloody act of the Redemption its pathetic "presentness." It keeps men from forgetting the sufferings of God and from believing that we can easily be consoled because these sufferings began and ended in the past. It implants over again in each generation the true Cross, the Cross that is made not of two beams of wood nailed together but of the embrace of man by the God-man, of the conformity of each human will to the Will of the Father, of the humble martyrdom of our love. And in doing all these things, it parallels the particular vocation and the principal function of the greatest saint of modern times: St. Thérèse of the Child Jesus.

Obviously, there never has been a saint who set out to do anything other than to commune in the sufferings of Christ and in His Redemption. There has never been a founder who in the last analysis did not pursue a goal of the same nature. But while all members of the Church of Christ live by the same life, participate in the same graces, and strive toward the same end, there are untold and sometimes profound nuances and differences, even on points which we cannot consider secondary. Extremely rare are those whose particular mission has been to give the essential its supreme and in a certain sense its exclusive value. St. Francis of Assisi, St. Thérèse of Lisieux, yes. But the former could not refrain from adding to the essential message of the Gospel his very personal cult of Lady Poverty. The latter had to conceal from certain eyes, through accessory aspects of her religious life, her life as a contemporary of the Crucified[8] and as a dispenser of the Redemptive Blood.

Paul, for his part, never wanted to see anything but the Cross. No contingency ever induced him to modify in the slightest degree the exclusiveness of his purpose. This emphasis is all the more striking in that it contrasted sharply with the attitude of the period in which Paul Danei lived. Born the same year as Voltaire, he died three years before him. What an antithesis! In the century of the enlightenment, to dream of the Gospel in its purity! We cannot exaggerate the importance of such a plan or stress too forcefully its permanent currentness. This absolute return to the absolute of love in the *Fiat* of Calvary seems to confer upon the one who accomplished it a practically absolute originality.

A judge far better informed and incomparably more qualified than all historians taken together could not refrain from situating the creation of the humble lover of the Cross in its historical context. In approving the Rule of this new Order which had been so bitterly opposed, the Sovereign Pontiff pointed out that "the Congregation of the Passion should have been the first founded by the Church, and behold, it comes last."[9] The Pope who spoke thus was Benedict XIV.

Coming from the lips of His Holiness, such a declaration did more than point to the merit of the Founder. It made clear to his sons wherein their duty lay. By these few words, so simple and so true, the Founder was reassured that he had not been misled by false visions. His exemplary humility and charity had truly led him to innovate in the only way that is valid in the holy Church of Christ, by allowing himself to be drawn by the Holy Spirit to the Source, and by founding, even if after seventeen centuries of incredible waiting, the congregation that should under normal circumstances have germinated at the very foot of the Cross.

The Passionists, for their part, saw the specific value of their vocation being defined. Last, and yet first among all the others, it was not unlike the vocation of a Carmelite nun who, although herself a relative late-comer, rooted herself in the tuff of the Church's origins. To salt the salt that has lost its savor, to give the laborers of redemption the supernatural vigor without which there can be no efficacious co-operation: such is the purpose of this intensely apostolic contemplation. As St. Thérèse of Lisieux understood and fulfilled it so admirably, this is the highest vocation open to those who cannot be priests: to be the love in the heart of the Church, our Mother. But to draw from the heart of the Church our Mother the Love Who is the Spirit, and to allow oneself to be nailed by Him upon the mystical cross where the fullness of the priesthood is shared in common by the One Priest and by each of those to whom He grants the privilege of participating in His priesthood, and thus live the mystery of Passion, death, and Redemption so completely that one truly communicates its fruits to the sinful multitudes — this outstrips the greatest saint of modern times in the very line of her deepest aspirations. For it is being in very truth what she would have wanted so much to be but could never become: a priest of Jesus Christ.

Nothing has ever been more necessary to the world than the most perfect participation in the priesthood of the Son of God. Nothing has ever been of more burning current interest in every generation. Nothing has ever possessed such beneficent fruitfulness. The greatness of Paul of the Cross and of his work must be measured in terms of this supreme necessity, this current interest, and this fruitfulness.

It is from this point of view that we should evaluate the merits of Father Alméras as a biographer. His book is sound, captivating. But it would be feeble praise merely to enumerate his qualities, for they are the service of a higher cause. May the excellence of his work draw the attention of many readers to this Saint whose soul was so profound and whose mind was so clear, this Saint with a heart of fire. May he inspire everyone with the resolution to commune more closely than ever with Jesus Crucified. Above all, may he kindle in many young men the desire to become really or at least in their hearts true *Passionists*. If he succeeds in making them rank *first* the authentically Christian ideal that too often remains *last*, he will have won the most enviable of rewards.

And why would he not succeed? We are in a still better position than our ancestors to know from experience that "he who would save his life will lose it." Why hesitate to "lose one's life" since it is the only means of keeping it safe, as well as many other lives, and even many earthly things besides?

Many around us close their eyes to these truths and continue to grope. They are too eager to seek in a revival of humanism the remedy to the ills of our time. That is reversing the essential order of things. Salvation does not lie in the maximum development of our human potentialities. Salvation is in the Cross. Whoever rejects the Cross, or even pushes it aside, refuses by that very fact the primordial condition of his salvation. We cannot help being distressed to see the Cross disappear more and more from our liturgical ornaments, even when embroidered by religious hands. What aberration can be inciting this unfaithfulness to a tradition heavy with wisdom? Man becomes fully man only at the foot of the Cross. If dedication to the City of God inspired as many sacrifices as does the defense of temporal fatherlands, would not the face of the world be changed? Men often die in vain for a mortal fatherland. No one ever runs such a distressing risk when he wants to live and die by the Passion of Christ. Jesus has told us: "He who believes in me, even if he die, shall live."

To live and to make others live, this is the function that properly belongs to the saints. That is the perfect definition of the program of St. Paul of the Cross and of his Passionists. There is none more beautiful. There is none more opportune. This book, which brings us close to such an ideal, is a great book. Our gratitude to its author should be all the greater since it is joined to a magnificent hope.

ANDRÉ COMBES
Neuilly, October 3, 1956
The Feast of St. Thérèse of the Child Jesus

Prologue

THE PREPARATION

(1694–1720)

"Men resemble their times more than their fathers," the Arab proverb says. It is true of men, but it is not altogether true of the saints, who resemble their mothers more than their times.

Chapter I

THE FAMILY AND CHILDHOOD
OF ST. PAUL OF THE CROSS

"May God make saints of all of you."

PAUL DANEI was born on January 3, 1694, in Ovada, Italy, a few days before Voltaire, who was to outlive him by three years.

Ovada is a large village at the junction of the Stura and Orba rivers, the latter flowing into the Po by way of the Bormida and the Tanaro. Situated about thirty miles northwest of Genoa, Ovada is reached from the coast by a road that climbs up the Apennines with many sharp turns, cutting through infertile farmlands and terraced pastures. These terraces, held up by simple grass levees, rise in strata up to the denuded summits. Here and there, gray farmhouses and a few hamlets lie hidden in the earth's folds. A striking contrast, this, with the luxuriant Riviera and its shining villas surrounded with fragrant oleander.

Rather abruptly, the road follows the Stura's course downward amid a wooded landscape of chestnut and other trees. Then it comes to a valley spreading out into cornfields and vineyards.

Ovada dominates this valley. As in all ancient towns, its buildings are crowded together, its narrow streets lined with well-patronized shops. It was on one of these streets, now Via San Paolo della Croce, that our Saint was born. His parents lived in a third-story flat. Their home, preserved with pious care and now a shrine and museum, consisted of three pleasant rooms with the rafters showing: a dining room with a large stone fireplace, and two other rooms.

The room where Paul Danei was born is now a chapel, with his portrait above the altar. The other two rooms are rich in mementos: among them his breviary, his instruments of penance, the bricks he used for pillows, his few books, and the death mask revealing his energetic features.

The baptismal register preserved here shows that he was baptized on January 6, 1694, as Paul Francis. His godfather was John Andrew Dannia, a great-uncle on his father's side; his godmother, Maria Catherine Massari, who was his maternal grandmother.

It was only "by accident," as he himself has said, that Paul Danei was born in Ovada, then part of the Republic of Genoa. He thought of himself as a Lombard, which indeed he was through his father if not through his mother.

The Daneis originally came from Castellazzo, a small town of some four or five thousand inhabitants, a few miles south of Alessandria. Before becoming part of the Piedmont and of the Kingdom of Sardinia in 1705, it had been one of the Lombard towns grouped around Milan.

Castellazzo is in the broad plain of the Po, with its rich crops of corn, prosperous vineyards, and fruit trees, as well as its silkworm industry and model dairies where Parmesan cheese is manufactured. The agricultural community sprawls out around its ancient shrines, which, like Ovada, treasure memories of St. Paul of the Cross. Notable is the church of St. Charles, which has preserved the small shelter where Paul remained for forty days to meditate upon the Constitutions of the Congregation he was to found.

The Danei family had belonged to the nobility, and their manor — adorned with the Danei coat of arms — had become the city hall of Castellazzo. But they gave little thought to their noble past. In fact, at the canonization process our Saint's sister affirmed she did not know if the city hall had ever belonged to her family.

This has seemed rather strange to Paul's biographers. The explanation is quite simple to anyone who knows the history of the internal struggles of the Italian city-states, at least of those where democracy won out.

What happened in Florence is well known. There the mercantile bourgeoisie and the artisans monopolized all power. "Whoever did not belong to a guild had no civic existence. And the sorry condition of the nobles, who were deemed unworthy to deal with the workers and merchants, excluded them from the corporations. This amounted to banishing them from all public functions. If they felt weary or degraded at being considered outcasts, pariahs, they could hoist themselves up to the common level of society only by becoming merchants or artisans, by repudiating their aristocratic birth in order to take up the weaver's shuttle, the apothecary's pestle, or the draper's ell."[1]

In Castellazzo, the Daneis must have been reduced to the same course of action in order to enjoy equal rights with the traders and artisans.

In fact, Paul's parents were clothing merchants.

Luke Danei was the last of seven children. He had an uncle and a brother who were priests. The uncle lived in Ovada and took Luke into his care when he was a small child. In 1685 the good priest arranged for Luke to marry the niece of the pastor of Ovada, Catherine de Grandis. After five years of marriage Luke was left a widower and childless.

Two years later, on January 6, 1692, Luke Danei married again, this time to Anna Maria Massari, who was born at Rivarolo, near Genoa.

Sixteen children were born to them. The eldest, a girl, lived only three days. The second was to be St. Paul of the Cross. History has preserved for us the names of several of the younger children — John Baptist, Teresa, Anthony, and Joseph, whom we shall meet again in our narrative.

We are also fortunate in knowing something about the temperaments of the parents and their relationships with their children.

Luke Danei was a man of strong faith, the enemy of frivolous amusements. He forbade his sons to play cards or hunt. But his robust good sense recoiled at the sight of some of the mortifications his children thought up. One day he caught Paul and John

Baptist by surprise, each holding in his hand a rudimentary discipline made of heels studded with nails. Looking at them, he exclaimed: "So you want to kill yourselves?"

Luke was harder on himself than on his children and even aspired to martyrdom. He died from the aftereffects of a fall caused by a neighbor, but on his deathbed he counseled his children to forgive and forget.

Anna Maria Massari's faith was as staunch as her husband's, but in addition she was endowed with an imperturbable meekness. When her children vexed her, she was content to sigh: "May God make saints of all of you!" Humble, devout, and avoiding luxury, she was considered by everyone to be a little saint. And Father Paul was the first to think so. "Would to God," he used to say, "that I had the virtue of my mother!"

The Danei family was richer in virtue, however, than in money. Theirs was an illustrious origin, but either because the family had fallen from its ancient splendor or because the right of primogeniture had been unfavorable to the last-born, Luke was constantly in financial difficulties and often changed his residence. From Ovada he moved to Cremolino, and from Tortona to Castellazzo. This would seem to indicate a lack of stability in his business.

Paul was even obliged to make an urgent trip to Alessandria to pawn his clothes so that he might help his father out of his straits. Indeed, for several years he thought it his duty to defer the fulfillment of his desire for solitude in order to help his parents in a material way.

And yet the family was not in abject want. Rather it experienced periodic hardships as the result of business difficulties. We know that at certain times the Daneis lived from the income of their properties, and that "casa di San Paolo," where Paul was born, is an upper-middle-class dwelling.

It was in this milieu, strangely reminiscent of young Francis of Assisi's (less the element of wealth), that the precocious virtue of Paul Francis Danei was to blossom.

What was this virtue like? We almost wish we could say that

he was a child like any other, mischievous, even noisy and undisciplined, and that he heard God's call a little sooner or later than usual. It would satisfy our need for naturalistic interpretations, aggravated by the modern rationalistic and scientific spirit that imbues us even without our knowledge. Besides, there is a certain type of pious literature that deserves to be discredited.

But without writing another *Golden Legend*, we must admit that young Paul was among the predestined.

We shall attach no importance other than as an explanation after the fact to his sister Teresa's statement that "their mother had already recognized marks of future holiness in him from the fact that during the months that preceded his birth — and only *his* birth — she never experienced any of the sufferings and discomforts of expectant mothers."

And we shall be equally unimpressed by the circumstance, carefully noted by Paul's first biographers, that as an infant he nursed every four hours instead of the customary three. They called this "a predisposition to mortification." We prefer to see in it vigilance on the part of his mother in the presence of a congenital hepatic insufficiency.

But this wise mother was a great Christian besides. And her vigilant education obtained amazing results that we shall not call into question despite their precocity. Did not St. Thérèse of the Child Jesus also write: "From the time I was three years old, I never refused God anything"? The marvels of grace begin early in a receptive soul.

Disentangling tousled hair is always a difficult if not painful operation. Mrs. Danei used to make it more pleasant for Paul by telling him stories from the lives of the saints. The child would listen with delight. When tears came to his eyes after a sharper tug of the comb than usual, she would show him the crucifix and say: "Look, my child, how Jesus suffered." Much later he declared that after listening to his mother's stories while she was combing his hair he would have stood still "even if she had pulled off his scalp."[2] "From this I conceived a great desire to belong wholly to God, and I have always remembered it."[3]

His recreation consisted in setting up a small altar together with his brother John Baptist, who was a year younger. They would place a wax Child Jesus upon it and adore Him.[4] These were rather ordinary games. But it was not child's play to get up during the night and pray for three hours. And this Paul did from the time he was eight years old.[5]

Moreover, Paul was as good at his lessons as he was devout. From 1701 to 1709 his family made many sojourns in Cremolino. One of these was forced upon them. Luke Danei had been falsely implicated in an attempted crime about which we know nothing. Until he could prove his innocence he had to flee Ovada. Cremolino is a suburb across the Orba from Ovada, but this river was then the frontier between the Republic of Genoa and the Duchy of Montferrat.

It was there that young Paul received his first schooling. But the schoolmaster soon declared "that he no longer knew what to teach him, because the child already knew as much as he did."[6]

Paul was therefore sent for a time to Genoa to follow a more complete course of study, but only until he was thirteen or fourteen years old.[7] What were the reasons for taking him out of school? We do not know. His parents had returned to Ovada. Perhaps their business in Cremolino had not prospered and their resources were insufficient.

Be this as it may, Paul then followed his family in another change of residence. This time they remained five years at Campo Ligure, a small village about halfway between Ovada and Genoa, in one of the valleys of the Apennines.

That is all we know about this period of his adolescence (1709–14), except that it did not belie his pious childhood. "He abstained from playing with the other boys"[8] and "his favorite occupation was to go to church, to help the priests sing the divine praises in choir, to learn the ecclesiastical ceremonies,"[9] and to serve as many Masses as possible.

Habit did not blunt his spirit of faith, since he declared: "If the angels took bodies and came to live on earth, they would spend their time doing two things above all others: serving Masses and helping the sick."[10]

He was an excellent young man, therefore, more devout and mortified than usual, but still giving no dazzling signs of holiness.

Chapter II

THE CONVERSION

"Paul was eagerly listening for God's call."

PAUL DANEI had reached his twentieth year. He was a handsome boy, as we can easily imagine from the portraits of his mature years. He was tall, strapping, with dark complexion and eyes. A broad forehead and aquiline nose were the distinguishing marks of his intelligent and virile countenance.

He had kept himself pure in body and soul. He would one day admit to one of his religious that his greatest immodesty had consisted in an involuntary look at his body during an illness.[1]

And in later years, during a violent temptation to despair, he was heard to whisper when he thought he was alone: "Lord, You know that thanks to Your help Paul does not remember sullying his soul by any voluntary sin."[2]

And yet when he was almost twenty he was profoundly disturbed by a sermon given by his pastor. He saw his wretchedness as in a sudden illumination, and when the allocution was over he threw himself at the priest's feet to make a general confession. Armed with a stone, he beat his breast and wept profusely, for in his own eyes he was a great sinner.[3]

An exaggeration, perhaps, to our way of thinking. But the exaggeration of a saint can be profound truth. Under the light of divine grace Paul Danei had just come to understand, as only privileged souls are permitted to understand, what God is and what man and sin are. He saw the misery that every child of Eve carries within himself, the stirring of unclean instincts, the outcropping of ideas, fugitive desires — the beast that sleeps within.

When he rose absolved, he decided to consecrate himself totally to the service of God[4]; that is, to pursue his flight from sin with still greater zeal and to give himself wholly to God.

This is what he has called his "conversion." And even if it was not a conversion in the same sense as St. Augustine's, it was, according to the deepest meaning of the word, a tearing away from nature in order to turn to the one and only Good.

He was twenty years old. From that moment on his virtue, already remarkable, became exceptional.

He pushed the spirit of mortification to a heroic degree. He often left his bedroom to go to the attic, where he would spend the night lying on the floor with a few bricks (which have been carefully preserved at Ovada) as a pillow.[5] When he slept in his own bed, he would get up two or three hours before dawn. Then he and his brother John Baptist would devote themselves to their spiritual exercises. Their mother would weep when she heard them taking the discipline, and their father was worried by their juvenile violence.

In the matter of drink, Paul shunned wine. He quenched his thirst with gall and vinegar. But as this would have seemed too admirable or too unreasonable to his parents, he drank from a gourd made out of a scooped-out pumpkin which did not reveal its contents. And he kept his supply of gall hidden in a small earthenware jar. After he had left home his sister inadvertently broke the jar and discovered his secret. In picking up the pieces she noticed the strange smell that they emitted.[6]

He went still farther in developing his spirit of mortification. One day as he was walking in the garden he yielded to the temptation to eat a few muscatel grapes. During the period of mental prayer that followed, he was filled with such remorse at the thought of this act of greediness that he made a vow to abstain from all superfluous satisfactions and to eat only the food that was strictly necessary.

His body, so harshly coerced, came to experience a strange satisfaction in a diet of dry bread. This gave rise to scruples. Wisely, the vow was commuted.[7] Indeed, his health could not resist such a way of life. To use his own words, "he was just skin and bones,"[8] and he became seriously ill.

His humility kept pace with his appetite for privation. We have seen his profound sentiments of contrition and unworthiness. He accepted scorn even from those who knew him intimately and should have admired him.

We cannot help being amazed at the insults one of his confessors heaped upon him. This priest never missed an opportunity to reprimand him aloud in church and in public. Sometimes he would drive Paul out of the choir when he was waiting to serve a Mass, telling him that he was unworthy to remain in a place reserved for the ministers of the Lord. On other occasions he would make him kneel, like a child, in the middle of the church. At such times Paul envied women whose veils concealed their embarrassment.[9]

One day the priest decided to come up suddenly behind the young man, who was lost in contemplation and had hidden his face in his coat to conceal his tears. The priest roughly pulled the coat away from his face and exclaimed: "Is this the way one behaves before the Blessed Sacrament?"[10]

Sometimes he ostensibly refused to give Paul Holy Communion. It was also his usual practice to relegate him to the end of the line when he was waiting to go to confession. And when Paul finally entered the confessional, he would rebuke him harshly.

We are told that this priest had a very austere and melancholy temperament which led him to mortify his penitent.[11] We can judge for ourselves. "He happened to meet Paul outside the village one day. He thereupon hung long flowers on his ears and commanded him to enter the village bedecked in this fashion."[12] On a carnival day when this "melancholy" man was making merry with a few friends, Paul happened to pass by in the street. The "austere" priest called out to him, made him come in, and commanded him to dance.[13] Paul consented, just as he had accepted all the other humiliations.

Paul rejected as a temptation the desire to abandon this strange confessor. To hearten himself, he used to say: "The devil will not win the day. This is the right kind of confessor for you. He will make you bow your head."

As it happened, Paul's confessor was the first to grow weary. When he finally realized that his docile penitent was leading him into spiritual paths where he could not follow, he sent him to someone who was more experienced than he in such matters.

Even these humiliations did not satisfy Paul Danei. He sought ways of his own to be the laughingstock of the crowd.

One day, for example, he tied a rag to his hat and went through the streets, the rag floating in the wind, followed by a band of hooting children. The housewives stood on their doorsteps, laughing. And he rejoiced in his heart to be vilified for Jesus' sake.[14]

This brings to mind St. Margaret of Cortona, who went about in rags, her face slashed with knife cuts. But she wanted to make everyone forget her fascinating beauty and the scandal of her loves.[15]

Paul Danei, who was considered a saint, wanted to pass for a madman. Had he not vowed to obey *anyone* who commanded him to do anything whatsoever that was not contrary to the law of God? People learned about it and treated him like a simpleton to be made fun of, until a prudent director commuted this too general and unduly difficult vow.

Toward the end of his life Paul admitted to his brother infirmarian that he had had another motive for making himself contemptible as a young man. He was the eldest son in his family. Although because of their virtue his parents had resigned themselves to his extraordinary behavior, the same was not true of his paternal uncle, Dom Joseph Christopher, priest though he was.

By right of seniority this uncle had inherited the Danei patrimony. He wanted to leave this inheritance to his nephew, but only on condition that he marry a young lady he picked out for him. He chose a beautiful, rich, and virtuous girl for his nephew. As Paul's parents were in straitened circumstances and had many children, they accepted this most honorable plan. But Paul refused, giving various excuses.

Dom Christopher would not accept his nephew's reasons. He had made a fine match for him. The qualities of the young girl were undeniable, and through her his family would regain its past splendor. Cornered, Paul agreed. But he had made a vow of chastity. This proved no obstacle. The uncle obtained a dispensation from Rome and commanded Paul to accept an invitation to dine at the home of the young girl's parents.

Bound by his vow of obedience, Paul could not decline. But during the entire meal he refused to raise his eyes, and he fled at the first opportunity.

The young lady, deeply hurt by this scorn and perhaps impelled by love, tried to attract Paul's attention on many occasions. "Accompanied by her woman servant, she would take her place close to Paul in church. From time to time she would say to her companion in a low voice but loud enough to be heard by Paul: 'How can he remain kneeling so long? How can he endure this great cold?' Now and then she would blow her nose, or do something else to distract him, and say: 'How is it possible? How will he bear up under such an austere life?' "[16]

Paul had to repel other similar temptations, which had in view far less noble objectives than an honorable marriage.[17] And to this end he tried to make himself appear as despicable as possible so that no one could take pleasure in looking at him. He did not shave, file his nails, or wear a tie, and he practiced an austere modesty.[18]

Meanwhile Dom Christopher died on November 16, 1718, liberating Paul from his pressing demands but still leaving him all his property on the express condition that he marry. Paul solemnly renounced the inheritance, simply asking for a breviary in the name of charity.[19]

Does this not call to mind the Poverello of Assisi stripping himself of his patrimony? At that moment Paul espoused "Lady Poverty" just as Francis had, although he did not put it into words. From then on he refused to wear anything but coarse clothing, and sometimes begged his bread on his knees from his family to make it clear that he had renounced his birthright.

There was another reason for his behavior. Paul was becoming less and less interested in material occupations. He continued to help his parents when they were in financial difficulties, and he himself tells us that this duty of charity prevented him for several years from following his inclination for absolute solitude.[20] But otherwise "he practiced no profession"[21] and spent much time in prayer, visiting the sick, and instructing the ignorant.[22]

This program for living the perfect life in the world continued for more than five years, from the time which he himself speaks of as his conversion until his final departure from his father's house. It was a life of prayer, charity, and apostolic action.

A life of prayer — in the full sense of the word. Guided by increasingly enlightened directors, sustained and reassured by the study of the great masters of the spiritual life, Paul's soul continued to progress in God's intimate friendship.

The strange confessor of the first hour turned his penitent over to a wiser man than he, Father Jerome of Tortona, a Capuchin. The latter welcomed Paul and quickly realized to what heights of contemplation he had already attained by himself. In short order he recommended that Paul entrust his soul to another Capuchin, Father Columban of Genoa, who was particularly well versed in the ways of mysticism.

Endowed with great talent for directing souls, Father Columban understood this chosen soul and helped him to find nourishment in the works of the great mystics. But he resided in Ovada, about twenty-one miles from Castellazzo, or at Savona, which was still farther away. Paul therefore decided to place himself under the direction of Canon Cerrutti, attached to the cathedral of Alessandria, which was only five miles from his home.

Canon Cerrutti was a man of great learning and excellent judgment, as our Saint was to testify. In fact, the young men whom the canon later sent to him for his Congregation were accepted with complete confidence.[23] But the canon's common sense led him to distrust the extraordinary paths upon which his penitent was entering.

He used to test Paul's patience by making him wait for him entire mornings. He listened skeptically to his disclosures on the divine illumination he received during prayer, and commanded him to remain in the purgative way, meditating simply on sin, death, and judgment.

Paul, always submissive, obeyed. He would consider sin and say to himself: Consider, O my soul, that sin offends God! But instead of ordinary meditation with its reasoning processes and its personal applications, he was suddenly rapt in God, Who communicated His ineffable secrets to him. "My son, in heaven the blessed will not be united to Me as someone is united to his friend, but as iron is penetrated by fire."[24]

What mattered the caution of the prudent canon? Paul, nourished by the mystical writers, could freely embark on the extraordinary ways of the spiritual life.

And yet a question arises. What was the extent of Paul's education?

We know that his formal education ended early. The totality of his secular knowledge consisted of the rudiments he had learned at Cremolino and perhaps a bit of Latin he had been taught at Genoa. However, he made remarkable intellectual progress, under what precise conditions we do not know. Although his sermons have disappeared, those of his letters that have come down to us show by their perfectly appropriate Latin quotations that he knew the fine points of both Italian and Latin.

Where had he learned his use of language? Very little in class. In his studies he was aided by the similarity between Latin and Italian, and above all by his quick intelligence and his prolonged meditations on the sacred texts.

The fact remains that, while Paul Danei's profane knowledge was rather mediocre, he attained to a profound understanding of ascetical and mystical theology.

He studied the works of St. Francis de Sales with particular attention. One of the friends of his youth who became a Capuchin affirms: "It was he who instructed me on the purgative, illuminative, and unitive ways of mental prayer. He made wide — indeed exclusive — use of the doctrine of St. Francis de Sales, which he possessed wonderfully well."[25]

If we did not have the testimony of others, even a superficial study of his own doctrine would reveal the influence of the Bishop of Geneva. *The Introduction to the Devout Life* taught him the elements of asceticism, and *The Treatise on the Love of God* the elements of mysticism.

Almost as well known to Paul Danei was St. John of the Cross, little Brother John beloved of St. Teresa of Ávila for his common sense, his spirit of penance, and his courage. It was reading St. John of the Cross that led him to make the vow depriving his body of all superfluous satisfactions and to resolve to imitate Jesus Christ in all things. These were the two great principles set forth by the Spanish reformer for the soul that aspires to divine union. Paul was to speak of St. John of the Cross as "the prince of mystics." He does not seem to have studied the luminous works of St. Teresa with as much care, although he affirmed he had read the book of the *Foundations*.[26]

Even more than these great mystics, Paul's favorite author was Tauler, about whom he spoke with so much unction that "when he so much as mentioned his name his face would light up."[27] This enthusiasm may seem surprising, especially when we remember Luther's infatuation for the same author, to the point of proclaiming him the greatest of theologians.

Luther and St. Paul of the Cross, both disciples of the most famous mystic of the fourteenth-century Rhenish school! The comparison is provocative. Luther drew from Tauler a code of morals that was, to say the least, quite broad. Paul of the Cross was inspired by him to embrace a rule of life whose austerity is sometimes terrifying. The fact might seem paradoxical if it were not true that from the same good earth parsley draws its pungent perfume and hemlock its deadly poison.

Finally, in our rapid enumeration of the masters of St. Paul of the Cross, we must not forget St. Francis of Assisi, so popular in Italy. Paul's mother had given him St. Francis as his second patron in baptism and had often talked about him to her son. Besides, the Capuchin Fathers whom Paul visited regularly must have made Francis' way of life familiar to him. Have we not already pointed out close similarities between the life of the Poverello and that of the man who was to love to be called "the missionary of the poor"? We shall come across other similarities as we go on.

When we remember that Paul's knowledge was drawn from sources such as these, we can better understand the statement of one of the companions of his youth: "If anyone wanted to find Paul, he had to go to church."[28] Paul spent long hours in church kneeling in prayer, sometimes hiding his head in his coat to conceal his tears of joy or repentance.

He meditated upon the teachings of the masters of the spiritual life; he delved into the secrets of the intimate and direct relations between the soul and God. Sometimes God revealed to him the ineffable sweetness of His love, and then he would weep for joy. Again He would disclose the sufferings of the Passion and the consequences of sin, and he would shed tears of repentance.

Later our Saint confided: "How many things I understood then concerning the power, the wisdom, the goodness, and the other attributes of God! It is impossible to talk about it, for there are no words with which to express oneself adequately!"[29] In the last analysis, this is the explanation of his astonishing knowledge of the mystical ways.

The long hours Paul spent praying in church did not keep him from devoting himself to works of charity and to apostolic action.

The poor never turned to him in vain. He used to give them alms, on his knees. His sister Teresa found him one day in this position before a poor woman and thought for a moment that he was venerating her like a saint.[30] He even gave his clothes away. His mother dared to reproach him gently for it: "Someday you will come home without anything on at all."[31]

Paul did not draw back before the most unpleasant tasks. He even carried on his shoulders cadavers left unburied for fear of contagion. And in the company of his friends who had been inspired to follow his example, he lingered beside the open graves, meditating upon these lifeless bones and on the vanity of passing pleasures.

His charity for souls was greater still. He began by practicing it with his brothers and sisters, teaching them to meditate upon the Passion of our Lord Jesus Christ,[32] to which he already had the greatest devotion.

He belonged to a pious association of young men who met in the oratory of St. Anthony, near Castellazzo. Quite naturally he was elected prior. From that time on he addressed an exhortation to his fellow members every Sunday morning. On Sunday afternoons he taught catechism to the children in the same oratory. Soon adults came to hear him, and he was invited to explain the catechism in the church itself.[33] Sometimes some of his hearers would irreverently engage in private conversations. When this happened he would not call them down but went and knelt before them, begging them to have more respect for the house of God.[34]

He also knew how to make excellent use of fraternal correction. Was it that he already had the gift of reading souls, as Don Bosco is said to have had, or was he a keen observer? In any case, he was known to warn one or another of his companions and to direct him to a confessor to set his soul at peace. He even foretold the premature death of certain impenitent sinners.

After being pelted with insults he was now surrounded with respect.

When he came upon a group engaged in licentious talk, they would say: "Here comes the saint!" The conversation would stop, and some of them would slip away.

A few friends agreed to group themselves around him. They formed the habit of accompanying him on walks into the country on Sunday evenings. He spoke to them on spiritual subjects and taught them methods of prayer.

Many young men found their vocation in this way. Some became Capuchins, others Servites of Mary, and still others diocesan priests.[35]

Why didn't Paul follow his companions into the priesthood then and there? Was he not more devout than they, their model, and already a master in the mystical ways?

The reason is not far to seek. The religious orders in existence at that time — and in Castellazzo there were three of them: the Augustinians, the Servites, and the Capuchins — had not escaped a certain relaxation of their Rule. They lived too close to the world and opened their doors too freely to visitors.

Paul felt drawn to solitude, which alone permits intimate conversations with God. He did not know quite where to find it. One day when he was crossing the Italian Riviera near Sestri, he caught sight of a tiny, isolated church on a mountaintop. He experienced a violent desire to retire there, but his parents still needed him. Out of charity he postponed his plan.[36]

Other difficulties arose while he was seeking his way of life.

We have tried to sketch the portrait of Paul Danei in the flower of his twentieth year. No doubt the reader has found him more admirable than imitable, for he practiced virtue so perfectly and with such apparent ease. The reason is that he was always tight-lipped about himself. Moreover, the witnesses of his life and his early biographers chose to remember only the most striking manifestations of his interior virtues.

But who can tell the daily effort, the struggles, and even the painful temptations that this life of prayer, charity, and apostolic action presupposed?

We can surmise these things in a letter he wrote twenty years later to a hesitant young man, to encourage him to follow his vocation: "Oh! If you knew the combats I had to wage before embracing my present mode of life! The devil used to suggest great fears to me. I was moved with compassion for my parents, whom I was leaving in great penury and whose only hopes according to the world rested on me. I experienced interior desolation, melancholy, and dread. I felt that I would not succeed in holding fast to my mode of life. The devil gave me notions that I had been mistaken, that I could serve God in another way, that this was not the sort of life for me, and other great apprehensions that I pass over in silence. To make matters worse, I lost all sensible devotion. I was tempted in every way imaginable. The very sound of bells was loathsome to me. Everybody seemed happy, except me. I shall never be able to explain these great struggles. They assailed me still more violently when I was about to take the habit and to abandon my poor home. This is all pure truth, and there are even many things that I am leaving out for the sake of brevity."[37]

St. Paul of the Cross may have been alluding in this letter to an episode that has been vividly remembered by the Passionists of Genoa in particular. It is an episode that gives this man, who might seem unduly ethereal, a profoundly human aspect.

Paul happened to be near Genoa, haunted by his desire for solitude and renunciation. As he looked over the city, night fell and the great city was lighted up by the fires on its ships and by its street lamps. In the calm of the night the sounds of the throng were wafted upward, and songs burst forth. Paul's lively imagination showed him the various houses of pleasure where the crowd was hurrying, easy pleasures.

"Everyone seemed happy, except me," he wrote.

He was seeking his way amid great interior struggles, but also in prayer. And his outward countenance was such that even in times of dryness he edified those who saw him.

A great lady, Countess Canefri, noticed this young man, whom she did not know, kneeling for hours in prayer near a column. She asked who he was, and when she went home she told her family what she had seen. She added: "This young man must have been contemplating some extraordinary resolution."

She was right. Paul was eagerly listening for God's call.

Chapter III

GOD MAKES HIS WILL KNOWN TO PAUL

The real superman is the mystic. HENRI BERGSON

COUNTESS CANEFRI was right. Paul Danei was formulating great plans.

At the time of his conversion he had resolved to consecrate himself totally to the service of God. What was he going to do? He did not know yet.

All of a sudden, like Francis of Assisi before him, he thought he heard the call of God. He had been living his life of penance

and prayer for about a year when the Pope issued his appeal for
a new crusade. In 1715 the Turks had declared war on Venice
and had won victories in Greece. The Pope was calling on all
men of good will to save Christendom once more.

Paul was then twenty-one. Would he not have an opportunity
to serve God and the Church if he joined the crusade? He en-
listed in the Venetian Army. He was sent to Crema first and then
to Parma and Ferrara. For several months, as an unpaid volunteer,
he devoted his efforts to learning the soldier's profession.

One day as he was at prayer before the Blessed Sacrament exposed for the Forty Hours' Devotion, Paul understood, as Francis
of Assisi had under similar circumstances, that God was calling him
not to bloody battles but to battles of another sort. In obedience
to the divine inspiration, he abandoned his project.[1]

Perhaps for lack of resources, he did not return to his family
immediately, and for a year he remained in Novello, in the diocese of Alba, where he had stopped to ask for hospitality. There
a fine family, having no children of their own, welcomed him
like a son and wanted to make him their heir. He refused, for his
were not earthly ambitions. When he returned home, he found
his family at last established in a prosperous business in Castellazzo. At once he resumed his life of penance, with far greater
ardor than before. He was waiting for God's hour, listening
intently for inspirations from above, meanwhile practicing all the
virtues and ever greater detachment from earthly things.

God's plans were not revealed to him immediately. Such is
ordinarily His way. Joan of Arc's voices at first told her merely
"to be devout, sweet, and good."

A few months after his return home, his desire for solitude —
which for all its vagueness had kept him from entering one of the
existing religious orders — became more precise. One day as he
looked at the little church of Our Lady of Gazzo on the isolated
mountaintop near Sestri, he crystallized his resolution to retire far
from the world. He was unable to carry it out immediately, but
a short time later he felt a still more powerful inspiration to withdraw into solitude.

We must let our Saint tell us about it in his own words. On the command of his confessor, Bishop di Gattinara of Alessandria, he has written about it in matchless terms:[2]

" . . . God gave me these inspirations together with great interior consolation. At the same time, the thought came to me of wearing a tunic of coarse black cloth, made of the most ordinary wool of the region, to walk barefoot, to live in the greatest poverty — in a word to live, with the grace of God, a life of penance. After that, the thought never left me. An ever more compelling attraction was leading me to withdraw, now no longer to the little church of which I have spoken, but to any solitude whatever, so that I might follow the loving inspirations of my God, whose infinite goodness was calling me to leave the world.

"As I could not carry out this holy inspiration because I was needed by my family, that is, by my father, mother, and brothers, I kept my vocation a secret except when I consulted with my spiritual father. I did not know what God wanted of me. That is why I thought of nothing but liberating myself from domestic problems so that I could withdraw from the world. But the Supreme Good, Who in His infinite mercy had other plans for this wretched earthworm, never allowed me to have my freedom at that time. Whenever I was about to be completely free, new difficulties would arise. They merely increased my yearnings.

"At times the idea came to me to gather together companions so that we might live in community and promote fear of God in souls. That was my most compelling desire. I did not take this notion of finding companions seriously, and yet it remained fixed in the depths of my heart.

"In short, so as not to expatiate further, I shall say that these desires and inspirations persisted until I received the new inspiration of which I shall speak. I cannot tell precisely how long it was, because I kept no record of it. I shall say that at most it lasted about two and a half years. . . . "[3]

A persistent and increasingly vehement desire for solitude and penance which was thwarted by circumstances, a yearning for apostolic action, and the purpose of founding a new congregation — a purpose that frightened him, as he was to admit at the end of his life:[4] these were the thoughts that filled Paul's mind upon his return from Novello. It was a rather contradictory state of soul, but at least Paul was eagerly waiting for God to show him the way.

It was in these circumstances that Paul received the Sacrament of Confirmation on April 23, 1719, from the hands of Bishop di Gattinara. The fact that he was twenty-five when he was confirmed may cause considerable surprise nowadays, but it was the custom at that time. St. Alphonsus was the same age when he received this sacrament.

We can well imagine, without fear of exaggerating, the sentiments with which Paul Danei received the gifts of the Holy Spirit that made him a soldier of Christ in a special way. He was still looking for his vocation, not yet knowing what God wanted of him. But God found him ready to receive the mission He had prepared for him.

Paul's vocation was revealed to him in a succession of visions that were increasingly precise, as he himself has related.[5]

The first vision took place during May or June 1720. On December 7, 1720, he wrote: "Last summer, I do not know exactly when, as I do not remember the month or the day, not having written them down — I know only that it was at the time of the harvest, a weekday — I received Holy Communion in the church of the Capuchins in Castellazzo and I remember that I then entered a state of deep recollection. After that I started home, and I walked through the streets as recollected as during mental prayer. When I was at the corner of the street next to my house I was raised up in God in very deep recollection, in oblivion of all things, and with great interior serenity. And in that moment I saw myself in spirit clothed in a black garment that touched the ground, with a white cross on my breast. On the cross, the Name of Jesus was written in white letters. In that same instant I heard these very words spoken to me: 'This is a sign to show how pure and stainless must be the heart that is to bear written upon it the most holy Name of Jesus.'

"This vision and these words made me weep, and then I stopped."

The vision had come to an end. Another followed. "Shortly

afterward, I saw in spirit that I was being presented the holy tunic with the sacred Name of Jesus and the pure white cross. The tunic, however, was black, and I kissed it with a joyful heart."

The invitation was clear. Paul was henceforth to wear a similar garment.

But it is not clear who the person was who presented the tunic to him. The Saint continues:

"Whoever reads this account should know that when I saw the holy tunic presented to me, I did not see any corporeal form, as for example the figure of a man. That, no, but I did see in God. The soul knows that it is God because He Himself makes it understand by the interior movements of the heart and by the light that He pours into the mind. But He does this in such a sublime manner that it is difficult to explain it. What the soul then hears is something so great that it cannot be spoken or written."

Is this not like an echo of St. Paul's famous vision, relating what no human eye has seen nor ear heard?

Our Saint tries his hand at it nonetheless, for he continues: "In order to be better understood, I shall say that this is a sort of spiritual vision, such as God has deigned to grant me several times in His goodness when He wanted to send me an unusual trial."

He cites one of these trials as an example:

"While I was at prayer, I saw a whip in God's hands, and this whip had cords like disciplines. Above it was written: *Love*. In the same instant the Lord raised me to a very high contemplation, my soul understood that God wanted to scourge it, but out of love. . . . "

He interrupted his account to explain, with masterly skill, these extraordinary phenomena:

"I write these things to explain what I want to say and to declare . . . that I hold what I see in spirit through the sublime light of faith to be more certain than if I saw it with the eyes of my body. My eyes could seduce me by some phantom. Here on the contrary there is no danger of error because of the understanding that God gives me, and also because I trust to the judgment of my superiors, accepting the decisions that the Holy Spirit inspires them to make.

"Thus, when I said that I had seen it in the hands of God, I do not mean to say that I saw. I mean only that the soul senses in a very elevated way that it is in the One Who is immense, and that is what happened to me in the case of the holy tunic."

After having clearly set down his mystical states and explained how, without the help of the senses and of the discursive intellect, the soul perceives God and revealed realities in the mystical state, Paul goes on:

"To continue my account of the wonders of God after the vision of the holy tunic and of the sacred sign, God gave me a greater desire and attraction for gathering together companions and founding, with the approbation of Holy Mother Church, a congregation which would be called: *The Poor of Jesus.*

"After that, God impressed upon my mind the form of the Holy Rule that was to be observed by the Poor Men of Jesus and myself, His very humble and unworthy servant. . . . "

Our readers will no doubt be lenient with us for giving these long citations. We had to let the Saint speak for himself, for fear of betraying the divine message in the process of transposing it. Who can fail to admire the mastery of this young man, scantily educated and yet rich in mystical experience, as he explains his intimate relations with God?

He had other visions that confirmed him in his vocation, although we have no detailed account of them. There was one, however, which he revealed toward the end of his life and which shows the role the Blessed Virgin Mary chose to play in his mission.

He had seen her, he said, dressed in black and wearing the emblem of the Passion on her breast.

"Oh! How beautiful she was, how extremely beautiful! I did not dare look at her!"

"Paul," she had said to him, "you must adopt this uniform and found a congregation that will wear perpetual mourning for the Passion and death of my divine Son."[6]

45

God's plans, so long in preparation and so patiently awaited, were now clear.

How could he hesitate? The path seemed to open up before him, straight and simple, even though hard to follow. He lovingly kissed the hand that held the whip, his eyes fixed on the one word *Love*, and he accepted the divine mission. He was twenty-seven years old.

He had no idea that the drama of his life was just beginning.

Drama? This is a big word when it is taken to include tragic catastrophies. Paul was to die in his eighty-third year, revered and surrounded by his spiritual sons.

But there are interior dramas more poignant than bloody trage-dies. Paul had been chosen by God for a very specific mission. Of this he was sure in his soul and conscience. And yet he was to see the most unexpected obstacles rise in his path. Although he never doubted his mission, he was at times to fear that he himself, by his sins, was placing obstacles to the fulfillment of God's plans.

Part One

THE ERRANT LIFE
FROM DEFEAT TO DEFEAT

(1720–1730)

Chapter IV

RECEIVING THE HABIT
AND THE FORTY-DAY RETREAT

"Sorrow at leaving his father's poor house forever."

"I PUT my trust in the judgment of my superiors, submitting to the decisions that the Holy Spirit will inspire them to make."[1] These words, which Paul wrote soon afterward, reveal the attitude that guided his conduct from the start.

Deeply convinced that he had been called by God to an extraordinary vocation, he went to see Bishop di Gattinara of Alessandria, made a general confession to him of his entire past life, revealed to him the visions he had had, and expressed his ideas to him orally and in writing.

The Bishop was a learned man, as well as a devout and prudent one. His portrait, which can still be seen at the "casa di San Paolo" in Ovada, shows him to be a kind and gentle person. He did in fact have a tender heart. Although he was a fiery and moving orator, he was easily moved to emotion himself. The saying was current in those days, and it was not without a barb of malice: "We don't know whether he pours out his sweat or his tears in greater abundance."

His charity was proverbial. His entire income was distributed either as alms to the poor or as bounties to religious institutions. He was later transferred from his see in Alessandria to the see of Turin. He died in Turin in 1743, offering up his life for his people, who were then afflicted by the War of the Austrian Succession.

In 1722 he was still Bishop of Alessandria, whose extent was no greater than that of a modern French deanery. This would explain, for lack of other reasons, why he was able to take a direct and active interest in Paul Danei's projects.

He listened to the extraordinary account of Paul's visions, had him put them in writing, and was moved to tears by his heavenly communications.

However, being prudent, he sent Paul to consult with enlightened directors and then asked their opinion. The results of these many examinations were favorable, and Bishop di Gattinara promised to clothe him with the penitential habit of the hermits.

Paul received as a gift, perhaps from the very hand of his Bishop, some coarse material which he had dyed black and made into a long tunic held in at the waist by a cord. This was indeed the habit contemplated in the visions, but not the complete habit of the proposed Institute. It did not bear the insignia of the Passion.

The reason for this omission was that Bishop di Gattinara wanted to proceed by prudent stages, protecting the rights of the Holy See. He had no jurisdiction over the foundation of a new institute with distinctive marks, nor over the right to gather companions together. However, he allowed Paul to devote himself officially to a life of penance in a solitary place. This was the vocation of the hermits and recluses.

We must not confuse the hermits and the recluses. They pursued the same goal of penance and prayer, to be sure, but by different means. The former lived close to nature, far from inhabited areas. The latter had voluntarily vowed themselves to religious reclusion; that is, to voluntary confinement in a walled-in cell containing only one aperture through which indispensable food was passed to them.

There were many women recluses, but few women hermits. The solitude of the woods was not suited to the feminine sex.

The eremitical life dates from the early days of the Church and flourished in the deserts of Egypt. From the sixth century on it was practiced in the West, where the hermits followed the Rule of St. Benedict. Hermits were under the control of a neighboring monastery at first, but soon afterward came under the jurisdiction of the bishops.

Their entrance into solitude was often inaugurated by the emission of vows of chastity and obedience before their bishop, who imposed the habit while reciting a formula. The habit and the formula were variable.

In general the hermits wore tunics and capes. Their bare legs and feet, their long hair, and their abundant, unkempt beards gave them a venerable and yet shabby appearance.

The formula invited the hermit to live a chaste, sober, and holy life, amid vigils, fasts, labor, prayer, and works of charity.

Whether clerics or laymen, they retired near an existing chapel or built their own oratory. And close by they built themselves a small cell with a door and a single window. The site was always preferably deep in the forest.

Completely surrounding the cell and chapel was a clearing in which the hermit cultivated vegetables, maintained an orchard, an apiary, and a few vines. He often had a *famulus* who shared his solitude, a fellow penitent or disciple; for it is written in Scripture: "*Vae soli* [Woe to him that is alone]!" (Eccles. 4:10.)

In this rustic environment the hermits devoted themselves to manual and intellectual labors, but above all to prayer and mortification. They tortured their bodies with chains and coats of mail worn on the bare flesh. They considered salt superfluous, in accordance with the words: "*Quia cinerem tanquam panem manducabam* [For I eat ashes as bread]." (Ps. 101:10.)

Having no witnesses to their austerities, they were protected from vainglory. And yet they had some contacts with the world. They gave shelter to travelers who were alone or who had lost their way. Many came to them for counsel, and literature has given us accounts of their role.

Thus Isolde, under the spell of the love potion, confided in the hermit Ogrin:

> *Sire, por Dieu omnipotent*
> *Il ne m'aime, ni je lui*
> *Fors par un herbe dont je buis*
> *Et il en but: ce fut péché,*
> *Pour ce, nous a le roi chassés.*

> Sire, by almighty God
> He loves me not, nor I him
> But for a potion which I drank
> And he, too: there was sin,
> And for this the king has banished us.

Revered as men of sound judgment, they were more popular during the Middle Ages than the monks who lived sheltered behind monastery walls. These hermits were out in the open view of passers-by.

But they were not safe from temptations. Sometimes solitude weighed too heavily on them and they became vagabonds. And so they were obliged to receive episcopal authorization before changing their domicile. Finally the Council of Trent commanded all hermits to enter religious orders.

However, with the Church's tolerance, there have been hermits even until the present era. Who has not heard of the hermit of the Sahara, Father Charles de Foucauld? And even though there are hardly any hermits left in the world, many hermitages remain that give us some idea of their mode of life.[2]

In the presence of a vocation so extraordinary, Bishop di Gattinara orientated Paul Danei toward the eremitical life. While this life did not correspond completely with Paul's visions, it did satisfy his burning desire for solitude and penance and left the future uncommitted.

Paul would have liked to receive the habit on November 21, the Feast of the Presentation of the Blessed Virgin Mary in the temple, but since the next day was a Friday he chose that day in memory of the Passion.

The day before the clothing ceremony, Paul visited the churches of Castellazzo, had his hair cut short as a mark of renunciation, bade farewell to his loved ones, asked forgiveness of all the members of his family, and invited them to join with him in reciting the *Te Deum* and the psalm *Miserere*.[3]

The next morning he set out for Alessandria, not joyfully as we might have expected, but amid "great struggles" and filled with sorrow at "leaving his father's poor house forever."

The goal he had so eagerly desired now seemed repugnant to him when he was about to attain it. Even stranger than his interior combats was the fact that he who loved to walk barefoot, as so many peasants in the Apennines still do, went from Castellazzo to Alessandria well shod; yet he suffered so much from the cold on the way that he feared he would not be able to live barefoot from that time on.

When he arrived, he was told that the Bishop was absent and would not be back that day. Paul obstinately waited, and Bishop di Gattinara returned to keep his appointment with him.

The prelate blessed the habit, which was of such coarse material that it seemed to be woven of horsehair or goats' hair. Paul put on the tunic, which, together with the simple underpants of equally rough material, must have caused scabs on his arms and legs. He put a heavy cord around his waist and a cross on his breast. This completed the attire of the "poor man of Jesus."[4]

It was not until twenty years later that Paul added a coat, hat, and sandals to his habit, at the express desire of Pope Benedict XIV.

After receiving the habit, Paul should have gone directly to some isolated sanctuary or chapel to live his hermit's life. However, he obtained a delay from Bishop di Gattinara and left Alessandria the next day to return to Castellazzo.

Without stopping at his father's house, he took up his abode outside the church of St. Charles, in a damp, narrow shelter between the apse and the sacristy. The dwelling consisted of a ground floor and an upper story joined by a narrow wooden stairway. The ground floor was lighted by a small window high on the wall. It has been preserved just as it was then. An altar has been placed in it, around which are gathered mementos similar to those in the "casa di San Paolo" in Ovada. There are a portrait of the Saint, a death mask, his instruments of penance, his breviary, devotional books, and letters written in his own hand.

This abode was temporarily assigned by the Bishop to the new hermit at his own request. Paul wanted to spend forty days there, evidently to commemorate Christ's sojourn in the desert at the start of His public life. But he also wanted to meditate upon the mission that God had revealed to him, set it down in writing, and compose the Rule of the future Congregation, so as to provide Bishop di Gattinara with the information he needed to evaluate and approve these projects if he saw fit.

Paul remained in the shelter from November 23, 1720, until January 1, 1721, living solely on bread and water, sleeping a few hours each night wrapped in a blanket and stretched out on vine branches spread out in a narrow trough.[5]

He occupied his days and a part of the nights as sacristan, sweeping the church, adorning the altars, reciting the divine office. His free hours were spent in mental prayer, keeping a diary, and drafting the Rule of his Institute.[6]

A copy of this diary, written at the express request of Bishop di Gattinara, has been preserved.[7]

Without literary pretensions, often repeating the same words, and even using incorrect and incomplete sentences, from day to day he noted down with great precision his impressions, graces received, and interior trials, in order to enlighten the director of his soul.

Thus on November 23 he wrote: "Saturday, which was the first day of my retreat at St. Charles, I received Holy Communion, unworthy though I am. I was neither particularly recollected nor distracted. The remainder of the day I was inwardly sad, with a melancholy of a special kind which is not like that experienced amid the trials of the world. But it is a certain interior suffering of the mind and heart, mingled with secret temptations that are scarcely understood and, because of that, greatly afflict the soul. One no longer knows where he is, so to speak, inasmuch as there is no sensible sign of mental prayer. I know that God makes me understand that they purify the soul. I know that through the mercy of our dear God, I do not want to experience anything else, or enjoy any consolation, that I want only to be crucified with Jesus."

"Tuesday, the 26th. I made my night prayer, unworthy though I am, and was dry except at the start when I experienced a very subtle and delicate interior sweetness. I then received Holy Communion and was raised up in God in a special way with a very lofty sweetness and a certain warmth of heart. . . . "

"Wednesday, the 27th. I made my night prayer. At the start I was very recollected, and this lasted for some time. Then I experienced anxiety of mind and temptation which lasted only a short while. Holy Communion was accompanied by a very lofty sweetness and elevation in God, mingled with tears. And then I remembered having heard that people were saying I would not be able to withstand this deprivation; at that instant my joy and my desire for sufferings were so great that the cold, the snow, and the frost seemed sweet to me, and I desired them with great fervor. . . . I know that I also experienced a special urge to go to Rome for the sake of this great wonder of God [the future Congregation]. I also asked my Supreme Good if He wants me to write the Rule for the poor of Jesus, and I felt a strong urge accompanied with great sweetness. I rejoiced that our great God wants to make use of this great sinner, and on the other hand, I didn't know where to cast myself, seeing myself so worthless. . . . "

A new vision confirmed Paul in his plans:

"Thursday, the 28th . . . I remember that I was praying to the Blessed Virgin in union with all the angels and saints, and especially the Holy Founders, when all of a sudden it seemed to me in spirit that I saw them prostrate before the Most Holy Majesty of God and praying for that end. It happened to me in an instant like a lightning flash of sweetness mingled with tears. The manner in which I saw it was not with any corporeal form. It was in spirit, with the understanding of the soul that I cannot explain, and almost at once it disappeared. . . . "

On December 2, the tenth day of his retreat, Paul began to draft the Rule of his proposed Institute.

He recited Matins before daybreak, engaged in mental prayer, and then started to work. He himself has admitted: "I wrote as quickly as if someone had been dictating to me from the pulpit. I felt the words come to me from my heart. Certainly all this proceeds from a special inspiration from God. From my own person, there is only iniquity and ignorance."[8]

On December 7 everything was completed. It consisted of a preamble in which Paul told of the mission that he had received from God, and of a dozen chapters inspired by the life of St. Francis of Assisi and his own attraction to solitude.

The Rule lacked precision, perhaps, as they had to be retouched later in order to be approved. Perhaps, too, they did not make sufficient allowances for the universal weakness of human nature. But our Saint tells us that they were maintained intact "as to their substance, just as he had received them from the Lord."[9]

All that actually remains of them is the preamble and a few fragments.[10]

Once the Rule was written, Paul continued his retreat. It was interspersed with sensible consolations, dryness, physical and moral temptations, and trials. "I was tempted to gluttony, I used to get very hungry, I felt the cold more than usual, and my flesh yearned to be comforted, and this made me want to omit mental prayer. . . . The devil had his part in it, too, because I know he is very jealous of anyone who devotes himself to mental prayer. And then, as I have said, my resistance made my heart pound, I would shake from head to foot . . . but through God's mercy I said I want [sic] to remain as I am, even if I had to be carried away in pieces. . . ."[11]

Sometimes his meditation would broaden out. On December 26, before the Blessed Sacrament, he thought of those who deny "this most adorable mystery. I desired the conversion of heretics, especially of those in England and its neighboring kingdoms, and I prayed especially for this intention during Holy Communion. . . ."[12]

He dreamed of martyrdom. "The yearning is always with me to die a martyr, especially for the Most Blessed Sacrament, that is, in some place where people do not believe in it."[13] This he added on the twenty-ninth.

And the diary closes on January 1 with an effusion of love for "Jesus, present in the Blessed Sacrament."

That same day, his soul radiant and transfigured, he set out for Alessandria. His diary in its sincerity would complete the briefing of Bishop di Gattinara. The inspired Rule was ready to be approved. The companions about whom he already had presentiments could not fail to come. The "Poor of Jesus" were going to gather together, to live and preach the Passion of Christ.

We can imagine Paul's joy as he journeyed to Alessandria, unmindful of the stones that wounded his bare feet, completely engrossed in his interior dream, attuned to the vast expanses of the plains of the Po River.

Inebriated by the sharp air after his forty days of claustration, he walked with a light step, unaware that he was going straight toward his first disappointment.

Chapter V

THE HERMIT

"God, being pleased with His servant and in order to authenticate his mission, marked him with His own sign."

BISHOP DI GATTINARA received Paul with great kindness. But with his customary prudence he decided not to give his approbation to his plans.

During Paul's retreat near the church of St. Charles, the Bishop had indeed received a letter from Father Columban, Paul's spiritual director, warmly recommending two young men to be his companions: Anthony Schiaffino and Michel-Angelo Michellini, who were likewise favored with extraordinary graces and eager to become Paul's associates.

However, the Bishop hesitated to express himself. When Paul insisted, invoking the light he had received and the mission God had entrusted to him, the Bishop made the common-sense reply:

"How is it possible that you should be the only one to receive all the light? I should like to have some myself."[1]

Endowed with at least human insight, the good Bishop sent his penitent to Genoa to seek counsel "from a great servant of God widely renowned for his wisdom and extremely competent in discerning genuine inspirations." All we know of this holy man is contained in the above evaluation of him by St. Strambi, St. Paul's disciple and first biographer. It may have been Father Columban himself, who was then staying at the Capuchin monastery of Ponte Decimo near Genoa.

It was the coldest part of the winter. The distance from Alessandria to Genoa was about forty-seven miles, cutting through the Apennines, including the Bocchetta Range and the deep ravines of Scrivia. Today a magnificent motor parkway with sumptuously lighted tunnels makes this journey a picturesque drive. "Paul Danei made the trip on foot in the heart of winter, without any hat, coat, or sandals, in a wind that blew so violently it sometimes catapulted horses and carriages into ravines."[2]

On the night of Epiphany, January 6, he was in the Bocchetta Range. The cold was intense, and the wind howled. Paul did not even have any bread to eat. He met several sentries on their rounds and begged their charity on his knees. They had pity on him and gave him something to eat.

Paul always preserved a lively memory of his meeting with those sentries. Later he liked to retell this episode, and on his missions he always took a special interest in riflemen. If they have no other patron saint, they can certainly look to St. Paul of the Cross as their protector.

When Paul reached more populated areas, he did not receive any such welcome. Seeing him in his pitiful garb, people would say: "That man must have committed some terrible crimes. See what a penance his confessor has imposed on him!"

Upon arriving in Genoa he encountered the ridicule of two religious who laughingly cried out when they caught sight of him: "*Quare fremuerunt gentes et populi meditati sunt inania* [Why do the nations rage and the people devise vain things]?" (Ps. 2:1.)[3] Chilled to the bone, unshaven, he no longer needed any disguise to arouse scorn.

When Paul later narrated these facts, he concluded simply: "I must admit that these scoffs and jeers were very salutary for my soul."[4]

In Genoa he was offered hospitality by Count Caesar Nicholas Canefri, who also had a country home in Castellazzo. Two Jesuit Fathers came to visit him, either spontaneously or at the command of Bishop di Gattinara. They listened to him and interrogated him for an hour and went away with an excellent impression. They told Count Canefri, according to his son's statement at the canonization process: "Make allowances for him. There is good in him."[5]

As for the "personage renowned for his wisdom" whom Paul had come to consult, we do not know what his opinion was. At any rate, Paul returned to Castellazzo and established his abode near the chapel of the Holy Trinity, about a half hour from the center of the town.

He stayed there only two weeks, until January 25. It has been asked why this sojourn was so short. He was probably awaiting the decision that he was sure Bishop di Gattinara would make after he received the report on his interviews with the Jesuits in Genoa.

The decision did come, but it was not the one Paul was hoping for. His Bishop was assigning him as a hermit to the chapel of St. Stephen on the outskirts of Castellazzo. He was permitted to devote himself to apostolic action but not to associate companions to his way of life.

Paul settled down in a narrow room, whose only furnishings were a straw mat and a blanket, a crucifix and a discipline on the wall.

At the door he hung a small basket with the inscription: "Give alms to the Poor Man of Jesus." Into the basket passers-by deposited a few pieces of bread and some onions. A well nearby furnished him with an abundance of drinking water.[6]

Paul's brother, John Baptist, who had followed in his footsteps from early childhood and had continued to live a penitential life, often came to share the hermit's poverty. One day their father came upon them in a state of total destitution and had help brought to them.

Another devout young man, Paul Sardi, came. He too aspired to enter the future Congregation, but he found less than satisfaction in the "inexhaustible wine cellar," as the hermit archly called the well. Sardi said "it made him sick to drink water in the morning." Later he became a canon.

The Marchesa del Pozzo, a great lady who owned much property and was to remain Paul's protectress, liked to discuss spiritual matters with him. She sometimes accepted his invitation to share his meager meal of bread, salad, and onions.[7]

The fact is that, almost as soon as he was settled at St. Stephen's, Paul began to devote himself to the apostolic ministry. His conquering zeal accomplished wonders.

He started by teaching catechism to the children. The archpriest of Castellazzo advised him to wait until the carnival was over, and Paul acquiesced. But the next day, during his mental prayer, he inwardly heard the Lord's voice reproaching him severely.

Without a moment's delay he went through the streets of the town and to the public places, holding up his crucifix and crying out: "Come to catechism class in St. Charles Church."

This behavior was less unusual than might at first appear. In the life of St. Alphonsus Liguori we read that he acted in the same manner in the streets of Naples.

Paul's call was heard not only by children but also by adults. Either out of devotion or curiosity, crowds filled the church and kept coming day after day. The clergy, therefore, took over the catechizing of the children. Bishop di Gattinara authorized Paul to preach to the adults from the pulpit, just as Innocent III had once done for Francis of Assisi.

Paul was assigned to preach the sermons for the four Sundays preceding Lent (the Lenten season having already been assigned to a well-known preacher) and also to preach a triduum during the carnival.

Paul chose to announce his sermons by going through Castellazzo with his crucifix in one hand and a bell in the other. Sometimes he wore a rope around his neck and a crown of thorns on his head. Usually a group of children followed him, singing popular hymns.

Once he had his congregation before him, Paul would preach a fiery sermon. There was nothing very polished about it, but it was spoken with such conviction and interspersed with such poignant apostrophes either to the crucifix or to sinners that the crowd would cry out with one voice: "We repent!"

For two hours he held his audience under his spell. If a hysterical or possessed woman threatened to disturb the gathering, he was not afraid to command the devil to be quiet, and silence would be restored, to the amazement of all present.

He commented with such heart-rending accents on Jesus' prayer for His executioners that enemies became reconciled. The results were remarkable. The carnival was canceled that year in Castellazzo, and the triduum closed with a general Communion.

For obvious reasons Paul did not hear confessions. He did, however, prepare perplexed penitents for the sacrament when they came to him for counsel. This was his first bitter encounter with the sinfulness of men, and he later admitted: "Until then I had imagined people lived better lives."[8]

But he also discovered the intoxicating joy of the spoken word, in all humility, to be sure: "Souls belong to God, the fruit comes from God, and I can claim no credit."[9] He became aware of the magnificent and gratuitous gift he had received to communicate his conviction, to make his soul enter the soul of the crowd: "It now appears evident to me that it is the Will of God that I devote myself to this holy occupation."[10]

Paul's conquering enthusiasm did not wane with the coming of the Lenten season. He left the great sermons to well-known preachers. For himself, he chose to give a daily talk in the form of a meditation on the Passion at the oratory of St. Stephen. He spoke to the women in the morning and to the men at night.

His renown spread even to cloistered convents. The canonesses of St. Augustine wanted to hear him. He asked authorization from Bishop di Gattinara to speak to them[11] and obtained serious reforms in their convent.

The nuns had been in the habit of relaxing their regulations at carnival time and allowing masked persons to visit them in the parlor. To anyone who has read the life of St. Teresa of Ávila before her total conversion, these strange practices will cause no surprise.

Paul delivered the message through one of his aunts, who was a nun at the convent. "If you don't tell them," he said, "I shall come publicly, crucifix in hand, to give a severe reprimand."[12] She delivered his message and the abuse ceased.

Consumed with zeal, he would have carried out his threat without a moment's hesitation. Similarly, he did not hesitate to appear, crucifix in hand, at a ball, where his presence soon dispersed the dancers. Nor did he fear to intervene in a fight where men were throwing knives at each other.[13]

God, being pleased with His servant and in order to authenticate his mission, marked him with His own sign.

In his leisure moments between sermons Paul devoted himself to works of charity. He buried the dead who were abandoned for fear of contagion, and he visited the sick.

It happened that Charles Vegetto, who supplied the hermit with firewood, injured his leg. He neglected it and the wound became infected. Paul visited him, untied the bandage, and told the patient to turn his head away. He then licked the purulent sore. The next day the doctor found the wound free of pus, and it soon healed completely. Paul had begged Charles Vegetto not to tell anyone, but the latter lost no time in publicizing his cure.[14]

This brings to mind the kiss Francis of Assisi gave the leper. It also explains the extraordinary influence exerted by Paul Danei, marked by the sign of God.

How could he have failed to plan to complete the divine work by founding the Congregation that he had so clearly foreseen?

This was always in his thoughts, despite his recent disappointment. The two young men recommended by Father Columban had not been accepted by Bishop di Gattinara. As soon as Paul was settled at St. Stephen's, he reported to his Bishop on the first successes of his apostolate and asked him to allow Paul Sardi, a devout young man of Castellazzo, to join him. He gave him the highest praise, saying: "His example will do me great good."[15]

John Baptist, our Saint's brother, often came to visit him and wanted to share his life. Other friends of their youth were eager to join the two brothers. But there were already three religious houses of men in Castellazzo — the Augustinians, the Servites, and the Capuchins. All of them clung to their privileges, and the last-named were neighbors of the hermitage at St. Stephen's. Quite naturally they feared lest a new congregation should siphon off some of the alms on which they all depended.

Once again the Bishop's answer was "No." And he was never to change his mind.

At first Paul, no longer daring to intervene himself, let his friends renew their requests. Later he counseled them against it, saying: "Nothing can come of it."[16]

In the end the Bishop did impose the habit on John Baptist, but on condition that the two brothers be accepted in another diocese.

And yet God's command was quite explicit. Paul had not reached the stage where he could write, as he did later: "I have not the slightest concern or worry lest this plan for the foundation of a retreat should run aground on a sand bar. I let the water flow where God wills. It goes toward the sea, its outlet."[17] He had a definite mission to fulfill.

Chapter VI

IN PURSUIT OF THE VISION

"I have so much trust in my crucified Lord, that I have absolute certitude everything will succeed."

FACED with the checkmate of his plans for a foundation in Castellazzo, Paul immediately set out to find a locality that would welcome him and to obtain authorization from the Holy See.

He remained under the jurisdiction of his Bishop, however, and the movements of hermits from place to place were strictly regu-

lated to avoid temptations to vagrancy. Paul thus had to explain
his new plans to Bishop di Gattinara:

"I must make known to Your Excellency that I feel increasingly inspired to leave for Rome. But before going, I should like
to go out of devotion to the holy mountain of Varallo; for I cannot alas! visit Jerusalem where my beloved Jesus suffered so much
for me. I had this desire to go to Varallo when I was still a layman, but at present it is more pressing. . . ."[1]

The purpose of his journey to Rome was obviously to obtain
the authorization to found a new congregation. He made no secret
of it and showed complete trust in the Bishop: "When I am
at the feet of His Holiness, God will reveal His mercies to the
whole world. I have so much trust in my crucified Lord that I have
absolute certitude everything will succeed. . . . What have I to
fear? I would be afraid of sinning through infidelity if I
doubted. . . ."[2]

The purpose of the pilgrimage was not specified, and Paul could
scarcely reveal it to Bishop di Gattinara, inasmuch as it was apparently his intention to find a place during his travels that would
be favorable to his foundation plans. In short, he was planning
to leave the diocese of Alessandria for good.

Varallo is a charming little summer resort among the lakes in
the heart of the Pennine Alps. Its Way of the Cross on the Sacro
Monte was a pilgrimage shrine. Built at the beginning of the six-
teenth century, it consisted of a series of chapels sheltering groups
of life-size terra cotta statues. The walls were adorned with frescoes
by Gaudenzio Ferrari representing scenes of the Passion.

It was here that St. Charles Borromeo had loved to come and
meditate at each Station of the Cross. Paul Danei had long wanted
to make the pilgrimage out of devotion to the Passion. The idea
now came to him that it also offered him an opportunity of dis-
covering a suitable retreat. It was best for him to know where he
could settle before asking Rome for the authorization to found
a new congregation.

Bishop di Gattinara was finally persuaded to allow Paul to absent
himself from his hermitage. He gave him a safe-conduct dated
April 18, 1721, recommending him to the charity of the faithful.[3]

Not much is known about the pilgrimage to Monte Varallo, except that Paul passed through Turin, where the future Cardinal Delle Lanze noticed him in his shabby hermit's attire, hatless and coatless and without sandals.[4] It is also known that he made this trip before the end of winter, since the snow and cold deterred him from establishing his proposed foundation in the Alps.[5]

The pilgrimage over, Paul returned to the hermitage of St. Stephen near Castellazzo, to await an opportunity to go to Rome. Meanwhile, consumed once more by his thirst for souls, he preached missions in various places, including Retorto and Porta-Nuova, on the lands of the Marchesa del Pozzo.[6]

Won over by the preacher's burning faith, the Marchesa followed one of the penitential processions barefoot. She also kept in her palace as a precious souvenir the heavy cross that Paul had carried on his shoulders as he led the throng.

Even the clergy were moved by the hermit's fiery eloquence, and one of these hearers reports that "he was trembling with fear and respect" when he officiated at the closing of one of the missions.[7]

Early in September, Paul left for Rome. He went to Genoa first, where the princely Pallavicini family offered him hospitality and helped to arrange sea passage for him to Civitavecchia.

His brother John Baptist had come in the hope of joining him, but Paul sent him back to Castellazzo. The latter consented, but not without a strange warning: "All right, go. But you will not find any rest without me."[8]

Paul embarked alone, and the voyage was without incident except for a forced stop at the foot of Monte Argentario. It was September 8, the Feast of the Nativity of the Blessed Virgin Mary. The wind had fallen suddenly, leaving the ship motionless. While the sailors disembarked on the narrow beach to pick wild grapes, Paul gazed at the solitary mountain in wonderment. From the depths of the thickets the rocky cliffs loomed, and he caught glimpses of their grottoes.

Did he know that these grottoes had once sheltered the monks whose virtues St. Gregory proclaims in his *Dialogues?*[9] In any case, he felt a strong desire to live there in solitude and resolved to settle there if he did not receive Rome's approbation for his projects.

We know what his plans were. It is therefore probable that he had already chosen the precise site for his foundation. It could not have been Castellazzo, where "there was nothing to hope for."

The wind again swelled the sails. Sailors and passengers embarked, and the next day the ship touched the port of Civitavecchia.

Before entering the lazaretto for the obligatory quarantine, Paul wrote to his brother, whom he had rather abruptly sent home. After reassuring him that his crossing had been pleasant except for the first day, he added to console him: "When I am in Rome, I shall give you news about everything. I hope that we shall be together both during our life on earth and in heaven. . . ."[10]

During the quarantine, which according to custom lasted about ten days, Paul lived on the alms of two buns given him by the administration. He spent his enforced leisure copying the Rule he had written in the church of St. Charles, and also catechizing his companions in the lazaretto.

When the doors were opened, he set out for Rome on foot, following the Via Aurelia, a distance of over fifty miles. An innkeeper gave him lodging for the night, and a Spanish traveler bought him some food.

As he approached the Holy City, he fell to his knees and kissed the earth sanctified by the steps and the blood of the Apostles and martyrs, then went straight to St. Peter's.

His prayer at St. Peter's brought him only dryness and interior desolation. Was this an omen?

He sought lodging at the almshouse of the Holy Trinity, the hostel for poor pilgrims from the Piedmont and upper Italy. At this hostel Cardinal Tolomei washed the pilgrims' feet and had alms of money and two buns distributed to each one. Paul was willing enough to have his feet washed, but he left the money for the other paupers. Of the two buns, he kept one for the next day.

Early that morning he went to the Vatican to seek an audience with the Holy Father. Had not Francis of Assisi approached Innocent III on his own initiative?

Paul was received in the Papal Palace by an usher, or perhaps — as some claim — by the Pope's own chamberlain. It really does not matter except that he was almost immediately shown out as a dangerous vagabond on the strength of his wretched appearance. "Don't you know how many ruffians come here every day? Leave! Go!" This was the answer he received to his naïve request.

He returned to the street discomfited but not discouraged. "I experienced no displeasure on this occasion, but went out quietly and with bowed head. I had an interior illumination telling me that the time for the approbation of the Rule had not yet arrived."[11]

Inwardly consoled after his humble acceptance of this rebuff, he felt the pangs of hunger. He sat down near a fountain beneath the balcony of a neighboring house and was just about to take a hearty bite of the bun he had saved from the night before when a pauper came up to him for alms.

He had the courage to share his bun at once. Later he told his religious about it good-humoredly, to amuse them: "I was hungry enough to eat two buns instead of one. Consider my plight before such a request." And as they pressed him to know what wonders he had admired in Rome, he answered ironically that, "being barefoot, he had to look at the ground to see where he set his feet."[12] How could he admit that his modesty and detachment had kept him from enjoying works of art?

At the Church of St. Mary Major he prayed for a long time before the painting of the Blessed Virgin attributed to St. Luke. It was there that he made the vow to promote devotion to the Passion in the hearts of the faithful and to strive to gather companions around himself.[13] Had not the Virgin Mary already confirmed his mission? At her feet his confidence was restored.

Paul then left Rome. The hour had not yet come for the fulfillment of his plans. He decided to go to Monte Argentario, the sight of which had so enthralled him on his way to Rome.

The return journey was to entail even greater hardships.

Paul had lost his initial enthusiasm. And now new humiliations were in store for him which he was to accept in silence.

He found passage on a ship that was going down the Tiber. He was deep in mental prayer, no doubt engrossed with God's impenetrable designs, when a priest became enraged at him for some unknown reason and poured insults upon him.

Later the boat ran aground on a sand bar and another ship took him aboard. This time it was a lay brother who began to affront him. Paul for his part, "considering himself a sinner, thought people were quite right in treating him in this manner."[14]

Landing at Santa Severa, about twelve miles from Civitavecchia, he reached the town on foot and took refuge in a church to pray. A laborer took him for a vagabond and drove him out. Paul spent the night under the portico of the hospital, and the next morning resumed the fifty-mile journey to Monte Argentario.

At Corneto the Augustinian Fathers offered him hospitality. At Montalto, a Corsican priest took him in. But in the Maremma — an area of vast rolling plains broken by marshes and thick woods and plagued by malaria — night caught him by surprise in the open country. Paul took shelter in an abandoned shepherd's hut overrun with vermin, an annoyance he did not get rid of until he was back in Castellazzo.

The last stage of his journey was the hardest. His soul, inwardly desolate, seemed attuned to the melancholy and unwholesome landscape.

Finally he reached Port'Ercole, one of the three ports of the peninsula. There he was cordially received by the archpriest, who pointed out the spot on the mountain about two miles from town where the hermitage and chapel of the Annunciation were located and which he felt would be most suitable for Paul's plans for retreat and penance.

Paul went at once and remained several days. The site pleased him. In order to settle there permanently, he would need the authorization of the Bishop of Soana. He set out to find him, which was no easy matter.

The Bishop ordinarily resided at Pitigliano, about forty miles away. There were very few dwellings in these parts. Sometimes when our poor hermit reached a crossroad he had no idea which way to turn. His only recourse was to fall on his knees and recommend himself to his guardian angel. "He never lost his way."[15]

As he neared Pitigliano he learned that the Bishop was then at Bienza, a charming little town with a beautiful episcopal palace near a handsome cathedral. For Paul this meant sixty more miles to walk. He went forward without hesitation.

At Bienza the Bishop gave Paul a cordial welcome and gladly permitted him to establish himself on Monte Argentario together with his brother.

Now Paul had to return home by sea and first of all to find a charitable boat owner to take him on board. Being far from the sea, he had to go to Pisa where he embarked on the canal for Leghorn.

The insults began again. Two Spanish priests on their way home from Rome, where they had obtained certain privileges, boasted about their success publicly, with little respect for the Roman congregations. Paul, who had just been so piteously turned away, thought it his duty to admonish them charitably. His remarks infuriated them. A gentleman came to his defense, and he arrived in Leghorn without further incident.

Even before looking for passage home, he had to beg for some food. A Jewish merchant gave him a few pieces of silver, enabling him to buy a bit of bread and wine. With the memory of his Roman experience in mind, he kept half of his ration for the next day. On his way to the port he stopped near a fountain and found his half portion of bread delicious.

There was a ship at the dock loaded with cowhides, ready to sail for Genoa, and the owner agreed to take Paul on. In order not to interfere with the sailing of the ship, Paul had to remain close to the cargo, which gave off a terrible stench. The vermin that still covered his body caused him great suffering. In addition, he imagined that others had become aware of his plight, and this humiliated him.

His bed was simply a board, and he ate whatever the sailors were willing to share with him. Even the ship boy taunted him for eating the bread of others.

When they arrived in Genoa, Paul was quarantined aboard the

launch. As he looked out on the city shining in all its beauty, his own poverty seemed unbearable to him. Then he thought of the agony in the Garden, of the chalice accepted, and the temptation vanished.

Finally he was on the road back to Castellazzo.

What sort of welcome did he receive? What did he say about his journey? We have no idea. We know only that he now realized he needed to have his brother John Baptist with him to live his life of prayer and that he intended to ask Bishop di Gattinara for him.[16]

He was received by the Bishop of Alessandria and no doubt told him about his disappointment in Rome, which must not have greatly surprised the prudent prelate. Then he told of his plans to establish himself on Monte Argentario with his brother.

Bishop di Gattinara agreed to impose the habit of penance upon John Baptist and made no objection to their departure from his diocese. After all, was he not perhaps well rid of the responsibility of such extraordinary vocations, since he himself had not yet been favored with lights from heaven?

On November 28, 1721, the Octave of the Presentation of the Blessed Virgin Mary, John Baptist was clothed in the habit of the Passion. The two brothers remained at St. Stephen's hermitage until the worst of the winter was over.

Paul had asked the Bishop of Soana permission to bring other companions, but had been refused. Bishop Fulvio Salvi said he could come with only one companion, "to live in holy solitude. To act otherwise would require the approval of Holy Church."[17]

Paul had just learned from bitter experience that it was not easy to obtain this approval. The horizon thus remained blocked, perhaps more so than ever before. For "to live in solitude" seemed to exclude even the apostolic ministry of preaching.

Chapter VII

GOLD IN THE CRUCIBLE

"Regnum Dei intra vos est."[1]

ON FEBRUARY 22, 1722, Paul and John Baptist left Castellazzo, to the regret of their compatriots.

They sailed from Genoa for Civitavecchia and retraced their course on foot to Monte Argentario. As they were passing through the locality where Paul had slept in the hut filled with vermin, night overtook them. The wiser for his experience, Paul sought shelter under a tree.

The winter was not over yet, and the following morning they awoke to find themselves covered with white frost. It was Holy Thursday. They had fifteen miles to go before reaching Port'-Ercole. They covered this distance without breaking their fast, so they could receive Holy Communion. The archpriest was just as gracious as on the occasion of Paul's first visit and kept them until the end of Holy Week.

Before settling down in the chapel of the Annunciation, the two brothers went to Pitigliano to see Bishop Fulvio Salvi, who confirmed the permission previously granted.

The provisions they took with them to their hermitage consisted in all of one sea biscuit and a few dried raisins. They suffered from hunger, and one wonders what they lived on until their poverty was made known to the surrounding countryside.

A devout lady from Orbetello supplied them with a small provision of dried beans, which they softened in water and ate raw. To this they added some more or less edible herbs. They felt rich the day a royal official allocated a daily ration of bread to them, as "soldiers" of the garrison of Port'Ercole.

Sometimes a benefactor brought them a few fish and a little wine. They kept the wine for feast days and roasted their fish on small sticks in lieu of a grate. The sticks burned, of course, and seasoned the fish with ashes.[2]

John Baptist slept on a table, and Paul slept on the stone floor. They rose at midnight to recite the divine office and for mental prayer, lying down again at the end of three hours. But often the nightingales' song delighted Paul's Franciscan soul and he would rise again to praise God in his turn.[3]

The day was divided into prayer, meditation, reading of the Bible, and some manual work. Each day they went barefoot to gather fagots, and found God in His works and His beauty in the splendid panorama that spread out before their eyes. In the distance lay the island of Elba, and on the horizon the rugged peaks of the Apennines. Closer to them were the blue hills of the Maremma. Below, on either side of Lake Orbetello, which was bordered by narrow strips of land, lay the perfect curve of the two gulfs that separate Monte Argentario from the peninsula. When the sun rose above the Apennines, they could imagine they were witnessing the birth of the world.

In this charming landscape which Francis of Assisi would have loved, temptation sometimes sought to force its way into Paul's heart. But when he heard the drums of the Austrian garrisons of San Stefano, Orbetello, and Port'Ercole, the three *praesidii* that guarded the precious peninsula, he would chide himself, saying: "Listen to what the soldiers of earth do to guard four walls. What must you not do to guard the spiritual kingdom of your soul!"[4]

Having recovered his serenity, he would resume his intimate conversations with God, which were scarcely interrupted even by a few catechism lessons in the church of Orbetello.

But perhaps the time has come to set aside this anecdotal account and turn to the history of this predestined soul, now dazzled by fulgurant light and again plunged into the darkest night. Otherwise the best part of his life — the quality of his mental prayer and his mystical ascent — would escape our scrutiny.

Need we preface our remarks by a call to prudence in dealing with these matters? Shall we say that it is at least as wise for us to admit the existence of mystical states as for someone blind from birth to accept the existence of the colors of the prism? Certainly the wonderful common sense of the great mystics (and of St. Paul of the Cross among them) is, as Bergson thought, our guarantee of the credence they deserve.

But is it possible to explain and understand mystical phenomena? Yes, if we are willing to be taught by these privileged ones of God and to record their own confidences.

In order to rediscover and follow the itinerary of the spirituality of St. Paul of the Cross,[5] we shall follow the classical method of St. Teresa of Ávila. We know her famous comparison of the soul to a magnificent palace, such as a fervent reader of tales of chivalry might dream of. We know of course that Teresa was talking about her own soul and that in writing *The Interior Castle* at the command of her confessor she was revealing the whole experience of her life of contemplation.

Teresa of Jesus compares the soul to a castle built of diamonds or very clear crystal, having a great number of rooms grouped into seven dwellings. In the seventh, which is at the very center, God Himself resides as King, resplendent with glory. In the others dwell creatures: the senses and faculties, the devil, and temptations.

By a sort of distinction the soul which is this castle is also the wayfarer who must successively go through these dwellings before reaching the seventh, where resides the King of Glory. It is mental prayer that opens each successive door:

Meditation on the last ends, on sin, heaven, and hell, opens access to the first dwelling and preserves the soul from serious sins. The light that emanates from the King's chamber is diffused but sufficient to draw the soul toward the next dwelling.

Affective prayer enables the soul to pass though the second door, even though temptations and fear redouble. But the soul submits its will to obedience.

The prayer of simplicity brings the soul to the third dwelling. The soul is detached from the world, mistress of its passions, prompt to obey.

73

This is the first stage, more negative than positive. Hence it has been called the purgative way. Each one of us, with the grace of God, can aspire to it.

The great adventure begins in the fourth dwelling. Here the King lavishes His graces "when He pleases, as He pleases, and to whom He pleases."

The prayer of quiet introduces the soul into this fourth dwelling, where the great concern is to love more than to reason.

The prayer of union introduces the soul into the fifth dwelling. The soul is betrothed to the King.

The ecstatic union that leads the soul to the sixth dwelling is close friendship between the soul and God through an ineffable mode of knowledge.

Finally spiritual marriage consummates this union. "The soul is in God, and God in the soul. The soul and God delight in one another amid immense silence."[6]

We shall see these desiccated classifications spring to life as we follow the spiritual itinerary of Paul Danei.

From his childhood until his twentieth year — that is, until what he calls his "conversion" — Paul practiced the first three stages of the mystical ascent. It is no exaggeration to affirm that even in his first lisping words he begged his mother to tell him about the sufferings of Jesus.

Very early in life he learned how to meditate upon the Passion by himself. When as an adolescent he leaned over the edge of graves to gaze at the fleshless bones of the dead and at human skulls, this was no mere game of his imagination but meditation on the last ends.

At the same time that his religious convictions were being strengthened, his soul was being purified through a painful crisis of scruples which was overcome by blind obedience to his director. His will wavered so under the assaults of doubts against the faith that he was reduced to letting his head rest on the altar rail for lack of other means of defending himself. And yet this same will abandoned itself to total obedience to God, and his terror before the mystery of predestination was dispelled by his loving submission to the Will of God.

This crisis left him with a horror of sin itself, the only real evil. And so he ran with a rock in his hand to throw himself at the feet of his pastor. Striking his breast, he made a general confession to him.

He called this his "conversion." He had gone through all the stages of the purgative way. He was now in the third dwelling: detached from the world, master of his passions, prompt to obey, on the threshold of the great adventure of mystical experience.

For twelve years he was to live this wonderful adventure. He, the poor hermit, unknown, rebuffed, in pursuit of a visionary ideal, was to live a hidden life filled with interior light and sweetness.

We know that immediately after his conversion Paul entered the fourth dwelling. His spiritual directors could no longer keep up with him. One of them, who did not want to make much ado about the graces which Paul was evidently receiving, simply turned him back to meditation upon the last ends.

Always obedient, Paul devoted his best efforts to it, but in vain. His reflections would quickly come to an end. He no longer needed to reason. He saw and was lost in love for hours at a time, without experiencing any bodily fatigue or lassitude of mind. This is the mark of the prayer of quiet.

It is impossible for us to state exactly at what moment he passed into the next dwellings, but we know some of the ecstasies and ineffable communications he received from God.

Thus he was transported in spirit to heaven and permitted to contemplate the Blessed Trinity, the choirs of angels, the cohort of the elect, the Blessed Virgin Mary, and Jesus.[7]

He was also transported into hell. Terrified and unaware of what he was saying, he muttered the blasphemies of the damned. Many years later he wept at the thought of this eternity of desolation.

The Blessed Virgin Mary herself opened the doors of purgatory for him. There he saw souls suffer more than do the damned in a certain sense, for they suffer from their separation from God, the sole object of their love.

And our readers certainly remember the direct revelations he received concerning the Congregation he was to found and the Rule he was to write.

Amid these graces of light accompanied frequently by inexpressible joys, there was room for crosses and trials symbolized by the discipline that Christ presented to him surmounted by the one word *Love*. These trials were a sign of love and were rooted in love for Christ crucified, the Victim of charity for His Father and for men.

It was then that the doors of the last dwelling were opened to Paul, the dwelling where the King of Glory resides in a realm of light and consummates the union of spiritual marriage.

This marriage took place for Paul on November 21, 1722, the day when the entire Church celebrates the Feast of the Presentation of Mary in the temple.

That day Paul "saw appear before him the most holy and lovable Mother of God with her divine Son on her bosom. She was accompanied by many saints. . . ." They were St. Paul, St. Teresa, St. Elizabeth, St. John the Evangelist, St. John of the Cross, St. Magdalen of Pazzi, as well as some of the holy angels. Before this spectacle he threw himself on his knees, his face against the ground. Meanwhile he heard the voice of the Blessed Virgin Mary resound in his ears, as well as that of her Divine Son. They asked him if he agreed to contract the mystical marriage of his soul with the Divine Word. At this question he was dumfounded and unable to utter a word, although he declared inwardly that he was not worthy of receiving such a signal favor. Still engrossed with these reflections he felt and saw himself elevated from the ground by St. Elizabeth, St. Magdalen, and the holy angels. They urged him to co-operate with the great grace offered by the Lord and to accept the mystical ring. Simultaneously this ring was placed on his finger by the Blessed Virgin Mary and St. Elizabeth. It was a gold ring in which the instruments of the Passion were engraved. The Child Jesus finished putting it on his finger. Then he heard said to him that in virtue of his espousals "he must continually keep in mind the most painful Passion of Jesus Christ, as well as the great love of the crucified Redeemer for his soul."[8]

This is the mysterious scene, and Paul's own account of it rivals in simplicity those we read in the lives of St. Catherine of Siena or St. Magdalen of Pazzi.

Each year he secretly celebrated its anniversary, if possible at Monte Argentario, where it had taken place during his first sojourn there.

Need we recall Bergson's reasons for believing in the reality of mystical experiences, and in the confidences of those who have been permitted to enter the interior dwellings of the "Castle of their souls"?

We shall see that throughout his life Paul Danei was endowed with robust common sense and perfect equilibrium that protected him from all danger of hallucination.

And it will perhaps surprise us, but at the same time satisfy us, to know his attitude toward extraordinary favors:

"We must neither seek, nor love, nor desire visions, revelations, or other similar favors. We must even flee from them for fear of being deluded. If God is their source, we do no wrong in rejecting them, and God will not fail to produce His effects in the soul even though we cleave to faith alone."[9]

This is the very doctrine of St. John of the Cross, recommending the rejection of all extraordinary phenomena without inquiring whether or not they come from God.[10] Paul put this doctrine into practice himself and counseled it to others:

"He often admitted that he repelled the illuminations of God even though they were genuine, so as to walk securely in humility. Many times he heard interior words spoken by God and received very clear illuminations from Him, but did not give them immediate credence."[11]

To one of his religious who was going to preach a retreat to some nuns, he wrote: "I know that in that convent there is a visionary Sister. Beware of believing what she tells you."[12]

When he wrote to women under his spiritual direction, he was still more explicit. To one of them he said: "The devil knows how to imitate like a monkey. He even knows how to transfigure himself into an angel of light. He can take the form of the Blessed Virgin, of the saints, and of Jesus Christ Himself. He can even elicit false peace and false consolations. That is why we must never rely on them."[13]

Elsewhere he wrote: "It has even happened that saints have sometimes mistaken illusions of the devil or of their own imagination for the operations and illuminations of God. In reality, they were not. Among others, Catherine of Bologna was tricked for five years by the devil; and if God had not come to her rescue, who knows where the devil would have led her with his deceits?"[14]

He even dared to write: "When these splendors present themselves to you, make the sign of the cross with a lively faith, and disregard them, spit at them once or twice, and then recite the Creed. Do this and fear nothing. . . . Do not give up mental prayer . . . for you would make the devil laugh."[15]

This man who was transported in spirit to heaven and there contemplated, as his glorious patron St. Paul once had, what "eye has not seen nor ear heard" (I Cor. 2:9) was not a visionary in the vulgar sense of the word. His testimony is prudent and reliable.

But the gold thrown into the crucible had been purified through trials and love. With the grace of God it was now ready for the divine alloy in the intimate fusion of the mystical marriage. This union took place on the Feast of the Presentation of the Blessed Virgin Mary, November 21, 1722, in the grandiose solitude of Monte Argentario.

According to St. Teresa of Ávila, the communications of Christ to the soul admitted to the seventh dwelling "bear fruit within us."[16] "This is the end toward which spiritual marriage tends: to give birth to works, works, always works."[17]

Even though for St. John of the Cross love is above all the annihilation of "self" in contemplation, for Teresa love is act, it unites Martha to Mary, "for how would Mary, always at the feet of the Lord, have anything to eat if her sister did not help her?"[18]

Paul Danei, condemned to be a hermit at the highest degree of contemplation, is more closely related to Teresa than to John

78

of the Cross. Imprisoned in solitude by the Bishop of Soana, he aspired with his whole soul, which was a raging fire of love, to act, to accomplish the mission entrusted to him by Christ and confirmed by the Blessed Virgin Mary.[19]

Chapter VIII

GOD'S VAGABOND

We have already felt the iron rod, but we have not yet caught a glimpse of the Holy Spirit.   JOHN BAPTIST DANEI

BISHOP FULVIO SALVI had granted the two Danei brothers permission to establish themselves on Monte Argentario on the express condition that they live there in solitude. And he had not relaxed this condition. At the utmost Paul as a devout layman was allowed to teach catechism to the children of Port'Ercole.

Afire with divine love and consumed with zeal for souls, how could Paul remain indifferent to the letter he received from Archbishop Pignatelli of Gaeta, accepting him in his diocese: "At Our Lady of the Chain you will find a place favorable to your vocation, and you will be able to give yourself extensively to work for the glory of God and the salvation of souls."

At Our Lady of the Chain, about a mile or so from Gaeta, there were already several hermits. Among them were the two young men who had been the first to seek, without success, to be associated with Paul: Anthony Schiaffino and Michel-Angelo Michellini.

Paul hoped at last to find the companions he had so long desired, and he saw an opportunity to help many souls.

The two brothers did not hesitate. On June 27, 1723, they obtained the authorization of the Bishop of Soana to leave Monte Argentario and go to Gaeta. They apparently spent only a short time in Gaeta and did no more than establish contacts there, for in the fall of that same year they were back in Castellazzo.

Why did they make this sudden trip to their native region? "Solely for the purpose of winning one of their relatives away from sin. Paul succeeded fully." Such was the explanation given by a witness at the canonization process.

Once this work of charity was accomplished, the two brothers were preparing to sail for Gaeta from Genoa when John Baptist was laid low with a fever. They were able to return to Castellazzo but were obliged to wait until spring before setting out again. Meanwhile they lived at the chapel of St. Stephen. It was from there that Paul wrote to the Spanish Cardinal Cienfuegos, Austrian Ambassador to Rome, to inform him of his brother's illness and of why they wanted to leave Monte Argentario and take up their residence in Gaeta.

Monte Argentario was then under Austrian domination. It would not be surprising, therefore, if Paul had needed the help of the powerful Cardinal in order to establish his hermitage at this strategic point.

The skill the humble hermit displayed in finding protectors is worth nothing, however. The works of God often need the co-operation of men. The lesson of his brutal dismissal from the Vatican had not been lost on him.

The Cardinal's answer was more than gracious: "Your very kind letter would have filled me with joy had it not informed me of the indisposition of your brother John Baptist. However, I know that the visitations of the Lord are always welcome and pleasing to your good heart. I recommend myself earnestly to your best prayers and wish you the abundant graces of the Lord."[1]

In February 1724 the two brothers set out for Gaeta, where they resumed their austere and mortified life. We have the testimony of a priest who, when he was still a seminarian, had been sent to them as a companion to be trained in the spiritual life: "At noon they ate a little vegetable and herb soup, without any seasoning. Often this soup was sprinkled with ashes.

"At night they ate a small quantity of biscuit or a few dried fruit, or a bit of chicory. They drank only water. . . .

"In order to have more time for mental prayer, they slept

very little, and then on the ground with a stone for a pillow. They had hair shirts armed with iron points, which they wore on their bare skin. They often scourged themselves to the blood with iron disciplines."[2]

They rarely talked among themselves. However, Paul had managed to find even greater solitude by setting up a retreat in a cave in the mountain. There, before an image of the Blessed Virgin, he meditated upon Holy Scripture and, nourished by the inspired word of God, he prepared his fiery sermons. For he was now permitted to give free course to his zeal.

The Archbishop of Gaeta even called upon him, a simple hermit, to give spiritual exercises to his ordinands. This caused not a little surprise. He went so far as to send priests to make their retreats under the direction of Paul at the Madonna of the Chain.

The hermits liked to kindle their solitary piety by making pilgrimages. After they had been in Gaeta a year, the two brothers wanted to go to Naples to venerate the relics of St. Januarius at the time of the feasts of the Translation in May, when the blood of the martyr, preserved in a phial in the Chapel of the Throne, usually becomes liquefied.

Having obtained permission, they made the journey by sea. The sailors were edified by their religious conversations. The Neapolitans, too, quick to enthusiasm, were inspired by their demeanor and piety. When they prepared to sail back to their hermitage, a crowd eagerly pressed around them at the port to kiss their hands and their habits. But they hid their hands in their sleeves. Thus their renown for sanctity was spreading beyond the limits of the diocese of Gaeta.

Upon returning to Gaeta, they received an invitation from Bishop Cavalieri of Troy and Foggia to reside in his diocese. This prelate, the maternal uncle of St. Alphonsus Liguori, was known for his knowledge, austerity, and holiness. He had already tried to found a community of priests dedicated primarily to the reformation of the clergy. The community had been dissolved, however, at the death of Father Louis Mary Calio, who had been its moving spirit. Bishop Cavalieri hoped to give his project a fresh start with the help of the Danei brothers.

As it happened, the two hermits had found in Gaeta both

solitude and the opportunity to devote themselves to the apostolic ministry. But as they had not succeeded in grouping companions living with them under a common rule, Bishop Cavalieri's call seemed providential. After seeking the advice of Cardinal Cienfuegos, they left Gaeta in August 1724.

The journey proved to be a hard one, because of both the heat and the lack of charity they encountered. As they traveled bareheaded and barefoot, John suffered a sunstroke which jeopardized his life and Paul caught a fever. The reactions they elicited from others were far from cordial. People refused to give them alms and showered them with insults, while ruffians threw stones at them.

Once started, however, they struggled on until they reached the Basilica of St. Michael on Monte Gargano, a famous shrine, where they spent the night praying before the grotto. John Baptist has said that they had time to meditate upon the words of the prophet: "*Visitabo vos in virga ferrea et dabo vobis Spiritum Sanctum.*"[3] The iron rod, he added, smiling, "we have already felt, but we have not yet caught a glimpse of the Holy Spirit."

After this detour they arrived in Troy, where Bishop Cavalieri lodged them in his own palace. They talked about Paul's divine revelations and the foundation of the Congregation.

The holy Bishop was enthusiastic. He read the Rule written by Paul during his forty-day retreat at Castellazzo, annotated it with care, and even added to its already great austerity.

But the Bishop had in mind the foundation of a diocesan congregation directly under his authority, and he wisely indicated what seemed the most prudent course to follow. How could the two brothers, simple hermits, expect to found an institute that Rome would approve?

Besides, the Rule anticipated priests as members. These priests could be ordained only by a bishop, a bishop authorized by the Holy See to ordain priests *ad titulum pauperitatis*, to use the technical expression in Canon Law; that is, authorized to live on charity. For a priest cannot be ordained unless his subsistence is legally guaranteed.

Bishop Cavalieri offered to be their bishop and to ask for the necessary authorizations from Rome.[4] Paul, for his part, could not agree to have his Congregation imprisoned within the limits of a diocese. Had he not been dreaming of a universal missionary order that would rekindle the memory of the Passion throughout the world?

Bishop Cavalieri's enlightened advice made Paul realize his situation and the humanly insurmountable obstacles to the fulfillment of his plans. As he would need the authorization of Rome in any case, he decided to return to the Holy City, encouraged by Bishop Cavalieri, who was unable to go himself because of illness.

Paul was still as poor as ever, but he was no longer the naïve beggar of a few years earlier. He was carrying in his beggar's wallet several precious recommendations from the Bishop of Troy and Foggia, addressed to cardinals and other important personages.

It was a splendid opportunity for a pilgrimage to Rome, for this was a Jubilee Year. The two brothers set out in the spring of 1725.

There are no details on their journey. But when they were at prayer in St. Peter's near the Confession of the Prince of the Apostles, an incident occurred which, though outwardly commonplace, was to have important consequences.

One of the canons of St. Peter's, Bishop Crescenzi, happened to pass by and was amazed at the attire and piety of the two hermits. He summoned them, asked them where they had come from and what their plans were. Paul answered these kindly questions effusively, for they contrasted so sharply with his brutal dismissal on his first visit to Rome.

Bishop Crescenzi was completely won over. He promised to help, and left the hermits to their prayers after having arranged to meet them later.

John Baptist grumblingly reproached his brother for his loquacity. Paul defended himself, pleading that he thought it best to be polite.[5]

Here we can see at a glance not only the difference in temperament between the two brothers but also the human explanation of Paul's success. The younger brother had a more austere and rigid virtue, while the elder was of a more affable disposition. Beyond this, Paul had the gift of winning hearts, of inspiring lasting good will, which he cultivated for the glory of God and the fulfillment of his plans.

Bishop Crescenzi kept his word and introduced the two brothers to Cardinal Corradini, who, won over in his turn, arranged an audience for them with Pope Benedict XIII.

This audience took place not in one of the sumptuous audience chambers of the Vatican but on the occasion of a visit by the Pope to the church of the Navicella. The two brothers were able to kneel at his feet and ask his permission to gather companions around them. The Holy Father agreed to this orally.[6]

There had been no question of securing approbation of the Rule or Constitution of the future Congregation. Nonetheless, the first step had been made, a prudent one which might prove decisive.

Paul's problem now was to find companions. He thought it wiser to make the attempt at Gaeta than at Troy or Foggia. At Our Lady of the Chain there were already several hermits who might well be interested in entering an austere congregation. There the expansion of the Congregation would not be hampered by the particularistic views of Bishop Cavalieri of Troy and Foggia.

There were soon seven hermits living at Our Lady of the Chain, devoting themselves to penitential practices.

The two brothers gave the example, but they were not always imitated. One day, for instance, a magnificent cake was given to the community. Paul had it placed on the table and invited his companions to assemble around it and convince themselves that they were not worthy of such a delicacy. When he thought they were agreed, he commanded one of them to go and offer the cake to the first poor man who passed by. This was easily done. A poor peasant soon came down the road. At first he thought it was a joke, but when he realized it was a serious offer he took the cake and ran off with it lest the giver change his mind.

Meanwhile Brother Blaise, one of the companions, had slipped

84

away from the others. Taking a short cut, he quickly caught up with the peasant and demanded his share of the cake. Paul learned of this and severely admonished the overly greedy brother.

But they were still in the novitiate, and there was much good will in the group. And now three new companions, two of whom were priests, presented themselves.

We know of these propitious beginnings not from Paul's letters, which have been lost, but from Bishop Cavalieri's answers to them. It was without resentment, if not without regret, that he saw the Danei brothers prefer Gaeta to his own diocese. But he did not despair of having them return to him, even as he wished them success in their efforts.

The favorable start did not last. Six months later Bishop Cavalieri's letter preached patience and "hope against all hope." Discord arose among the companions. It seems quite certain that Anthony Schiaffino, who came from the same region as Paul and John Baptist, was a party to it. It seems even more certain that Paul was having difficulties with the "patron" of the chapel of Our Lady of the Chain.

The right of patronage conferred privileges upon the donor and upon his heirs, and this often brought about friction and sometimes even lawsuits against the "users" of the church.

When Bishop Cavalieri learned of it he counseled prudence to Paul, for even bishops had no jurisdiction over the rights of patronage. He also renewed his offers of hospitality with greater insistence than before.

Paul did not yield to Bishop Cavalieri's warm invitations. Soon afterward the good Bishop died. During the Easter season of 1726, Paul left Our Lady of the Chain in the company of John Baptist, going to the shrine of Our Lady of Civita near Itri, also in the diocese of Gaeta. This shrine, situated on a high mountain, was then the object of frequent pilgrimages.

The two brothers remained there only three months, mingling in the life of the priests assigned to serve the shrine. This was only a temporary stage. After his failure at Our Lady of the Chain, Paul could no longer see any way out of his impasse. He had obtained permission to gather companions around him, and his companions had gone away.

His protectors in Rome, Bishop Crescenzi and Cardinal Corradini, offered him refuge at the Hospital of St. Gallicano, so that he might dedicate himself to the care of the sick. He had no choice. He agreed to enter the royal road of total charity, even though it seemed to delay the fulfillment of the magnificent visions of his youth.

During August 1726 the two brothers set out for Rome with these discouraging thoughts in their hearts. It was the path of Providence.

Chapter IX

THE DEFINITIVE STAGE

"That is what he thought it was. It was supposed to establish him permanently in Rome. It brought him back to Monte Argentario."

IN SEPTEMBER 1726 the two brothers arrived in Rome. Paul thought that he was done with his life of wandering in pursuit of the ideal he had once glimpsed: "We shall not make any more journeys. God has so ordained. We are stopping at the holy hospital which seems more and more the auspicious place for us to sacrifice ourselves totally to Divine Love."[1]

The new Hospital of St. Gallicano was inaugurated shortly after their arrival, and they immediately dedicated themselves to the care of the sick. Specifically, they were entrusted with the spiritual welfare of these poor folk. They were wonderfully successful in this work, especially Paul, who had much experience teaching catechism and preaching. In fact, they were so successful that Cardinal Corradini decided they would be even more useful if they became priests.

Paul was readily convinced, but John Baptist did not think he would be able to attain this high goal, as he knew much less Latin than his brother. In the end, however, they both agreed.

After taking lessons in theology from a Capuchin Father, they successfully passed the required examination.[2] Paul was thirty-three, and John Baptist thirty-two. During that year, 1727, they received in quick succession the various minor and major orders, and on June 7, Pope Benedict XIII ordained them to the priesthood in St. Peter's Basilica.

After the ceremony His Holiness granted them a short audience. He allowed them to keep their penitential habit and to change nothing of their mode of life, but they were to wear sandals when they celebrated Mass.

From that moment on they dedicated themselves exclusively to the religious instruction of servants and of the sick. The results were excellent, but everything did not always go smoothly. There were abuses, as in all human works. Paul took up the defense of the sick and drew upon himself the anger of those who were exploiting their misery.

The superior of the hospital, Father Emilio Lanii, a good priest more in sympathy with the charitable activities of Martha than with Mary's contemplation, did not appreciate the life of prayer and interior recollection the two brothers were leading. Nor did he spare them criticisms and humiliations. One day when a great lady, the Marchesa del Vasto, was visiting the hospital, the superior first pointed out to her the charitable attention which the sick received, then said to her: "Would you like to see how we practice virtue here?" Thereupon he called Paul and John Baptist and harshly reprimanded them.

The two brothers knelt in silence, and when the irascible superior was finished they kissed his hand and withdrew. The Marchesa was profoundly edified and conceived the highest esteem for their virtue.[3] We do not know what she thought of the superior, who on other occasions required the two brothers to use the linens of scurvy persons and imposed other similar mortifications on them.

Their health could not withstand it. They were ill the entire summer.[4] They then left Rome for several months, not for reasons of health, however, but because they had received news of their father's death.

They wrote to their mother, announcing their return home: "The news of our father's death has, you may be sure, caused us great sorrow, especially as it has reached us without any details. It is true that at the very instant we received the news we adored the holy Will of God. We come to beg you to stop grieving. Dear Mother, rejoice, for we have the firm trust that he is in heaven. Have the whole family share in this joy. I do not write you at length. I am telling you simply that we shall both leave here very soon and seek means of helping you in your need for the glory of God.

"Today, the same day that we received your letter, we shall ask permission to go home. Then we shall see what is most expedient for us to do, and we shall leave at once. We hope it will be in the beginning of September. Pray for us. Tomorrow and the following days we shall say Mass for the soul of our deceased father. — Rome, August 16, 1727."[5]

They were gone for two months, and upon returning to Rome they were laid low with malaria. For eighteen days Paul was too sick even to say Mass.[6]

That entire winter Paul was ill. The climate of Rome did not seem good for his health or his brother's, and the atmosphere of St. Gallicano was still less propitious to their particular vocation. They therefore took advantage of the elaboration of a new rule for the hospital to ask permission to return to their solitude.

A curious article of the new rule required all nurses, including priests, to take care of patients suffering from scurvy. And they were to do this by pulling out their patients' hair. It was a common practice.[7] The two Danei brothers could not make themselves do it. It was certainly not a matter of revulsion on their part but of pity.

Cardinal Corradini understood the excuse they gave and the underlying reason for their request. He obtained a brief allowing them to retire into solitude and to persevere in their mode of life.

They left Rome early in 1728 and went back to Monte Argentario. They were planning to return to their former hermitage of the Annunciation, but it was now occupied by their compatriot, Anthony Schiaffino, who had also left Gaeta after being ordained to the priesthood. Either because Anthony did not care to have them as messmates or for some other reason, the two brothers had to seek shelter elsewhere.

They found another hermitage about halfway up Monte Argentario, some quarter of an hour's walk from the first one and a little more to the west, but still in the area of Port'Ercole. It was situated in a hollow shaded by a few chestnut trees, close to a clear spring which watered two or three gardens whose grape arbors were terraced on the mountainside.

This was the hermitage of St. Anthony, consisting of a chapel a few feet square and two small adjoining rooms. Paul later described it as "*un povero tugurio*," a miserable hut. What is left of it today, amid surrounding farm buildings, does not contradict his affirmation.

It was a poor little oasis in the wilderness, but what solitude! It also commanded a beautiful view of the bay of Port'Ercole and of the waving plains of the Maremma. Entranced from the start, the two brothers settled down with a sense of recovered peace.

They took little interest in their lodging but gave all their attention to the chapel. A few months later, on the occasion of a pastoral visitation, a favorable report was made: "The chapel has but one altar, clean and fittingly adorned, surmounted by a painting of St. John the Evangelist and St. Anthony. The visiting dignitaries praised the two brothers for keeping everything so clean and in order. They merely recommended that an oil-cloth be placed over the altar stone. . . . All the sacred vessels are kept with great care. The two visitors expressed their satisfaction. Thank God, the chapel does not need any reparations. The visitors recommended the setting up of an iron grille on the women's confessional. . . ."[8]

A lay brother soon came to join the two hermits, relieving them of certain manual labors.

The life of prayer and penance began again, illumined as before by plans for a foundation. It was as it had been in the happiest days of their first sojourn in the wild and grandiose solitude of Monte Argentario. It was even better than the first time, for now the two brothers were allowed the joys and hardships of the ministry.

After his pastoral visit the Bishop granted Paul and John Baptist the right to hear confessions at their hermitage and in the entire diocese, and he urged them to preach. John Baptist, who was less well prepared and more austere, at first hesitated to make use of these faculties. However, he did agree to go to San Stefano once a week.

Paul immediately gave free play to his zeal for souls. Every Saturday he left the hermitage for Port'Ercole. He spent the night in prayer in the church and early the next morning entered the confessional. Later in the morning he preached and taught catechism.

On Sunday evenings the two brothers came back to their hermitage and humbly rejoiced in the fruits of their zeal, bought at the price of their sacrifice. For these trips were not pleasant strolls. They walked barefoot on paths bristling with thorns and strewn with rocks, and they sprinkled the road with their blood. In summertime the sun beat down on their bare heads.

They regained their strength in their solitude.

They did not remain alone very long. Their lay companion soon abandoned them, but their third brother, Anthony, who was already a cleric, came to share their life. Then two laymen arrived. And so they were five crowded in the little hermitage. But Paul thought there was plenty of room to build more cells, and his dreams of founding a religious community haunted him once more.

He threw all his fire into persuading Dom Erasmus Tuccinardi, pastor of the church of the Annunciation in Gaeta and his director during his sojourn in that city, to come and join them. He wrote to him, saying: "This is a narrow retreat, in which there are only two rooms and the chapel, but the holy recollection and silence would keep us at peace even if we were a hundred. God does not lack the means to have more rooms built. . . ."

On June 14, 1730, he urgently invited Dom Tuccinardi "to jump over the mountains, without allowing himself to be stopped even by reasonable objections." "As to financial help for your mother, you already know my view: Mass stipends, which I hope will not be lacking, will make it possible to produce this fine flower of charity. . . ."[9] He closed, asking him to bring another priest with him, Dom Angelo de Stefano.

Neither of these priests agreed to come. On August 15, however, three postulants presented themselves. And Dom Tuccinardi, while remaining firm in his own refusal, announced he had found two new recruits. One of them was Dom Angelo de Stefano.

Was this not the moment to have the Rule approved? Paul was ready to go to Rome without delay and throw himself at the feet of the Holy Father.

Paul's protectors, Cardinal Corradini and Bishop Crescenzi, considered such a step premature. The latter wrote him: "To act with prudence and wisdom, we must first examine the Rule. You may send it in an envelope addressed to Cardinal Corradini."[10] These were friendly counsels.

Meanwhile others were sowing weeds. It seems probable that Anthony Schiaffino, impelled by jealousy, was no stranger to the unfavorable rumors that were spreading as far as Gaeta concerning the Danei brothers.

Paul was informed of these calumnies. His only answer to them was a magnificent cry of confidence: "The ship is at sea, without sails or oars, but the great Pilot is at the helm Who will lead it safely into port. Winds and tempests assail it, so that the power and wisdom of the Great Pilot may shine forth even more brilliantly. Hail to Jesus Christ who gives us the strength to endure all trials for love of Him. The works of God have always been opposed so that the greatness of God may be made manifest. Indeed, when an undertaking seems to have failed completely, it is then that we see it succeed wonderfully."[11]

In fact, Paul's undertaking did seem to have failed completely at the end of 1730. Of the five postulants who had come to St. Anthony's during the year, not one remained.

The schedule of life at the hermitage, as it has been transmitted to us by one of the postulants, explains their rapid discouragement: "The hermitage consisted of a chapel and two rooms, one above the other. We all slept in the upper cell on small straw mats spread out on boards raised up a little above the stone floor. The mats were separated by linen curtains so that we could not see each other. At midnight we rose to go to the chapel. Father Paul and his two brothers recited Matins. Brother John Mary and I recited the Rosary and other prayers.

"After Matins we spent an hour in mental prayer. This was followed four times a week by the discipline. Then we could return to bed or devote ourselves to study or to some other praiseworthy labor.

"We rose before dawn to recite Prime and Terce in the chapel, and this was followed by an hour of mental prayer. Then the Fathers celebrated Holy Mass. After the thanksgiving they spent a while in the lower room reading and writing. Then Father Paul and Father John Baptist took their writings and each went his separate way into the forest. Sometimes Anthony followed suit. We two lay brothers occupied ourselves working in the small hermitage garden, cutting wood, and cooking a few vegetables in the kitchen, which was a shed facing the door of the hermitage. . . .

"About an hour before noon, the Fathers returned to the hermitage and went to the chapel to recite Sext and None. Then we had our main meal, the menu consisting of various kinds of bread obtained by begging, a little wine thinned with much water, a vegetable soup, and a small portion of fish, dried or fresh, likewise received as alms.

"After the meal they took a short recreation, either in the refectory or in the kitchen-shed. Then Vespers were recited, after which each one took his writings and returned to his hiding place in the woods.

"About an hour before sundown, they would return for Compline, which was followed by an hour of mental prayer for all. Then we recited the Holy Rosary. In wintertime, the Fathers would study another hour. Then came collation, for we fasted every day except on feast days. . . ."[12]

Such was the hand-to-mouth existence of the Danei brothers, hermits of St. Anthony's. Their companions soon got out of breath trying to keep up with them, although at times the monotony was broken by incidents worthy of the *Fioretti*.

One day Anthony left the hermitage early in the morning. As he was passing by a fig tree full of juicy fruit — the first of the season — he yielded to the desire to pick five or six of them. He secretly ate them and then carefully wiped his lips. As Paul was still deep in mental prayer, he thought there was nothing to fear. But the very next time he met Paul he heard him say severely: "Well! You ate figs without permission?" Surprised, he confessed.

"I see. But in a few days you will have a fever for your disobedience."

Frightened by this threat, Anthony answered: "I have heard said that it was good for the health to eat figs on an empty stomach."

"You will know soon," said Paul.

"And in fact a few days later he had an attack of fever, and as many more attacks as the number of figs he had eaten." So reports St. Strambi.

Another day the two brothers were walking in the country. Suddenly Paul asked Anthony what he was thinking about. The latter, too brutally drawn from his reveries, gave a false answer.

"Beware of lying," said Paul quietly. "I shall tell you myself what you were thinking of." And he did.

Anthony was still marveling at it when he reported these facts at the canonization process.

Paul gave his companions other cause for astonishment which could well discourage human frailty. It sometimes happened that one or another of them would catch him by surprise scourging himself to the blood with iron chains.

The rule of life and the example given were too hard to follow. One after another the companions went away, and the Danei brothers were alone once more.

Paul realized that he would have to mitigate the Rule.

He began to do this at once instead of sending it in its original form to Cardinal Corradini, as Bishop Crescenzi had advised.

The Bishop, apprised of the proposed changes, did not disapprove on condition that the spirit of the Rule remain unaltered. He even intimated that Paul would receive a kindly welcome in Rome and a serious offer of a hermitage in the principality of Piombino.

These were but hopes for the future. For the time being — and this was to continue for years — Paul was faced with total defeat, and a most painful one.

Very far indeed seemed the days of the sublime revelations, the visions of Christ and the Blessed Virgin Mary showing him the emblem of the future Congregation and inspiring him with a burning desire to gather companions together.

In those days he had written speedily, as if under dictation, a Rule that he must now laboriously edulcorate in the face of defeat and amid interior desolation. Soon after those days he had been plunged into the delights of the mystical marriage. Five years had passed since then.

These spiritual desolations had begun in 1725 and were to continue for forty-five years.[13]

He was spared nothing of the trials described by the mystical writers as being reserved by God for His saints. "Absolute dryness in prayer," he used to say. "I am like a camel bone." This did not cause him to abandon his meditation. On the contrary, he would stir up his courage by repeating the words of a Spanish officer who could not think of anything else to say when he visited the Blessed Sacrament: "*Acà sta don Diego* [Here is Don Diego]."

The night of the spirit, while it did not keep him from guiding others admirably, kept him from enlightening himself. He felt as if he were without faith, hope, and charity.

The apparent absence of God: "My most wretched state is not much less miserable than that of the damned, for I experience a veritable abandonment by God."[14] "It is a kind of punishment of the damned, a suffering that surpasses every suffering."[15] He often groaned: "I am in hell," and it was almost more than a figure of speech.

The attacks of the devil, who tried to take advantage of his discouragement, according to his confessor's account: "The evil spirits . . . tormented him fiercely on the subject of predestination. . . . Indeed the servant of God trembled with terror at the subject of his eternal state."[16] They sometimes filled him with such weariness and melancholy that he felt "vehemently impelled to throw himself out of a window."[17] At such times everything was repugnant to him: "Even the sun that I see depresses me."

He often said: "God preserve anyone else from such a state. I would not even want to see a dog in the state in which I now find myself."[18]

"Naked suffering" without consolation and without solace, like that of Jesus abandoned on the Cross. He admitted one day: "I then addressed myself to Jesus Crucified and to the saints, but the cross weighed down even more heavily on my shoulders and remained there for a long time."[19]

All these desolations and trials were the more painful precisely because he had received such an abundance of graces of light and a foretaste of heavenly beatitude. The memory of all those joys was very painful and not consoling. According to St. Teresa, when a soul suffers great dryness through God's permission, it forgets the visions and ecstasies of former days and loses, so it seems, even the memory of God Himself.

Having been in this state herself, Teresa wrote: "I then forgot all the favors that the Lord had bestowed upon me. All that I had left of them was like the memory of a dream which serves only to torment. My mind would become so darkened that I fell prey to a thousand doubts, a thousand perplexities. I used to say to myself that I had not understood anything of what was going on within me, that it was perhaps only reverie, and that it should be enough for me to have been mistaken without leading good people into error along with me."[20]

Paul thought rather that God was angry with him, that he had not co-operated with the extraordinary graces he had received: "Ah! What torment for a soul, after having experienced heavenly caresses, to see itself stripped of everything! Far more, what torture to feel, so it would seem, that God is abandoning it . . . that He is indignant with it."[21]

"I am becoming increasingly convinced that God is indignant with me, and because of that has withdrawn Himself and His graces from me, as a just punishment for my very great sins."[22]

These trials were simply the natural consequence of the divine espousals accepted on November 21, 1722, when he had heard said to him that "he must continually keep in mind the most painful Passion of Jesus Christ, as well as the great love of the crucified Redeemer for his soul."[23]

At any rate, he always accepted the cross under whatever form it came to him, with complete submission to the Will of God.

"God desires it, His will be done." Under one form or another, this is as it were the refrain that closes each of his sad confidences.

And in his grief he wrote, holding his crucifix in his hand: "You flee from me, Lord, but flee as much as You will, I shall always belong to You, I shall always pursue You, I shall always be all Yours."[24]

Sometimes Christ, conquered in His loving sternness by so much good will, lessened the weight of the trials by granting His servant a few periods of light and even of extraordinary graces.

One day when Paul was praying for sinners, he turned toward the crucifix and said to his Divine Master with great humility: "I am praying for others when my own soul is in the depths of hell." But he heard a voice answer: "Your soul is in My Heart."[25]

Step by step, the wandering hermit had found the ineffable joys of the presence of God in the silence of the seventh dwelling of his soul. Then interior trials[26] had come to compound his external defeats. He was thirty-six years old and he had not even one foundation to his credit.

His companions had abandoned him, rebuffed by his austerity. He still had his two brothers, his love of God, and his zeal for souls. He could already have been called Paul of the Cross.

Part Two

THE PAINFUL TRIUMPH

(1730–1769)

Chapter X

OFF TO THE CONQUEST OF SOULS

"He has sent me to preach to the poor."[1]

"To transmit to others the fruits of one's contemplation."[2]

WHEN everybody else abandoned him, Paul did not abandon himself. His whole soul "inebriated with love," he launched out upon the only road that remained open to him, the ministry of the word for the greater glory of God and the salvation of souls.

In the days of his adolescence he had loved to gather his brothers and sisters together to tell them about the Passion, and later he exhorted his friends to holiness. As a hermit he had devoted his best efforts to explaining the catechism and had even been authorized to preach from the pulpit. It was when he meditated aloud upon some episode of the Passion that his burning convictions bore wonderful fruit. His fiery tones touched hearts. But as soon as he turned away from the favorite subject of his own meditations, he found little to say.

After becoming a priest in Rome, Paul's natural oratorical gifts developed rapidly, nourished by his faithful reading of the Bible at St. Anthony's retreat and stirred by his painful enlightenment on the needs of souls gained through long hours in the confessional at Port'Ercole.

It was in 1730 that Paul of the Cross began his apostolic career in the strict sense, which was to make of him one of the greatest preachers of his time, the rival of St. Alphonsus Liguori, Father Bridaine, and Wesley, his contemporaries.

Until then Paul had preached only isolated sermons. He now devoted himself to preaching missions. And by "missions" we mean a series of instructions which are given in a single

99

parish morning and night for a period of one or two weeks and sometimes longer.

This practice is quite common even today in France and elsewhere. But if we are to understand — nay, evaluate — St. Paul of the Cross as a missionary, we must remember that he was addressing himself to an audience that was essentially made up of ordinary Italian folk.

Paul did not preach from pulpits like those of today, from which a preacher addresses a congregation that is more or less attentive and always mute. On the occasion of a mission, a great platform was erected in the choir or even in the middle of the church. This platform was dominated by a large crucifix with an armchair at its base. The orator walked back and forth on the platform with a staff in his hand, gesticulating freely. He was almost on the same level as his hearers, questioning them and receiving answers from them. When he became tired he would catch his breath by sitting in the armchair and then start preaching again. This could last for hours. It captivated the crowds of southern Europe, always eager for pageantry but also filled with a spirit of faith.

For thirty years Paul was to exercise this exhausting ministry, until his strength completely gave out.

He carried on three apostolic campaigns every year. That is to say, he carried on three series of missions preached one after the other without a break, from one parish to the next. The first campaign lasted from Christmas until Ash Wednesday, the second from Easter to the Feast of St. John (June 24), and the third from September 15 until Advent. The rest of the time he spent in solitude, to regain his physical and moral strength through prayer and study.

It may surprise us that Advent and Lent were periods of solitude for Paul. This was above all not to give offense to the great religious orders primarily dedicated to preaching. St. Alphonsus Liguori and his religious did the same.

It is for this reason also that Paul preferred to evangelize the rural areas rather than the cities, even without regard for his desire to go to the poorest and most abandoned. He liked to say:

"*Misit me evangelizare pauperibus* [He has sent me to preach to the poor]." But who can fail to admire the daring balance of this program of apostolic life?

Others before him had been able to nourish their zeal with a profound interior life, but the contemplative and the active order were widely separated. Paul harmoniously united the loving contemplation of Mary with the beneficent activity of Martha, first as a missionary and later as a founder.

This singularly wise view well in advance of his own time protected his disciples from the temptation of action for its own sake, from what the Europeans of the early 1900's called "Americanism" and what is today known as "activism." It is a part of the message of St. Paul of the Cross to the modern world, drawn, like all true messages, from the Gospel. And this is not the least important part of it.

Paul's first mission that we know anything about took place in the little village of Barca-dei-Grazi in the township of Orbetello. It was the center of a vast estate owned by the Grazi family. At this point a ferry crossed the Abbegna River, whence the name "Grazi's Ferry."

During the seasons of agricultural activity a temporary migration brought many workers to the large estates. The Grazi family wanted to give their autumn laborers the benefit of a mission and asked Father Paul to preach it.

We do not know what response he received from the workers, but we know that the Grazi family appreciated him. Agnes Grazi had lost her mother when she was twelve. Left to her own devices and being of a lively temperament, she dreamed only of dances and songs. During the mission she was conquered to the point of renouncing the pleasures of her age and condition. As it happened, she was suffering from a violent toothache when she heard Paul cry out with regard to the torments of hell: "That will be something very different from a toothache."

These words were like a flash of light for Agnes. She placed herself under the direction of the holy missionary and remained faithful to him during the remaining fourteen years of her life, which were to be years of sorrow and of extraordinary favors.[3] Her father, Captain Mark Anthony Grazi and her uncle, Canon James Grazi, became Paul's zealous protectors.

On December 30, 1730, Paul again left his hermitage in the company of his brother John Baptist and preached until Lent. So great was his success that the Bishop of the diocese, Bishop Palmieri, gave them the general authorization to preach throughout the diocese and the most extensive faculties for confession. Moreover, thanks to Bishop Crescenzi, two favors were granted to them by Rome.

The first of these made them missionaries in the official sense, with the canonical title of "priests assigned to preach missions." The second favor granted a plenary indulgence to all who attended the mission exercises they preached in the diocese of Soana. This last was granted for a period of seven years. On January 22, 1738, they obtained its renewal without any limitation of time or place.

In their new capacity the two brothers traveled all over the diocese of Soana. Then their field of activity spread into the diocese of Aquapendente in Tuscany, to the Papal States, to the islands of Elba, Giglio, Caprera, and so on. This was arduous labor, during the course of which our two vigorous Lombards ruined their health. We shall easily understand how this happened if we follow them on their apostolic campaigns.

In every kind of weather they went barefoot and bareheaded, clothed only in their simple tunics. Father Paul carried nothing with him except his staff and his sack of sermons. This flat two-handled bag of black leather has been religiously preserved together with his staff in the Passionist Fathers' monastery of Sts. John and Paul in Rome. The sack contained a few instructions taken, with no concern for originality, from a Spanish collection of sermons.[4] It also contained a writing kit.

When the two brothers approached a parish, the clergy and the faithful sometimes came to meet them in a procession while church bells rang out loudly. At the spot where the missionaries and the throng came together, Paul would give his first allocution, addressing himself directly to the crucifix. Then he would hold the crucifix in his hand and lead the procession toward the church, where he gave the opening sermon of the mission.

On other occasions their reception was simpler. The pastor might not even receive them in his rectory, even though they had been sent to him by the Bishop. They would then have to remain in the church until some charitable person offered them lodging of sorts. They prepared their own meals when they did not bring a brother-cook with them, and their fare was very meager, always meatless. Exhausted by the journey and by his constant mortification, Father Paul had to nibble on an onion to sharpen his appetite.

And then their work began. They had to attract people by going through the streets, stopping at the crossroads to address them. The missionaries sometimes were jeered at because of their pitiful appearance. But after Paul challenged the sinners in a loud voice to shock them out of their lethargy, and after he had been scourged to the blood at his own request, the scoffers were silent. They knew that an orator and a saint had come among them.

Sometimes the church would be so full in the evening that the crowd overflowed onto the public square. To be heard by all, Father Paul had the platform erected near the entrance of the church.

While awaiting the hour of his sermon, Paul would lie prostrate before the Blessed Sacrament or perhaps retire to a secluded place to mortify himself discreetly by penances known to himself alone. That was the way he prepared himself.

When the time arrived, he seemed to abandon his habitually humble demeanor and lose every trace of fatigue. Staff in hand and with a solemn air, he advanced from the sacristy to the platform. His tall stature was impressive, his serious expression and renown for austerity commanded respect, and his vibrant voice captivated his hearers.

In the first part of his sermon he simply set forth the eternal truths, rarely straying from his written text. In discussing the last ends he became excited when he spoke of the torments of hell, giving the impression that he was describing what he himself had seen — which he had indeed. "He sometimes trembled from

head to foot, and made everyone who was listening to him trem-
ble, too."[5]

When he explained the malice of sin, if he happened to be
aware of the presence of a public sinner or if he knew of
a vice that was peculiar to the locality, he would often interrupt
the thread of his prepared sermon. He would even point his staff
in the direction of the guilty ones, walking back and forth on
the platform, with beads of sweat on his brow. Wiping off the
sweat with the back of his hand and placing his hand against the
wall, where it left an imprint, he would cry out: "The walls of
this church that have heard my sermon will cry vengeance
against sinners until the day of judgment," paraphrasing the text
of the prophet: *Lapis de pariete clamabit* [For the stone shall cry
out of the wall]." (Hab. 2:11.)[6]

So that no one might accuse him of purely verbal exaggeration,
he would open his tunic and uncover his shoulders. Then he would
scourge himself to the blood with a discipline of sharp iron blades
or with convicts' chains until the breathless throng cried out:
"Enough, Father Paul, enough!" A priest would rush up to pull
the instrument out of his hands. If the Bishop happened to be
present and commanded Paul to stop scourging himself, he would
obey at once.[7]

While the crowd wept over its sins, he would rest for a few
moments on the chair placed at the foot of the crucifix. Then the
sermon would resume, but on another tone.

Now that he had aroused fear of God's judgments, he had to
inspire trust in divine mercy. At the end he completed the work
of moving all hearts by a quarter hour's meditation on the Passion
of Christ. His words were not merely cold reflections on the sufferings of our Lord but a vivid presentation, sometimes even a dialogue
with the crucifix. Paul asked questions of it and then communicated its answers to the people after placing his ear at the feet of
Christ, as if to hear secret words.

The crowd waited anxiously for the answer Paul would give.
"He says 'No!' He says 'No!'" the preacher would declare.[8]

And the crowd would beg and protest its sentiments of repentance. Sometimes one of the persons present would come forward

and confess his sins before the crucifix. For example, a great lady from Ischia declared that she had crucified Christ through her frivolousness and vanity. She promised to change her mode of life and remained faithful to her promises.[9]

There was an element of pageantry in all this that can be understood only in the context of the time and country in which it occurred. We should note, on the other hand, Paul's increasing concern to avoid all ostentatious gestures and even extraordinary ceremonies.

On some occasions he appeared on the platform wearing a crown of real thorns which made the blood flow from his temples, and he multiplied his scourgings. Again, in a transport of holy anger, he broke his staff as he walked franticly to and fro on the platform.

In the beginning of his career as a preacher of missions he organized penitential processions which he followed, "carrying a very heavy cross made of great beams, wearing an iron chain and heavy ropes around his neck, a crown of thorns on his head, and long chains on his feet." And at the various stations the crowd would listen to his passionate reproaches while he scourged himself.[10]

He soon put a stop to this exterior play, for as he himself said, "These processions tend to distract the people and turn them away from meditation upon the eternal maxims that they have heard preached to them. They are converted only when they are inwardly moved by these maxims, and not for having seen the paraphernalia of penance exhibited in processions."[11]

One of his hearers, apparently surprised at Paul's manner at Sutri in view of his reputation as a popular orator, said: "I noticed that he acted with great wisdom and common sense. There were no processions, which are, if I may say so, a waste of time. There were no pictures, no pious emotion, and no terror."[12] This comment was an allusion to certain customs of the time and contrasted our Saint with other contemporary missionaries.

For example, St. Alphonsus Liguori illustrated his sermons with real paintings. While he preached on hell, two priests went among the congregation, torch in hand, carrying a painting of a damned soul. When the orator spoke of the last ends, they would go about with a skull which St. Alphonsus would on occasion address. St. Leonard of Port Maurice did much the same.

During the same period Father Bridaine, preaching in France, came down from his pulpit one day and told his assembled congregation: "I shall now take you home." He led them to the cemetery, where he opened up the graves that were awaiting them. This was, to say the least, a concrete way of inducing them to think about death.[13]

But the question presents itself: Wherein lay the extraordinary appeal of St. Paul of the Cross? For when he preached, "the church would be filled with groans and cries of sorrow."[14]

It was certainly not the novelty or the beauty of the things he said. We have seen that the substance of his sermons was borrowed from a collection of sermons. Nor was it his oratorical gifts, although they were above the ordinary.

The secret of his appeal lay in his commanding appearance, his voice, and his gestures. But what captivated his hearers even more than his personal qualities was the burning conviction that they sensed in him. When he expressed strong emotion, it was because he really felt it himself. His tone, his voice, his gestures, all revealed his profound faith. He lived what he said.

All witnesses are agreed on this point. The Saint's emotion and unction touched the hearts of his hearers. He fulfilled the classical definition of an orator: "A man who is convinced and seeks to convince others."

And the enthusiasm he aroused was not merely temporary. He brought about many sincere and lasting conversions. After he had passed through a parish, the people would say of missions preached by other religious without great results: "It takes Father Paul to preach missions with great and lasting fruit."[15]

The story of his most brilliant conversions easily compares with those in the *Golden Legend*. This is not to say that he did not suffer some failures or that there were no relapses after his visitations. But such is the way of human frailty.

We shall relate both failures and successes, but each must be seen in its context. Together, they make up the painful triumph of St. Paul of the Cross.

Chapter XI

IN SEARCH OF A RETREAT SITE

The demons are attacking, men scourge me with their tongues. Within me battles rage, and on the outside there is fear and darkness. PAUL OF THE CROSS

DURING 1730, Paul's hopes of establishing a foundation at St. Anthony's hermitage were completely defeated when his first companions deserted. His only recourse was to throw himself totally into the ministry of the missions.

Amid his prodigious success, however, he did not forget his belief in his vocation as a founder. Besides, success could only increase his desire to find many workers to labor in such an abundant harvest.

Actually, by making him known and esteemed, by bringing him in contact with generous Catholics and influential persons, Paul's missions helped him to realize his plans.

One of the first of his missions — perhaps the very first — had the unexpected result of opening the way for a foundation. The Grazi family and other influential personages in Orbetello were so much impressed by Paul's success at Barca-dei-Grazi that they offered to help him settle permanently in their city. They were even ready to build a monastery for him.

Paul, who proclaimed himself to be "the poor man of Jesus," did not want a monastery. And being a passionate lover of solitude, he refused to establish his headquarters in a city. These two obstacles were removed in the simplest way possible. The proposed foundation would be a mere "retreat," without any artistic cloister or sumptuous chapter room. It would consist of a chapel around which individual cells (3.8 feet by 7.4 feet) would be clustered, all of them devoid of furniture. There would also be a few indispensable adjoining buildings. As for solitude, this was easy to find on the slopes of Monte Argentario within the very limits of Orbetello.

It is said that Paul discovered the site predestined for the first retreat under divine inspiration. He had left St. Anthony's hermitage and walked toward the west, following a path along the side of the mountain. When he reached a point where he could see Orbetello in the distance, he knelt down to adore the Blessed Sacrament present there. While caught up in ecstasy he received the revelation that the spot where he knelt was to be the site of his proposed foundation.

Indeed, the location was admirably chosen. It is a kind of promontory halfway up the mountain (at an altitude of about 850 feet), forming a sloping ledge. Above it Monte Argentario rises abruptly, covered with a thick copse of ilex, rosemary, and myrtle. Below lies a broad valley rich in farmland and olive groves all the way down to the lake, from which the ramparts and roofs of Orbetello seem to rise.

The horizon stretches far into the distance: toward the north, to Cape Talamone and the hills of Piombino that face the island of Elba; to the south, as far as Civitavecchia. Straight ahead the gentle hills of the Maremma reach all the way to Tuscany with its villages and towns hidden in greenery.

This little promontory was known as the "palazzaccio," the ugly palace. It might better have been called "Beauregard," for few places offer more glorious panoramas. Indeed, anyone who has ever had the good fortune to be there to watch the sun rise over the Apennines, set the sea afire, and suddenly make towns and villages shine out from the shadows could well think he had witnessed the fairylike birth of a new world.

The ledge itself was called St. Antoninus' field. It consisted of a field planted with chestnut trees and a garden near a spring. There had once been a hermitage here, but all that was left of it was its name and a chapel in ruins. The land had become the property of the Cathedral of Orbetello and was the benefice of one of its priests, who rented it out for sixteen crowns a year.

Paul's problem was to get the city of Orbetello to acquire this land by compensating the priest-beneficiary and thus make it available for the new foundation. His friends took the necessary steps, and the transaction was concluded to everyone's satisfaction. The beneficiary gladly accepted an income that was more certain than the rental of land. The town bought the ground and turned it over to Paul.

All that Paul needed now was the approbation of Rome, which was necessary for the transfer of ecclesiastical property. And of course he needed the approval of the Austrian court on matters relating to the city. The latter, however, was only an administrative formality. Rome's approbation was more difficult to obtain.

Orbetello was a dependency of the Abbey of San Pablo Tre Fontane, near Rome, which in turn was a dependency of Cardinal Altieri's. The Cardinal should have been informed before any negotiations took place, but either through ignorance or because of the need to conclude the matter quickly without noising the news abroad, Cardinal Altieri was the last one apprised. He was an old man, very much aware of his rights and duties. He felt he could not approve a transaction that did not respect canonical rules and might later cause disputes and lawsuits.

The whole matter had got off to a bad start, and petty intrigue added to the confusion. From muddled explanations to obstinate refusals, the debate continued for years.

Meanwhile the good people of Orbetello, little concerned about canonical rules, set their hands to the task and gathered the first building materials. When Father Paul, during a new mission which he preached to them, informed them quite frankly that the foundation would be delayed until conditions were more favorable, they would not hear of it. Gifts began to pour in from left and right.

So great was the people's enthusiasm that on March 4, 1733, the cornerstone was blessed. The occasion, which reminds us of the foundation in Rome years later, deserves to be retold. The lords of Orbetello and the benefactors were all there. Father Paul traced the plan of the retreat on the ground with his staff. The cornerstone was laid and blessed, and volunteers started working.[1]

It should be noted that as a matter of prudence the building was to be erected not on St. Antoninus' field but next to it, on town property. The ceremony had moreover been authorized by the Vicar-General, who represented Cardinal Altieri in Orbetello. But this very precaution confused the situation still further. When Paul continued to request St. Antoninus' field, in order to have the garden and field, Cardinal Altieri thought this property had already been transferred for the church and convent and that suspensions had been incurred.

Besides, as the people of Orbetello were in a hurry, the city had given a piece of community land without informing the King of Naples, upon whom the Praesidii depended directly. There were new complaints from that quarter which were temporarily quieted by a trip to Naples.

Obviously Father Paul had a better understanding of mystical ways than of those of administration. But he belonged to the lineage of St. Teresa of Ávila, who once quietly declared: "Three ducats are nothing, three ducats and Teresa are not enough, but three ducats and God, that is a great deal." Paul had started out with a single *testone*, which was a little less than two lire. And the walls were already rising up out of the ground.

Delighted, Father Paul left the new construction to preach a mission in Piombino, leaving Father John Baptist to supervise the work. The latter felt that progress was greatly slowed down by the difficulty in obtaining water. The spring was at the end of the meadow, and the construction work was on a higher level. The water had to be carried in two small barrels on a donkey's back, a slow and painful process.

Being of a fiery temperament, Father John Baptist decided to seek a better water supply. He grabbed a crucifix and set out, followed by his companions. A few hundred yards up the mountain from the construction work, he knelt down and, as if inspired by heaven, commanded the workmen who were with him to dig. Water gushed up. By the natural process of gravity a small canal soon brought the water down to the construction area. The spring is still flowing. In 1920 it was discovered that the pressure was sufficient to reach the upper floors of the monastery.

Meanwhile international events threatened to have unexpected repercussions on the new project, which was already some thirteen feet aboveground.[2] Rumors of war were current at the time of the imminent succession of the Emperor of Austria, who had tried to make Europe accept his daughter Maria Teresa as his sole heir through the Pragmatic Sanction. If war came, the Praesidii might well become one of the battlefields.

The Praesidii formed a tiny state of a few hundred square miles in area, but their strategic and historical importance is greater than their physical extent. They included the peninsula of Monte Argentario and the three townships of San Stefano, Port'Ercole, and Orbetello. About ten miles to the north, they also included Cape Talamone and the island of Elba, as well as the principality of Piombino.

In 1557, when Philip II, King of Spain, surrendered Tuscany to Como de' Medici, he kept these strongholds for himself. In 1708, at the time of the Spanish War of Succession, the Austrians seized these territories and held them after peace was restored. That is why in 1722, when the Danei brothers first sought to settle on Monte Argentario, they went to the Austrian governor to ask his permission. Not only did they obtain their request, but an Austrian officer, Alphonsus von Labar, went so far as to have a daily ration of military bread distributed to each of the hermits. He became one of the most enthusiastic promoters of their foundation.

Father Paul soon acquired such a reputation for holiness throughout the garrison that the soldiers followed his missions, and many of the Protestant Austrians were converted to the Catholic faith.

If the construction work had to be halted because of the threat of war, it would not be through the hostility of occupying authorities. The danger was that the Spaniards would try to regain their former possessions. Since the Austrians were much too weak to resist except in their fortresses, it was imprudent to expose the still unfinished retreat to the hazards of war and perhaps offer the enemy a stronghold of sorts. It was urgent, therefore, to set up defenses.

On February 20, 1734, war was actually declared by Austria on France, Spain, and Savoy. There were several more months of waiting, which Father Paul spent preaching missions. Then in April 1735, the Spaniards landed, and a patrol seized Paul near Talamone as he was en route for Monte Argentario from Santa Fiora, where he had been preaching.

It must be admitted that Paul looked very shabby in his hermit's attire. He was taken for a badly disguised spy. When interrogated by the officers, he did not appear suspect. They brought him to General de Las Minas. Being a fervent Christian, the general soon realized Paul was a man of God and gave him the place of honor at his table. He even wanted to have him hear his confession.

The fact is that Father Paul had the gift of being all things to all men. He soon won over his hosts, both officers and men. And these were uncouth troops, fresh from the conquest of Oran in Africa. Father Paul's ignorance of Spanish proved a handicap, but they managed somehow to understand one another. He would enumerate the commandments, and they would answer him by signs or words.

There was a more serious obstacle to overcome: human respect. Some of the men did not dare kneel in public before this poor padre. He put them at their ease by "walking with them through the camp or on the bastion, so that no one could notice what was going on."[3]

Everything would have gone according to the apostle's heart if he had not been separated from his old Austrian friends and from the people of Orbetello and Port'Ercole, all firmly barricaded behind their ramparts. As Father Paul could see only souls to save on both sides, he was able to convince the opposing generals to grant him a permanent safe-conduct.

Those were the happy days of wars that were not wars, and Paul was soon able to go freely from one camp to another. For him alone the drawbridge would be lowered, and the artillerymen held their fire to let him pass. He visited the soldiers in their entrenchments, and sometimes bullets at very close range splattered him with earth.

As he was a novice in the ways of war, a soldier was assigned to him to show him the safest approaches to follow and the moment when he should lie flat on his stomach. He practiced absolute discretion and always refused to reveal anything whatever about the preparations either side was making.

Apart from his purely spiritual ministry, Paul intervened only to obtain mercy for men condemned to death. In these armies of mercenaries there were deserters, and the law was ruthless toward them. He sometimes obtained mercy and sometimes not. But at any rate he managed to prepare these poor men for death. He would accompany them up to the firing squad, his hand raised toward heaven, where men receive their final judgment.

Meanwhile the war was going in favor of the Spaniards. They had already taken Port'Ercole and were preparing to take Orbetello. General de Las Minas laid siege to the city and decided to destroy it by having all its vineyards uprooted along the lower slopes of Monte Argentario and then to crush it with a massive bombardment. Mortars and bombards were already in place.

When Father Paul learned of this he rushed to the general to plead the cause of the inhabitants, vouching for their sentiments and assuring him that the siege would suffice to reduce the city to submission. For a long time the general refused to give in. Finally he agreed, saying: "All right, I agree. But I am doing it only for you!" The city surrendered, and the attitude of the inhabitants amazed Las Minas, who congratulated himself on having yielded to the hermit's entreaties.[4]

After the last important fort, Monte Filippo, had capitulated, the besieging army was repatriated to Spain. It was scheduled to sail from Pisa, and General de Las Minas asked Father Paul to accompany the men to the port. We can imagine the farewells of the victorious army to its impromptu chaplain.

The Spanish general's successors, garrisoned in the conquered cities, continued to protect Paul. We shall see them help complete the construction of the retreat that the war had so unhappily interrupted.

As soon as the war was over Father Paul hastened to resume his missions, first of all on the island of Elba. He liked this island and long nursed the hope of being able to establish a retreat there with the help of the Princess of Piombino. Although his plans never materialized, the island brought him excellent vocations.

Upon returning to Monte Argentario, Paul was surprised to find the long-abandoned construction work going ahead again. Despite the ravages of war, the inhabitants of Orbetello proved themselves grateful and generous. To speed up the work, a limekiln had been built at the site after the Italian fashion. Wood and limestone from the surrounding area were thrown into a great pit. A fire was kindled, and after the limestone had been burned, the quicklime was extracted.

The ordinary alms did not suffice, however, and Paul took his pilgrim's staff and set out for Naples. The court was not in favor of new congregations, yet Paul had such a reputation that King Charles II granted him an audience and had one hundred gold ducats given to him.[5]

Paul hurried back. In his joy he wrote to one of his confidants: "This summer our poor retreat will be completed, at least the walls. Let us pray God to fill it with His servants."[6]

But he was soon on the road once again, or rather on the sea, this time going to Pisa. On February 18, 1736, he wrote to Agnes Grazi from San Stefano, where he boarded the ship: "Here I am on my way to Pisa, with regard to this holy retreat. God knows what worry it is causing me. . . ."[7]

Things were not going as fast or as well as he had hoped despite the generous royal gift. Out of a scruple on the matter of poverty, the money had been entrusted to a devout layman, who was to provide for the expenses as they arose. The depositary felt himself authorized to spend some of the money temporarily for his own personal use. He later returned the loan and more besides, but for the time being the construction work was slowed down.

The poor Founder was obliged to postpone his plans for the inauguration. He had already announced it for November 21, the Feast of the Presentation, which he had many reasons to love. This date would no longer be possible. The windows and doors were missing, and he was reduced to beg a benefactor to send him some boards from the island of Elba.[8]

And other difficulties more serious than money worries seemed to make the necessary authorizations impossible. These difficulties were of long standing but became more pressing now that the work was almost completed. Reading between the lines of the veiled allusions and the reticences of Paul's first companions, we can see quite plainly the nature of these problems.

The new foundation was in a sense a competitor to certain existing groups and aroused jealousy. There were other hermits in the area, as well as other mendicant orders. Besides, an exempt congregation was by definition outside the jurisdiction of the bishops. This explains many of the calumnies and much of the opposition Father Paul encountered.

Paul's former companion, Anthony Schiaffino, rose against him. Playing upon the vanity of the inhabitants of Port'Ercole, he had a monastery built a little higher on the mountain than Paul's retreat. But his project failed, and only a few decaying walls remain today.

Paul always showed Anthony the greatest consideration, just as he graciously received those who came to heap abuse on him while he was supervising the construction work.

There was a more serious incident. A band of demoniacs tried to tear down the walls that were rising. Witnesses have affirmed that these possessed souls disappeared in terror when they saw the Archangel Michael towering above the structure with a flashing sword in his hand. One of the altars of the present-day monastery has been dedicated to St. Michael.[9]

Still worse, a curate from Port'Ercole did not hesitate to denounce Father Paul before the Inquisition, accusing him of laxity in morals. Others accused him before the Spanish authorities of being a hostile stranger who should not be allowed to settle on Monte Argentario but on the contrary should be expelled from the Praesidii.

Our Saint had to vindicate himself. He did so easily, but with a heavy heart. He had been chosen for a great work. Of that he could have no doubt. And now once more everyone was leaguing against him. Like the Master in the garden of Gethsemani, "his soul was sorrowful unto death."

Writing to Agnes Grazi, he said: "If God inspired me to abandon this retreat, how gladly I would do it! Who knows? I gladly await death." And a little while later: "I do not know what God wants nor where I shall end. Whichever way I turn I see only crosses, storms, contradictions, sinister noises. . . . Very often I see everything dashed to the ground. . . ."[10]

He kept fighting, and during November 1736 he left for Rome to negotiate directly with Cardinal Altieri. The Cardinal received him kindly and even promised to give his permission to have the church blessed. He kept his promise, but when he granted the permission in writing to his Vicar-General, he set unusually precise conditions. Some of them were quite ordinary, such as the condition that the church and the sacristy be suitably constructed.

The other conditions proved disappointing to Paul. He and his companions were to remain under the Cardinal's direct jurisdiction, and their Constitutions were to be approved by him according to his own ideas.

Paul did not then know the exact intentions of Cardinal Altieri, who had asked him only to transmit to him the Rule and the documents permitting the cession of St. Antoninus' field. But he came back from Rome filled with anxiety. Other trials were awaiting him, although we do not know precisely what they were.

Once again Paul's sufferings found expression in heart-rending terms: "Realize that I am in the most pressing need and amid continual, violent interior and exterior tempests. Ah! If God would give me the alms of the death that I ask of Him for His greater glory, how delightful the news would be to me!"[11] "I see that new battles are in preparation, and who knows how I shall come through? The storms continue, the shadows grow darker, fears never vanish, the demons are attacking, men scourge me with their tongues. Within me, battles rage, and on the outside, fear and darkness. . . . Ah! How much more desirable to me death is than life!"[12]

Perhaps he was thinking, as he would later, that his death would hasten the fulfillment of God's plans to which his own unworthiness was an obstacle. He was then forty-two years old.

Meanwhile Paul had sent the documents requested by Cardinal Altieri. Quite apart from the Rule to be approved, there was the matter of obtaining the ratification of the transfer of St. Antoninus' field in return for an income of sixteen ducats.

In examining the documents the Cardinal was under the impression that the church and retreat had been built on St. Antoninus' field, to which Paul had not yet obtained the rights. Whence a series of errors which were to delay the settlement of the transaction for months.

When the first misunderstanding had been cleared up by an exact explanation of the facts, a second difficulty arose: the town property had been ceded without the government's consent. Negotiations had to begin all over again. General Blom, commander of the Spanish troops, came to Paul's rescue, and the transfer of the land was approved by the court of Naples through his good offices.

At last Paul's undertaking was within the law. But his construction plans had not been prudent. The chapel, too hastily built, was in danger of falling into ruins, thus exposing the Blessed Sacrament to profanation. The expected income would be too small and not regular enough. The Constitution was too strict and could not be approved as long as the new Congregation had only three members.

After oral and written explanations, and the pledge of the Grazi family to maintain the church and the retreat, Cardinal Altieri yielded up to a certain point. He decided there would be no objection to Father Paul's moving into the retreat with his companions or to their celebration of Mass in the chapel as in a strictly private oratory, provided they received permission from the Holy See.

This was a very small concession and it must have considerably hampered Paul's ministry and that of his companions, since the faithful could not come to Mass, go to confession, or make retreats there. These restrictions grieved Paul so much that he still remembered them with sorrow at the end of his life.

Despite all his efforts to explain to Cardinal Altieri the serious disadvantages of his decision, and despite his intimations that he would leave Monte Argentario, the Cardinal remained adamant. Weary of fighting, Paul took up residence at the retreat with several companions and asked the Holy See permission to celebrate Mass in the church as a private oratory.[13]

The answer came without delay, and it was a pleasant surprise. Although Father Paul would not be allowed to reserve the Blessed Sacrament in the chapel, the faithful would be permitted to come to Mass. Bishop Crescenzi and Cardinal Corradini had obtained more than Paul had asked for.

This beginning of success was made manifest to all, both friends and foes, when the blessing of the church and of the retreat took place on September 14, 1737, the Feast of the Exaltation of the Holy Cross.

All of Paul's friends and benefactors were there. The Spanish officers, led by General Blom, came, accompanied by the regimental band. Boats streaked back and forth across the lake.

The assembled crowd paid little attention to the magnificent panorama they knew so well. They were waiting for the religious. Father Paul appeared at the door of the retreat with a rope around his neck and a crucifix in his hand. Behind him were eight companions, four priests and four lay brothers, clothed as he was in the coarse penitential tunic.

The band rolled its drums with all its might, stirring the hearts of all present. There was an allocution for the occasion. The Vicar-General then proceeded to the blessing of the church and offered up the Holy Sacrifice of the Mass.

Little by little the crowd thinned out, leaving Father Paul and his eight companions to their solitude.[14]

Not long afterward St. Antoninus' field, adjacent to the retreat, was turned over to him with full rights of ownership. After so many trials and contradictions, Paul might well have rejoiced. But he had obtained only one retreat. In a letter written about two months after the formal blessing of the retreat he wrote: "Now the biggest difficulties will arise. For I shall soon go to Rome to cast myself at the feet of the Sovereign Pontiff, to secure the approbation of the Rule. What terrifies me most is that I am not at all prepared."[15]

He had a bitter memory of his earlier trips to Rome.

Chapter XII

APPROBATION OF THE RULE

"Why don't they at least wear sandals on their feet?"

PAUL's difficulties over the foundation of the first retreat on Monte Argentario had interfered with his zeal for apostolic activity, without, however, lessening it. As soon as the blessing of the church was over, he started out on his autumn campaign. But the negotiations to obtain approbation of the Rule continued to hamper him in his missionary work. After Christmas he had hoped to preach a mission at Talamone, but he had to go to Rome instead.

Cardinal Altieri wanted to approve only a rule for secular priests, while Paul intended to found an authentic religious institute that would extend beyond the limits of a single diocese. Paul had to appeal to the Holy See.

Our Saint set out with fear in his heart, and his short sojourn in Rome did not restore his confidence. Back at Monte Argentario, he wrote: "I am in the waters of tribulation in view of the difficulties to overcome for the establishment of this Congregation. I fear, indeed I fear very much that my ingratitudes are an obstacle to it."[1]

While the motive for his fear was unfounded, he did have cause for apprehension. The Rule was not approved by Rome. It seems that the opposition came chiefly from Orbetello, where the clergy did not want a new religious community. In any case, Paul sought to disarm his enemies by showing himself as rarely as possible in the city which he had saved from ruin.[2]

His disappointment was lessened in some measure by two temporal advantages that came his way. First, St. Antoninus' field finally became the property of the retreat after much litigation and misunderstanding. Second, the King of Naples, through the good offices of General Blom, gave Paul an additional piece of land from the royal domain which provided the community with a vegetable garden. He also granted them the right of cutting wood over the entire area of Monte Argentario according to their needs. Later, when the royal domain was lost, the Passionists exchanged this right for full ownership of a wooded area.

When we remember how strongly prejudiced against religious orders the court of Naples was, we can see that this was no mean victory for Paul.

There were other consolations. Paul spent 1738 and 1739 giving an almost uninterrupted series of missions. We know how exhausting this proved to be, but also what wonderful results he obtained.

In 1739, an incident took place that seemed unfavorable for Paul but in the end proved to his advantage. Cardinal Crescenzi, his protector and friend, left Rome to become Nuncio in Paris. Before his departure, he placed Paul in contact with Cardinal Rezzonico, who was to become Clement XIII nineteen years later.

Cardinal Rezzonico gladly offered his good services to the Institute, and there was talk once more of the approbation of the Rule. Paul, for his part, kept talking about his hope for a "good and holy death,"[3] so insurmountable did the difficulties appear to him. He kept humbly begging for prayers, for he was still convinced that his own unworthiness was the greatest obstacle to the foundation of his long-dreamed-of Congregation.[4]

Once again disappointment and grief beyond words. Writing to his confidante, Agnes Grazi, he said: "I am convinced that the Divine Majesty no longer wants the work I thought I was to accomplish. The Lord is giving me the most manifest signs of it. . . . I foresee that very soon the retreat will be abandoned and that calamities will increase in such a degree that I shall remain crushed and dead under the heavy burden. . . ."[5] Two weeks later he wrote: "Never speak to me again about the retreat, and I shall never mention it to you either. I don't even want to think about it any more. It is not a work to be accomplished by me, who am a stumbling block. Pray that God may permit me to die contrite, humbled, and truly penitent."[6]

It was the crumbling of his soul's dream. His physical strength was completely exhausted too, and he was unable to preach many missions toward the end of 1739 and the beginning of 1740.

An event soon took place, however, which would prove favorable to Paul's plans. Clement XII died on February 6, 1740. Meanwhile the eager Founder, overcoming his discouragement, had already asked Cardinal Rezzonico to present a new request for the approbation of the Rule. When Benedict XIV was at last elected Pope on August 17, Paul had a presentiment of success that later proved correct.

Cardinal Rezzonico enjoyed the favor of the new Pontiff, and he quickly obtained an audience for Father Paul. A few weeks later Paul was impatiently wondering why Pope Benedict XIV had not yet made a decision.

When Paul learned that he had been called to Rome, he wrote to another of his confidantes, Sister Maria Cherubina Bresciani: "Our affairs are going well. The Holy Father, informed by the Cardinal Protector, has expressed strong satisfaction with this work. He summons us to His feet with the Constitutions."[7]

Once again he implored prayers so that he might not be an obstacle to God's plans. He still doubted he would succeed. Gone was the fine assurance of earlier days when, illumined by his visions, he had cried out: "Whom shall I fear? To doubt would seem to me a sin of infidelity."[8]

Since then he had lived through the drama of apparent abandonment by God. "Now we shall try one last time. It may be that by the defeat of my presumptuous plans God wants to force me to retire into profound solitude to save my soul. May the divine Will be done in all things."[9]

At the end of November 1740 he left for Rome, taking with him the Rule that he had somewhat modified.[10] Remembering the bitter lesson of his first journey to Rome, he took his brother John Baptist with him.

Cardinal Rezzonico put them up in his palace, but not until he had them discreetly watched to make sure of their sincerity and virtue. The investigation, carried out by his good friend Father Garagni, was all in their favor.

Father Garagni was greatly edified by their spirit of mortification. They would come back from their errands through the city of Rome, numb with cold, their feet bloody, and having suffered in silence the derision of the crowd. Some urchins even cried out as they passed: "Come and see two savage Jesuits!"[11]

But while Father Garagni admired the two brothers, he found their mortification exaggerated. "If only they wore sandals!" Nor did he see any need for a new congregation. He had been made secretary to Cardinals Rezzonico and Corradini, who had been requested by the Pope to examine the Rule, and he made no secret of his opposition.

Father Garagni had to be won over. Paul began to pray, and the moral miracle happened. Father Garagni sent for the poor hermit and promised to do what he could to help him.

The cause was won, and so the two brothers left Rome in order to arrive at Monte Argentario two days before Christmas.[12] Once there, Paul wrote to Father Garagni to express his gratitude and trust: "So many storms have beset the poor little boat. Blessed be forever the most sweet Name of Jesus!"[13]

Alas! Paul's bark was to run into many more hurricanes. For the moment, however, it faced only a heavy tide that came thundering against the cliffs of Monte Argentario, rough enough to keep him close to port.

And so there were very few missions during the early part of 1741. Father Paul at first hoped for a quick solution. But the delegates began an exhaustive examination of the Rule and proposed some changes. Paul defended his project doggedly. He himself had made certain mitigations and was obliged to accept others, such as the wearing of sandals on journeys as well as the wearing of hats and coats.

What was much more painful to him was that his Congregation would not be completely exempt from the authority of the bishops. He was unable to obtain the privilege of exemption. Moreover, the commission did not mention the wearing of the emblem of the Passion on the habit. This was a bitter disappointment.

Finally, on April 30, 1741, Father Garagni was able to announce to the Founder that the Rule had been approved. Pope Benedict XIV had given the order to transcribe it officially and to prepare the rescript of approbation.

The text elaborated by Father Paul and the commission was respected as far as its spirit was concerned. However, the secretary gave it a more juridical tone and omitted the moral reflections with which it was interspersed. Thus modified and transcribed in due form, it was approved by Benedict XIV on May 15 with great praise and many restrictions.

The Pontiff is said to have commented: "The Congregation of the Passion should have been the first founded by the Church, and behold, it comes last."[14]

In fact the Institute was not approved, but Paul and his companions were authorized to live in community and to follow the Rule and the Constitutions "with this clause that the clerks of this Congregation whose sole purpose is to preach missions are to preach them especially in places, villages, and hamlets where the air is less healthy, in uncultivated islands and areas where there are no other missionary houses. . . ."[15]

This amounted to assigning to Paul, through the use of learned circumlocutions, a mission field that few would envy: the Maremma. Of course bishops were allowed to call them elsewhere.

After so many futile efforts Paul had the wisdom to rejoice at this first modest result, and intoned his Magnificat from his heart: "Let every spirit praise the Lord and let all creatures exalt the infinite mercies of this great God, Who, not allowing Himself to be defeated by my wickedness, has deigned to bring to a happy conclusion this work that is His alone. . . ."[16]

Paul's obedience was soon rewarded. A few days later Cardinal Altieri granted permission to reserve the Blessed Sacrament in the church of the retreat. Together with this authorization he sent the authentic copy of the approved Constitutions.

Once again our Saint's heart overflowed with joy. Upon reading the Constitutions, "preserved in their essence just as God had inspired them," he was satisfied.

The new Congregation was entitled "Minim discalced clerks regular of the Holy Cross and Passion of Jesus Christ." The religious were to observe the three usual vows, and in particular the vow of rigorous poverty. They were to devote themselves to missions and to preaching the Passion above all else, by virtue of a fourth vow.

They were to wear the very habit that Paul had seen in his visions, with the emblem and the inscription "Jesu Christi Passio," which he had erroneously believed to be suppressed. They were to live by alms spontaneously given, not begged from door to door, observing a less rigorous fast than that envisaged by the Founder in his youth.

When they were at the retreat, the day and night were to be spent in a harmonious succession of hours of prayer, study, and rest, in absolute silence except during the evening recreation. Mortifications were specified by the Rule, and any additional penance had to be subjected to the prudent permission of the superior.[17]

Each religious was to have his own tiny cell, measuring about six and a half by thirteen feet, with a rotunda-shaped ceiling that could be touched with an uplifted hand, whitewashed, meagerly furnished with a bed and straw mattress, a bolster stuffed with straw, bed covers, a table of white wood, and a chair. The cell was to have a rather large window to provide air and light.

On May 30, 1741, the approved Rule was brought to the Retreat of the Presentation on Monte Argentario.

Paul and his companions — they now totaled six priests and two lay brothers — began a retreat. On June 11 they affixed the emblem of the Passion on their black tunics. The professed renewed their vows, and the new members pronounced their first vows.

Agnes Grazi, Father Paul's greatly loved spiritual daughter, was favored with his confidences on this occasion. His heart was bursting with gratitude: "Oh! How sweet and kind is our Jesus, Who, after the storms, gives calm, and after the clouds, serene weather. . . ."[18]

His visions had not deceived him. He and his companions were wearing the tunic presented to him by Christ and the Blessed Virgin. The Retreat of the Presentation stood in its gleaming whiteness on the shady slopes of Monte Argentario.

How he loved his cell which concealed so well his terrible mortifications. He had chosen the smallest cell of them all. How proud he was of the church, the most beautiful on Monte Argentario, where Jesus dwelt perpetually.

But he still loved the solitude of nature. He would often go to the end of the enclosure where a great oak stood that is perfectly healthy even today, with its enormous trunk and powerful branches. There he would pray, meditate, and dream of greater plans for the future.

Writing to a confidante, Maria Cherubina Bresciani, he said: "The society is not yet complete. It is still only a tiny infant, deprived until now of holy apostolic workers who will give it milk and the rest of the spiritual food it needs to make it grow. If they do not come, this Congregation will die soon after its birth. Pray God to send us holy laborers."[19]

From this time on Paul's great concern was to attract new recruits, to form fervent religious, to make his Congregation branch out into new retreats.

Chapter XIII

IN SEARCH OF VOCATIONS

From all sides retreats are offered to us, but we
do not see the apostolic workers arrive. I do not
understand this mystery. ST. PAUL OF THE CROSS

THE approbation of the Rule safely in his possession, Paul set out
to search for vocations to fill the Retreat of the Presentation
and the others he dreamed of founding.

When he informed the bishops of his acquaintance and his
friends about his newly approved Congregation, he begged them
to send him fellow workers. But it was soon evident that he
would have to depend above all on his own efforts in this matter.
He resumed his missions with renewed zeal and kept going until
he was completely exhausted.

Paul still had friends in Alessandria whom he hoped to win
over, and so he offered to evangelize the diocese where he was
born.[1] He even asked his mother to invite two priests from Castellazzo, former friends of his, to come and join him.

Without waiting for postulants, he began once more to make
plans for a foundation on the island of Elba. The site was
chosen, the court of Naples approached through Prince de Sangro, commandant of the Spanish Army, and money secured for the
purchase.

Despite Paul's request that the matter be kept secret, it was
noised out. As a result, "all hell was unleashed."[2] The religious
already in the locality opposed a new foundation. The poor
Founder poured out his grief in a letter to one of the women
under his spiritual direction: "Know, my daughter in Jesus Christ,
that tribulations are increasing as much on the part of the enraged demons as on the part of men who, I think, are motivated
by good intentions. If God does not give me great strength,
I fear I shall surrender under the attack. . . . The Congregation

is born, but I see clearly that it can die soon after its birth, for I do not know how servants of God are going to come to be the cornerstones of the spiritual structure. It may be that when I, who am the obstacle, have disappeared, the Divine Majesty will provide for it. . . ."[3]

Work and worry got the better of his robust constitution. In the spring he had been thoroughly exhausted. As soon as he regained some of his strength he resumed his missions to the garrisons of the Praesidii at the request of Prince di Sangro. But his stay in Piombino proved disastrous. This town is situated in the Maremma, which is infected with malaria. He at once began having attacks of high fever.

Between two attacks of malaria he tried to return to the Retreat of the Presentation to enjoy the quiet and the healthful air of Monte Argentario. At Orbetello he was obliged to stop, as he was too sick to go on. He remained there for three months and did not arrive at his monastery until January 16, 1742. From that time on he was subject to intermittent illnesses for the rest of his life: attacks of fever, painful sciatica, and rheumatism.

He was forty-eight years old, and his Congregation had just come into existence.

Illness proved a trial not only to him personally. It also had its effect on his foundation. A few of his companions, lacking the stimulus of his example and presence, became discouraged. They were abetted in this attitude by a physician from Orbetello who was too lenient with regard to their slight physical indispositions. He advised them to seek a change of air and to lead a less austere life.

Paul grieved over these defections but excused the persons concerned: "The poor fellow! He was willing enough, but he didn't have the strength. He helped me on the missions, and caught tertian fever too. He got over it quickly, but it was the straw that broke the camel's back and made him decide to leave. . . ."[4] Thus did he write about one of them.

In this way he lost three companions, including his brother Anthony. The departure of the last-named caused him the greatest sorrow, not only because of family ties but also because Anthony was really gifted for preaching and filled with zeal. Interestingly enough, while Paul had an equable, even a joyous, temperament and John Baptist was more stern and less expansive, Anthony had a tendency to melancholy. Giving health as an excuse, Anthony first made several more or less authorized visits to the island of Elba. Finally, on September 30, 1742, Father Paul placed love of the observance above personal affection and signed the act for Anthony's dismissal from the Congregation.

A year later Anthony asked to come back. He was accepted on condition that he begin his novitiate all over again. He persevered eighteen years and left again in 1761, this time for good. He remained a priest in good standing until the end of his life.

A few consolations came Paul's way. Two novices, one of them a priest and the other a layman, entered the Congregation. Paul, whose health was somewhat improved, resumed his missions in the diocese of Viterbo.

He had not been able to go to Vetralla during his illness. After Easter, 1742, he set out in that direction. Without a moment's rest he continued preaching until June, going successively to Vetralla, Oriola, Barbarano, and Bieda. By then he was exhausted and obliged to postpone his visit to Sutri which had already been announced. He returned to Monte Argentario instead.

All of these missions proved very fruitful spiritually, especially the one in Vetralla. First of all, in Vetralla he had the opportunity to enter into closer contact with an eminent servant of God who later died in the odor of sanctity, Sister Columba.

This Sister was a Carmelite, held in high esteem by the Sovereign Pontiff. During the course of a retreat he preached in her convent, Paul had several conversations with her. She counseled him strongly to carry on the work of his Congregation.[5] Even the Prioress of the Carmel of Vetralla chided him for his exaggerated fears and his lack of faith. Our Saint, tempted to discouragement in the face of obstacles, was greatly consoled.[6] Without waiting for new companions to arrive, he decided to make plans for other foundations besides the one on the island of Elba.

His mission in Vetralla had aroused popular enthusiasm.

The people wanted to have one of Father Paul's disciples among them. The community, which possessed the vast forest of Monte Fogliano nearby, even offered to build a retreat at its own expense.

Deep in the forest, there already stood a chapel dedicated to St. Michael, with an adjoining garden. With a few additions the hermitage would be perfectly suitable. The municipal council decided unanimously to give it to Father Paul.

Elsewhere he was negotiating to establish a retreat on Monte Cavo, close to Rome, where an abandoned monastery was located. This foundation appealed to him, since it would bring his Congregation close to the center of Catholicism.

But he knew it was easier to plan new foundations than to fill them with religious. This made him hesitate to take on any definite commitments. "From all sides retreats are offered to us, but we do not see the apostolic workers arrive. I do not understand this mystery...."[7]

Discouragement hovered over him once more: "I see the Congregation practically destroyed, but I preserve peace of heart, and am resolved to lead a very hidden life."[8]

His discouragement was only superficial. The moment a few recruits arrived, he wrote: "Subjects are increasing in number, and I have high hopes...."[9]

They were not yet twelve in all, and already Paul was planning to branch out. It is true indeed that the ways of the saints often deviate from ordinary human paths. But men see to it that they return to earthly ways.

Paul was brought back to earth by "well-meaning" people, so he tells us. Actually these were members of the regular mendicant orders or, as they were commonly called, the "Fratri." These various mendicant orders were for the most part born of the great Franciscan movement. To assure themselves of a monopoly on alms, they had obtained the privilege, among others, of prohibiting any new monastery from being built within a radius of at least four miles from their own.

As it happened, the foundation planned on Monte Fogliano

came within the prohibited zone. Whence the first skirmishes, which were to be followed by many more.

In addition, a difficulty arose in the case of Vetralla, located in the Papal States. The commune did not have the right to transfer any portion of its property without the consent of what would nowadays be called the Ministry of the Interior, represented by the prefect. In those days it was called the "Congregation of Good Government." At the instigation of the Capuchin Fathers, the Congregation of Good Government refused to approve the gift made by the city of Vetralla to Father Paul.

He hoped to remove this opposition through the good offices of the Bishop of Viterbo. Confident of his rights and of the spiritual advantages the new retreat would bring to the inhabitants, he wrote to the Bishop: "I want to leave everything in God's hands, to Whom all souls belong. If God chooses to open the way, I do not refuse the labor."[10]

Paul did finally attain his ends, but only much later.

His plans for the island of Elba were also thwarted. The court of Naples was more concerned with rumors of war than with granting its consent. And the support of the Bishop of Massa, upon whom the island depended, was suddenly withdrawn without any apparent reason. Paul had incurred his disfavor after laboring so hard in his diocese. He had no idea just what calumnies had influenced the prelate, formerly so cordial to him.[11] In any event, he had to put off this foundation until a later date.

Despite these defeats, Father Paul set out for his fall campaign of missions. He preached at Civitavecchia, where he met Mark Aurelius Pastorelli, an eminent religious, who was to become one of the pillars of the young Congregation.

From there he went to Sutri, where he spent a month evangelizing the people, the clergy, and the nuns. As never before, perhaps, he realized the efficacy of meditation on the Passion to convert the most recalcitrant souls.[12]

During Advent and the Christmas season he returned to his beloved solitude on Monte Argentario.

Early in January 1743 he took up his missionary staff once more and left for Toscanella in the diocese of Viterbo. He had his customary success there, and the people tried to keep the mortified and zealous missionaries in their midst by offering Father Paul a retreat.

A few miles from the town was the famous shrine dedicated to Our Lady of the Oak. Though in the care of a hermit, it belonged to the town of Toscanella. The municipal council offered it to Paul.

His only objection to it was its unwholesome climate. The shrine was located in a marshland, and in view of his own experience with malaria the Founder wanted to provide his companions monasteries in healthful sites. Since they were obliged to preach in the Maremma, they needed retreats where they could regain their physical as well as their spiritual strength.

This gives us a clear picture of Paul's common sense, of his moderate and well-balanced temperament. In all authentic mystics these qualities are combined with a contemplative spirit nourished by the most sublime visions.

Paul's objection to the unwholesome location of the retreat offered him by Toscanella was obviously well received. He was told he might build the retreat on a higher site nearby. The administrative formalities were quickly concluded. The Congregation of Good Government approved the transfer of property without restriction, and Paul accepted. However, he did not carry out his project immediately. He was to found the retreats of Vetralla and Soriano first.

After his very successful mission at Toscanella, Paul planned to go at once to Montalto. However, his brother John Baptist, who accompanied him, was taken ill, and both returned to Monte Argentario. Nevertheless, they were able to open the mission in Montalto on February 13, 1743.

After spending Lent and Easter as usual in solitude, they began their spring campaign, which they expected to preach in the diocese of Genoa, near the region of their birth.

They did in fact go to Chiavari, a pretty little town on the coast. But the Republic of Genoa was a private preserve. By law, no foreign missionary was allowed to preach missions there. The Lazarist Fathers appealed to this law to force the newcomers to interrupt their labors and leave the country.

History does not tell us whether Paul shook the dust off his sandals. But it was a bitter blow to him, for he had high hopes of stirring up vocations in this region where he already had friends.

At any rate, he had the consolation of returning to Monte Argentario to find it practically full: "We are twelve. There are only four cells free, or rather only two."[13] Among the new recruits was one who was to bring renown to the young Congregation, Father Mark Aurelius Pastorelli.

Father Pastorelli was born in Nice on September 27, 1693. As a young man he had entered the Congregation of the Fathers of Christian Doctrine. He became a professor of grammar and then of theology and made a name for himself as a preacher. He was given several important assignments in his Congregation: master of novices in Rome, then rector of St. Martin's, and finally rector of the college of Civitavecchia.

It was at Civitavecchia that he met Father Paul. He had been looking for a congregation with a stricter rule than his own. From the start he felt drawn toward the new Institute but wisely decided to think it over and ask advice.

On June 19, 1743, when he was fifty years old, he received the habit of the Passion and the name of Mark Aurelius of the Most Blessed Sacrament. After a fervent novitiate he rendered eminent services to the Founder, whose constant mainstay he became.

A month later Canon Cerrutti, Paul's former confessor in Alessandria, informed him of the arrival of four postulants, among them Father Anthony, who begged to be readmitted.

Paul accepted them with open arms, even his repentant brother, bearing in mind Jesus' words to Peter: "You shall forgive your brother seventy times seven, that is to say always." (Matt. 18:21.)

The Retreat of the Presentation on Monte Argentario was full. They were already fourteen and when the postulants arrived the four lay brothers had to be placed in a single room so there would be enough cells for the clerics and priests.

And what fervor! "Each one tries to be the one who humbles himself most profoundly, mortifies himself most, and arrives first in choir. . . . I have never seen such fervor before. O great God, how rich You are in Your mercies!"[14] Our Saint was in a transport of joy.

The time had indeed come to branch out into one of the retreats that had been offered and to think of a more complete organization of the newborn Congregation. Workers were coming.

Chapter XIV

FOUNDATIONS AND ORGANIZATION

Men will fight and God will give the victory. ST. JOAN OF ARC

FINALLY reassured on the score of vocations, Paul at once attacked the problem of new foundations.

He concerned himself first with Monte Fogliano, near Vetralla. As we already know, Paul's problem there was to get the Roman Congregation of Good Government to confirm the city's cession of St. Michael's hermitage to him.

Now he no longer had his usual protectors in Rome. Cardinal Corradini was dead, and Cardinal Rezzonico had become Bishop of Padua. Nonetheless, he stirred up the zeal of his friends in Vetralla. His efforts in this connection give us a compelling proof of his burning but practical faith. He trusted Divine Providence but did not neglect to explore every human means.

To Canon Blaise Pieri of Vetralla, who took an interest in his projects, he wrote: "Your Lordship must be its promotor for the greater glory of God and the spiritual welfare of your native city and of the surrounding areas. . . . And what is Sister Columba, that lover of the Cross, doing? This is no time for her to take a long sleep; rather is it time for her to act, wide awake in God. She should write to Rome. You have the Cardinal Protector of Vetralla, whose name I do not recall, and others. God makes use of these means. . . ."[1]

Another nun, the Venerable Gertrude Salandri, foundress and

superior of the convent of Valentano, intervened and won the governor of Vetralla to Paul's cause. When the devoted Father Garagni was alerted, he did even better. He got Cardinal Hannibal Albani and Cardinal Alexander Albani interested in the matter. These two prelates were powerful in Rome because of their authority, and in the rest of Italy because of their wealth.

From then on there were no more difficulties. The Sovereign Pontiff, when informed, approved the project. The Congregation of Good Government ratified the gift to Paul by the municipal council of Vetralla.

This success was due above all to the help of the Cardinals Albani, Princes of Soriano. Their influence stemmed from the ancient origins of their family and from their lands, which extended over a large area of the Roman countryside.

The cardinals' lands, unprepossessing and half deserted, were exploited by poor farm laborers and shepherds, who lived huddled in wretched villages. They had no organized parishes, and the spiritual needs of the people were great.

It is not surprising, therefore, that the Cardinals Albani became interested in a congregation which, according to its very purpose set forth once more when its Rule was approved, was called above all to work in the Maremma and in unwholesome and abandoned regions.

They therefore invited Paul to settle to the south of Rome, in Nettuno. But Paul was too deeply concerned about the health of his spiritual family to accept, as the region was infected with malaria. When Father Garagni wrote to him, transmitting the offer, he answered: "It would be a cemetery for our poor apostolic workers."[2]

As Paul's refusal was based on the soundest of reasons, the cardinals accepted it in good grace and then offered him a more favorable site near Soriano.

About two and a half miles from the town of Soriano was a shrine dedicated to St. Eutychius, Martyr, entrusted to a college of canons. It is not known whether candidates were lacking to the group or whether the Albani family had dismissed the canons.

In any event, the shrine and its adjoining house were placed at Father Paul's disposal.

The Founder went to Rome to negotiate the matter, and it was concluded without any difficulties. Although there was already a monastery of Fratri in Soriano, the donors of the new retreat obtained the necessary authorizations themselves.[3]

With the success of the ventures in Vetralla and Soriano, plans for a foundation on the island of Elba were put off until a later time. Only the project for a retreat at Toscanella remained pending.

At the start of 1744, therefore, Paul was faced with the task of carrying out as soon as possible his plans for three new foundations. He had to begin thinking once more about the religious who would populate these new retreats.

Actually the problem was less one of finding new postulants — since the retreat on Monte Argentario was bursting at the seams — than of hastening the religious profession of the novices and arranging for the ordination of his religious. And this was more difficult to do. It would involve obtaining new favors and effecting a more complete organization of the Congregation.

In order to understand the sequel and the course of action Paul followed, it is necessary to call to mind a few of the regulations of Canon Law:

The Church ordains to the priesthood only those who have a "title"; that is, a kind of guarantee that the candidate for the priesthood will have enough money to live honorably throughout his life without being obliged to earn his living in a secular occupation. This is what is called the "title of ordination."

This title may vary. It may consist of family property sufficient to provide a living — that is, the title of patrimony; a benefice or income from ecclesiastical property; the service of a diocese to which the priest is attached; the "title of the mission," for missionaries.

Religious who make the vow of poverty are ordained priests by reason of the title of poverty or of the common table; that is to say, they depend for their livelihood upon their Congregation. But this right must be granted to them by the Holy See. Paul had not yet obtained this right, which was indispensable for the extension of his Institute.

He discussed the problem first with Father Garagni by letter, and then in person with Cardinal Albani. Through the Cardinal's good offices he easily obtained the favor of shortening the novitiate of twelve of his subjects if he saw the need for it. As for the second favor — that is, the privilege of having his religious ordained to the priesthood with the title of poverty — this was restricted to six cases only.

At that time there was an oversupply of priests in Italy, and the Church was trying to limit their number to the actual needs of the dioceses. Besides, Paul's Congregation was still in its formative stages. If it should be dissolved, what would be the financial status of its priest-members?

Rome is prudent. However, the favor granted to six religious could be renewed. In 1746 Paul obtained the privilege of having ten of his religious ordained; in 1751, twelve; in 1756 and 1763, eighteen.

It was not until 1769 that the number of priests the new Congregation could ordain at one time was no longer limited.

Another restriction, as wise as the one discussed above, proved embarrassing to the Founder. The subjects he presented for ordination had to be ordained either by the Bishop or at least with his "dimissorial letters"; that is, with his formal authorization. This measure was designed to prevent abuses, but what an inconvenience for Father Paul! The bishops did not always know the young men in question and hence hesitated to give these testimonials. And if the prelate had been influenced against Paul, he might delay the dimissorial letters endlessly. In any event, everything took time in eighteenth-century Italy, cut up as it was into so many parcels of land, each with frontiers that slammed shut at the slightest rumor of war or danger of epidemic.

For the time being Paul had to make the most advantageous use of each individual favor as he obtained it. He set to work and founded the retreats of Soriano and Vetralla.

In Soriano he prepared the way for the foundation of the retreat by preaching a mission. He then went to Monte Argentario to prepare the religious who were to be assigned to the new retreats. In this connection he shortened the novitiate of his brother Anthony and of Father Mark Aurelius. He preached at all the spiritual exercises of his religious and arranged for them to elect superiors for the new retreats. For Soriano, Father John Baptist was elected, and for Vetralla, Father Mark Aurelius.

On Monday, March 2, 1744, Father Paul left Monte Argentario with nine religious, arriving in Vetralla at five o'clock in the afternoon. There was a solemn reception in the parish church, at which the archpriest gave a panegyric of the new Congregation.

The religious spent the night at the home of a certain Mr. Brugiotti, one of their outstanding benefactors, and they were treated with "princely liberality," to quote Paul. "It was most edifying to see the good canons and the principal lords of the town serve the religious at table. Before that, they had been so good as to wash their feet."[4] Decidedly, Paul's mission had prepared the way well.

The next day there was a procession from Vetralla to Monte Fogliano. When they arrived at St. Michael's Retreat, the installation ceremony began. The chief magistrate of the city read the official act of donation. This was followed by the *Te Deum*. Then there was a sermon, and the Blessed Sacrament was solemnly deposited in the tabernacle.

The superior-elect of the retreat, Father John Baptist, kept four religious with him. Four others went with Father Paul to Soriano the next day.

In Soriano the same ceremony took place at the sanctuary dedicated to St. Eutychius, a spot rich in catacombs where the relics of several martyrs rest.

Paul returned to Monte Argentario without taking possession of the proposed retreat in Toscanella, as the site was too unhealthy. "It would be a cemetery. If I had known, I would not have entered into negotiations."

Even the realization of his plans for two foundations did not fill him with joy. Writing to his confidante, Sister Maria Cheru-bina Bresciani, he said: "I find contentment in nothing. I am on the cross without consolation."[5]

This should not be looked upon as the all-too-human disappoint-ment that habitually follows overly high expectations. Rather it gives an insight into the desolation of his spiritual life after the enchantment of his ecstasies.

To these interior trials was added the recurrence of illness: "I have begun to have heart palpitations. If they persist, my poor life will soon be done for. I should take care of myself, but I cannot. If I am still alive in May, I shall take a cure by means of emollient decoctions, bloodlettings, . . ."[6]

In May he was still alive, but at death's door. A cure at the warm springs of Viterbo attenuated his attacks of arthritic rheumatism but did not heal his stomach or his chronic sciatica. He used to say of himself sometimes: "From the waist down, I am not worth anything."

Once or twice a year after that he was obliged to interrupt his work and remain in bed amid terrible sufferings which he endured with great patience. The instant he was on his feet again, he would set out to preach missions or to tend to the business of his Congregation.

So it was that at the end of 1744 he went to Rome to obtain a new and more complete approbation of the Rule, which would grant solemn vows and raise his Congregation to the rank of a monastic order.

From the start he had dreamed of these vows which involved a more complete gift of self on the part of those who pronounced them and would moreover give greater distinction and more priv-ileges to the Institute.

Rome had granted only simple, perpetual vows. But now the Congregation had three houses and enjoyed the protection of such powerful figures as the Cardinals Albani. Paul therefore set out for Rome confidently, but he was back on Monte Argentario by January 15, 1745. The only immediate result he had achieved was that three cardinals had been designated to examine the Rule once more.

It would be better to say that this trip to Rome had two very different results. The first was the winning of a new and brilliant recruit for the Congregation, Father Thomas Struzzieri.

On an earlier trip Paul had met this remarkable man, member of an association of diocesan priests dedicated to the preaching of missions. He was a powerful orator and had the gift of touching the hearts of his hearers. Although he knew Paul by name, he had made no effort to meet him. They met by chance in one of Rome's churches and were irresistibly drawn to each other. For the remainder of Paul's stay in Rome on that occasion they were together almost continually. As Father Struzzieri was to say himself: "We never had enough of talking about God."[7] When Paul left the Eternal City, Father Struzzieri accompanied him as far as Ponte Molle, where they separated after having knelt, known and blessed each other.

Paul was very eager to have Father Struzzieri at Monte Argentario. They had remained in contact after their first meeting. When Paul left Rome in January 1745, Father Struzzieri went with him. He was to be the first Passionist bishop, and the glory and honor of the young Congregation.

Quite different was the second result of this trip to Rome. On the way home Paul caught cold walking in the icy north wind, and his sciatica returned. He had to remain in Orbetello, where for five months he was flat on his back amid excruciating sufferings. It seemed to him as if a saw were bruising his lower back.

For forty days he did not get an instant's sleep. He prayed to the Blessed Virgin for the grace of an hour's sleep. When this was refused, he begged for a half hour's sleep, and finally for fifteen minutes. But the grace was refused him. He was in a state of absolute dryness of soul, and the demons tormented him constantly.

Instead of complaining, Paul sang of his pain in his magnificent bass voice, and the night watchman stopped on his rounds in the streets of Orbetello to listen to him. For five months Paul was unable to celebrate Mass, and when he did get up he could stand only with the help of crutches.

A great moral suffering was added to the others. One of his

religious priests left the Congregation. He had gone to settle a family matter at Chiavari. Advice, letters, entreaties — all proved futile. He never returned.

The revision of the Rule dragged on for a whole year. As soon as his health began to improve early in February 1746, Paul returned to Rome. For two months he multiplied his efforts, walked upstairs and waited in antechambers. "He was half crippled. We would see him, leaning on his staff, going about the streets of Rome. . . . He was reduced to the point of scarcely being able to stand up. Did he think that at a precisely determined moment someone would show him the other side of the medal?"[8]

Finally, on March 31, 1746, he was able to tell his religious that he had succeeded: "The Vicar of Jesus Christ has signed with his own hand the draft of the brief for the confirmation of our holy rules. He has affixed to it his *Placet Prospero*."[9] Prospero was the Pope's baptismal name.

Now the official transcription of the brief had to be made, and the chancery costs amounted to 140 crowns. Poor Paul thought that was expensive. He even dared to mention it to the Holy Father: "I thanked him for his kindness, and begged him to be a little lenient as to the costs."[10]

He was a bit more fortunate than had been St. Alphonsus Liguori's spokesman three years earlier, who in a similar situation received the answer: "You are all poor, but here we are poor too, and the Pope is the poorest of all."[11] In Paul's case, Pope Benedict XIV promised to talk the matter over with the Cardinal Secretary of Briefs. The costs were reduced to 120 crowns, and Cardinal Albani paid this amount.

The brief approved the Rule but reserved its approbation of the Institute.

Paul declared he was satisfied, although as he put it: "This does not complete the work; it is only an auspicious beginning."[12]

What did the papal brief provide?

It changed nothing as to the essentials of the Constitutions but mitigated the strictness of the Rule on a few points. The cells were to be a little larger and the beds not quite so narrow. Each religious was allowed to have the necessary materials for writing in his cell, and not only in the community room.

More important, the retreats were no longer subject to the authority of the local ordinary, except in matters that concerned the parochial ministry.

The religious were given the right to beg for alms, but their houses were not granted the right of ownership. The use of eggs and dairy products was permitted in localities where fish was not available, and the fast was limited to three days each week.

Finally, and this was the most significant change, the Superior-General was no longer elected by all the religious, nor were the local superiors so elected. Elections were to be made by the chapter, consisting essentially of the rectors of the various houses.

Meanwhile, without waiting to receive the new Rule, Father Paul was spontaneously and unanimously elected Provost General by the three retreats already founded, namely the Retreat of the Presentation, Holy Angel Retreat, and the Retreat of St. Eutychius. Father Fulgencio replaced him at Monte Argentario as local superior.

At Father Paul's request, the religious held a solemn triduum to thank God for the great favor of the new approbation.

Yet the papal brief of 1746 did not grant Paul everything he had hoped for. For one thing, the question of freedom in the matter of ordinations was not settled. He tried to obtain a solution by a direct request addressed to the Sovereign Pontiff. When he was told to specify the number of subjects, he asked permission to have fifty religious ordained. Although he did not expect more than a temporary authorization, he wanted to take care of the needs of the Congregation for a long time to come. Rome reduced the number to ten and continued to demand dimissorial letters from the bishops of the towns of origin.

Ten was a small number. Paul concluded simply: "I have ever stronger confidence that God will do great things. Contradictions are not few, and the devils are not on vacation."[13]

The commission assigned to study the Constitutions had discovered that there was no ceremonial for the clothing and profession of the religious. Such a ceremonial was prepared and approved without difficulty.

All in all, the young Congregation came out of the Roman furnace strengthened not from the trial but from the examination of the Constitutions. The Provost General felt new zeal stir up within him to establish new foundations, in view of the ever-growing number of subjects.

First he reconsidered the possibility of a foundation at Toscanella. The site had originally seemed unhealthy to him, and he had had no religious to send there. This was no longer the case. He revisited the spot with his brother John Baptist in the heat of summer, hoping to establish the retreat the following winter. A monastery of Fratri put up some opposition to the plan. Previously another group of religious had started a lawsuit against the Fratri but had lost.[14]

Paul finally decided against this foundation and so informed Father Fulgencio in blunt language: "The discalced Trinitarians who had hoped to establish a foundation on the same site lost their lawsuit to the Fratri. I have just read the decision. . . . Therefore let us not talk about it any more. It is a stroke of God's high Providence, for I would have been the first to leave my bones there. Deo Gratias!"[15]

The foundation on the island of Elba was still pending. Paul resumed negotiations. To be more exact, he let his friends resume them, for he no longer had his heart in the matter. He was thinking more seriously of establishing a foundation in Rome near the Church of St. Bibiana and of the construction work going on at Vetralla and Soriano to expand those two monasteries.

Besides, he had not yet completely recovered from his serious illness of the preceding year. Articular rheumatism kept his limbs swollen and in pain despite several cures of warm mineral baths. His attacks of fever also came more often. Paul wondered if the deplorable state of his health might not be due to the climate of Vetralla. Holy Angel Retreat was situated at an altitude of only about eleven hundred feet and was not so favorably located as the retreats at Soriano and Monte Argentario. As he himself said: "All my ailments cease as soon as I leave here, and so my case is clear."[16]

This did not keep him from making Vetralla his habitual residence. There were practical reasons for this decision. Vetralla was closer to Rome, where he had to go constantly, and offered him easier access to his other retreats. Moreover, it provided better mailing facilities for his ever-increasing and pressing correspondence.

For twenty-six years he occupied a little cell in Vetralla, 11.8 feet long, 9.1 feet wide, and 7.6 feet high, and having a tiny window measuring 13.8 by 22.5 inches. This was his little "prison," as he called it. It has now been transformed into a chapel.

A moral trial was added to his physical sufferings. His mother died suddenly toward the end of September 1746, so suddenly, in fact, that she did not have the opportunity to receive Holy Viaticum. In his letter of condolence to his brothers and sisters who were still living in Castellazzo, some of his human sorrow can be caught in the expression of his admiration for his mother and in the counsel he gave for following her example.[17]

At about the same time death struck one of his childhood friends, Anthony Schiaffino. Anthony, once one of his rivals in penance, later became his bitter enemy and the source of many calumnies against him. He later asked to be admitted into Paul's Congregation. The circumstances of this request are not known. The archives of the Congregation simply mention his death in Orbetello on October 13, 1746, strengthened by the sacraments of the Church, and his burial the next day at the Retreat of the Presentation.

Apart from this brief mention, there is complete silence in the archives concerning Anthony Schiaffino. His name is even replaced by dots in the summaries of Paul's canonization process; that is to say, the history of the Founder, his trials and successes.

Are we not permitted to see in the turbulent destiny of Anthony Schiaffino, who came to sleep his last sleep at his rival's retreat, one of the painful victories of Paul of the Cross?

There yet remained the task of complying with the new Constitutions on the matter of the election of superiors.

Father Paul had been elected Provost General by all the religious priests, and the rectors of the retreats had been elected by their own subjects for a period of three years.

To regularize all these elections, Paul convoked a general chapter at Monte Argentario on April 10, 1747. He was confirmed in his post. Consultors, the master of novices, and the rectors of the retreats were designated. The Congregation was at last organized.

Chapter XV

RENEWED IMPETUS AND SUPREME ATTACK OF PAUL'S ENEMIES

Everybody has taken up arms against the poor little flock
of these blessed lambs of Christ. . . . Prayers, prayers,
I beg of you, so that the Divine Majesty may grant us victory.

ST. PAUL OF THE CROSS

ENCOURAGED by the growing number of his religious, Paul turned again to his plans for new foundations.

As there was not much to hope for on the island of Elba, he looked once more in the direction of Toscanella. The opposition of the Fratri had made him fall back earlier. This time he had the ingenuity to forestall their attacks by having the clergy of Toscanella ask for a direct authorization from the Sovereign Pontiff. Benedict XIV granted the request.

It looked as if all problems were solved. However, the enthusiasm of the people had vanished by now, and the Founder encountered general indifference. This naturally hurt him deeply, but his reaction to it gives us still another proof of his profound common sense.

When he sized up the situation, he wrote to the Vicar General of Toscanella: "We shall all have to sleep in one room, whereas our rules require a cell for each religious so that he can devote himself to his exercises in silence and recollection. These are essential points of the Rule. The rules prescribe a study room, and there is none. The holy rules call for rooms that are well laid out — a kitchen, a steward's office, a refectory, etc., and there are none of these. Even the facilities for basic human needs are lacking. Under such conditions, how could we start a foundation? It is not with words that such holy works are accomplished. . . .

"In any case, I am altogether ready to found the Retreat and to fill it with as many religious as it can hold. They will all sleep in the same room. Patience! They will be very uncomfortable there. Patience! They will suffer everything for love of Jesus Christ. But such a situation cannot continue more than a few months. . . .

"Meanwhile, we would need for the new foundation eight to ten straw mats of solid hemp cloth, stuffed like mattresses. The cloth must be strong and closely woven so that the straw does not come through, for we sleep in our habits. These mats must be eight palms [hand's breadths] long and a little more than eight palms wide. The religious can thus use them by folding them double. Or else you can take twenty single ones, and we shall give two to each religious. You will find them for sale at St. Matthew's fair. We shall also need kitchen utensils. . . ."[1]

In closing he indicated that he did not have too many illusions about the results. After doing his part he left the rest to God. He must have been very eager to branch out to accept a foundation under these conditions.

Monte Cavo, near Rome, was still available, but its abandoned buildings were falling into ruins, and the humid climate offered no incentive to settle there. Cardinal Albani, who owned the monastery of Monte Cavo, agreed with Father Paul's objections and suggested that he found a retreat in the city of Rome, at St. Thomas-in-Formis.

Paul was delighted with this offer, which gave him a chance to establish a foothold in the center of Catholicism. He went to Rome, visited the site, and was so satisfied that on the way back he wrote down his impressions at the stagecoach's first halting place. Taking out the writing kit from the leather satchel which he always kept with him, he sat down and wrote to Father Fulgencio: "I am writing you in haste from the inn in Baccano. I left Rome this morning at dawn. Just like the Bohemians, I took care of my business in three days, visiting the church, the house, and the garden of St. Thomas-in-Formis. The church is lovely, with three marble altars. It is one of the most solitary spots in Rome. It is a place of great silence and recollection, almost a mountain: good air, a garden with water, larger than the one at St. Eutychius, where cabbages are grown. It is full of fruit for summer and winter, at least for a part of the winter: figs, grapes, artichokes, strawberries, cabbages, even enough to give to your novices. What does Your Reverence say? But I have not finished. There is a house like a good hayloft. Drafts go right through it, except through the door. Oh! What a lovely thing it would be to see poor Paul and his companions ventilated by the air of Monte Celio! What do you think? But let us stop joking. I am telling you only the truth. Despite this drawback, I do not know where I could find a better one in Rome. . . .

"As far as the Pope is concerned, everything is settled. All that is lacking is the consent of the chapter of St. Peter. I think this will be forthcoming before Christmas.

"I am waiting for the final decisions as to Ceccano, and I shall immediately inform Your Reverence so that you may send me the subjects needed. On my return I shall pass through Rome to take possession of St. Thomas.

"Meanwhile, you good people will stay in your snug rooms while I enjoy the fresh air of Monte Celio. It might well cure my sciatica. Oh! What a wonderful bath! But I should like to bathe in the bath of fire that the great God is preparing for my neighbor by means of this foundation. . . .

"We must go. . . . Adieu! Jesus bless you all! Amen." And he dated his letter as coming "from the great post-inn of Baccano where the birds die in the summer, from what I hear, December 16, 1747, your very unworthy and affectionate servant, Paul of the Cross."[2]

Paul was rejoicing too soon. The project was to miscarry. But his letter shows us the young and lively spirit of this man worn out by privations, sickness, and anxiety. His roguish allusion to Baccano becomes clear if we call to mind that this little town, situated near Lake Bracciano, was notorious for its unhealthy climate.

In this letter Paul mentioned another plan for a foundation at Ceccano. Things were progressing well there, owing to the influence of Father Thomas of Jesus' Side (Dom Struzzieri).

As a diocesan missionary priest, Father Struzzieri had labored in the Campagna Marittima Province, south of Rome. After he became a Passionist and returned to these regions, his prestige quite naturally reflected on his Congregation. In this way four foundations were established, at Ceccano, Paliano, Falvaterra, and Terracina.

Ceccano was a fief of the Colonna family. About two miles from town was an ancient abandoned Benedictine abbey, now the property of the Bishop of Ferentino. It boasted a miraculous statue of the Blessed Virgin, who was honored there under the title of Our Lady of the Dogwood Tree. The inhabitants of the area were grieved to see this beautiful shrine fall into ruins.

In 1736 the Capuchin Fathers had been obliged to give up plans to establish themselves there as the result of opposition from other monasteries in the vicinity.

One of Father Thomas' friends suggested that he ask to have the abbey transferred to his Congregation. The Bishop of Ferentino agreed from the start, as did the clergy and notables of the town. When Paul was informed of this auspicious beginning he sent Father Thomas to visit the site.

The latter found the place abandoned. Whatever buildings were not in ruins were being used as a stable for a herd of goats. The spring that once watered a beautiful garden was choked by a mass of brambles. Father Thomas, who was a better preacher than real estate man, did not look too closely at things. His report to Paul gave an enchanting description of the place.

Paul, for his part, was more concerned about the Capuchins'

past difficulties with the religious orders already established in the area. He therefore took precautions. First he asked the Bishop of Ferentino to advise the Fratri of his plans so that they might present their objections. As they declared they had none, he then asked and obtained the consent of the High Constable Colonna.

There was also the matter of compensating the Bishop of Ferentino for the loss of the abbey. One of Paul's benefactors, Father Pompey Angeletti, offered the Bishop a piece of property of equivalent value, and Rome accepted the exchange.

Paul then sent Father Thomas to take possession of the abbey officially. This he did on December 21, 1747. The community could now establish the foundation.

After Christmas, Paul took nine religious priests and brothers from Holy Angel Retreat and St. Eutychius and set out for Ceccano.

They traveled eight days in the middle of winter, barefoot and poorly clad, with no resources other than those obtained on the way from alms. When they came to a chapel they chanted the office, and the astonished peasants admired the fervor of these strange pilgrims.

On January 13 they approached Ceccano. As their arrival had been announced, groups of people came to meet them, forming the vanguard of the organized procession. They all went to the church, where a priest gave a short sermon. After Benediction of the Blessed Sacrament, Father Pompey Angeletti received the travelers with such kindness that they forgot the hardships of the journey.

The next day, the Feast of the Holy Name of Jesus, they proceeded with the solemn installation. The people and the clergy had assembled in Ceccano. Even the Bishop of Ferentino was there. Paul appeared, followed by his religious, wearing a crown of thorns, a heavy rope around his neck, and holding his crucifix. In this guise he led the procession.

Snow was falling in thick flakes, and it was an hour's walk to the new retreat. When they were about halfway, the abbey loomed in the distance. It was nestled at the foot of a mountain which towered two thousand feet above it. Even when the sun was shining, it could not help being in deep shadow.

When Father Paul saw the abbey his face became pensive, and by the time he arrived at the site of the abbey he was completely disillusioned. Father Thomas had given such an enthusiastic description, and everything was in a wretched state. The goats had been evacuated and a few wooden partitions set up. Beyond that, no other preparations had been made for the newcomers.

Paul wanted to take his religious back with him then and there. The Bishop and the notables begged him to be patient, promising to start work on the abbey without delay. Paul answered that he would give his decision after Mass. He wept during the Holy Sacrifice, and then in a fervent allocution he declared — to everyone's relief — that he was accepting the foundation.[3]

Paul's trust was not misplaced. When he came back ten months later, he found the installation greatly improved and the site a good one.[4]

Father Paul did not leave Ceccano immediately after the installation of his religious, for he had promised to preach a mission. He began his mission but fell ill after three days.

In his sickroom he received the visit of two Franciscans, who assured him that he had nothing to fear from the Fratri in the vicinity. They were personally sincere, but the facts were not as they presented them. Action had already been taken against the new foundation, and was to continue.

At the time, Paul knew nothing about these developments. Meanwhile other disappointments were heaping up. The project for the Retreat of St. Thomas in Rome was at a standstill, as the chapter of St. Peter had refused to give its consent.

Paul pretended not to be offended: "It is a high tower that has been taken off my shoulders."[5] He turned his efforts at once to St. Bibiana and, despite the serious difficulties in view, decided on the foundation of Toscanella.

As soon as his health permitted, he set out for Rome. First of all he negotiated the matter that had brought him there: the ordination of his priests. But he also discussed the proposed foundation at St. Thomas-in-Formis and accepted the "high tower on his shoulders."

The Sovereign Pontiff received him cordially. When Paul informed him of the successful foundation at Ceccano, the Holy Father blessed this retreat.

Paul was joyously departing from his audience when, in the antechamber, he was told that the Procurators-General of several religious orders had followed him into the Holy Father's offices to protest the foundation of Ceccano.

Paul's joy vanished. If he were accused in Rome, innocent as he was, it would be hard for him to obtain favors concerning ordinations. In any event, he was faced with the prospect of new anxieties and attacks.

He could not guess how serious these attacks would be. But he did not allow himself to pass the matter off lightly. Writing to Father Fulgencio, he asked for prayers: "The Fratri have taken up arms."[6]

Meanwhile it seemed best to press forward. Since his projects were making no headway, he decided abruptly to occupy Toscanella. He had delayed the foundation there, fearing the unwholesome climate of the site. A series of misunderstandings further complicated this dreaded foundation.

Paul went to Monte Argentario to get the religious assigned to Toscanella. They started out on March 19 and arrived at Montalto, the halfway mark, without incident. The second day a cold and violent wind made their march painful. They finally arrived, exhausted, but hoping to find the retreat prepared for them by Father John Baptist, who had been deputed by his brother to this end.

Father John Baptist had indeed come to Toscanella. But nothing was ready and the inhabitants had asked that the foundation be postponed until May. Since the good Father could do nothing about it, he had reported the situation to Father Paul and then returned to Holy Angel Retreat. As it happened, his letter had not reached his brother before his departure. When Paul and his religious arrived in Toscanella, therefore, they found the retreat un-fit for occupancy, without furniture, kitchen utensils, or other necessities.

What were they to do? It was already night, and they were utterly exhausted. Paul accepted the hospitality of some of the leading citizens in Toscanella, firmly resolved to leave the next day. During the night one of his religious had violent pains in his side. The physician advised against an immediate departure.

Meanwhile His Excellency, Bishop Abbati of Toscanella, came to visit Father Paul. The latter quite naturally told him of his disappointment and of his decision to delay the foundation. The Bishop summoned the notables of the town, begged them to make an effort, and set the example by donating a sum of money himself. "Have carpenters repair the windows, go out and buy straw mats, bed covers, etc." Such was his command.

For two days there were feverish preparations, and on March 24 the installation took place according to the habitual ceremonial. After the Bishop had given his blessing, all the guests dispersed. It was noon. The religious, left to themselves, went to the chapel to chant Sext and None, then gathered in the refectory. All they found on the table were a few cloves of garlic left over from their journey.

Paul sent someone to a neighboring hermit to borrow some bread, and to a nearby winegrower to get two bottles of thin wine. Each of the religious received a bit of bread, two cloves of garlic, and a few swallows of wine.

Thus restored they went to chant Vespers. Father Paul was thinking of the evening meal. He would be bringing famished young mouths to the table. He put the whole matter into the hands of the Blessed Virgin Mary. Toward dusk an unknown person brought five pounds of macaroni.

Now the meal was assured. But it was soon noticed that there were no forks. An industrious priest set about whittling reeds to serve in this capacity.

That night, so the chronicle tells us, Father Paul watered his food with tears of gratitude. For on the one hand he saw how merciful the Lord was, and on the other he saw the joy and contentment of his religious amid their privations.[7]

The workmen had not been able to accomplish much in two days. Curtains were hung in lieu of doors, and everything else was done in the same makeshift way. Writing to his habitual confidant, Father Fulgencio, Paul said: "We have never as yet founded a retreat in such extreme poverty, and never before had I experienced such interior sufferings."[8]

And yet he needed tranquillity of mind as never before. For the tempest was about to break against his poor little bark, as he loved to call his Congregation.

The Procurators-General whom Paul had passed in the Vatican had begged the Sovereign Pontiff to abolish the foundation of Ceccano as being detrimental to their monasteries. The Pope had transmitted the petition to the Congregation in charge of these questions, and it in turn interrogated the Bishop of the place for further information on the matter. Bishop Borgia of Ferentino, who had lent his support to the foundation of Ceccano, answered with a documented and justificative memorandum.

The matter remained pending, nevertheless. The budding young Congregation's success in planning and realizing a series of foundations in the same province of Campagna Marittima merely kindled the anger of the Fratri and increased the number of objectors.

The first of Paul's projects in this area was for a foundation at Terracina. Many years earlier, during his youth, Paul had had a presentiment while on a trip to Gaeta that someday a monastery of the Congregation he hoped to found would be located on the mountain that towers above Terracina.

And now, twenty-five years later, the opportunity for a foundation presented itself. It happened in this way: Bishop Oldo, a friend of Father Thomas, sent some dry beans to the retreat at Ceccano, where Father Thomas was then rector. Father Paul, who was visiting the retreat at the time, was not satisfied until he had personally thanked the generous donor, and in so doing he broached the subject of a Passionist foundation in Terracina.

The site seemed predestined. The city was situated on high and wholesome terrain. At the same time it bordered on the Pontine

Marshes. The proximity to this abandoned area offered the Congregation a chance to exercise the apostolate assigned to it: the apostolate of the rural poor, living on submarginal land.

Bishop Oldo was enthusiastic from the start. He promised to donate five hundred crowns and commanded that a suitable site be chosen. Monte Sant'Angelo seemed to meet all the requirements, except for the opposition to a new foundation on the part of a neighboring monastery.

In a spirit of conciliation the Bishop chose another site equally well situated. "At my age," he said, "people do not try to bully the Fratri, and do not bring on lawsuits that may last a long time." He thus averted the possibility of controversy and made arrangements to have the site prepared for occupancy. He spent at least four thousand crowns in the process, going so far as to stock the fishpond in order to provide food for the religious.[9] Paul did not want so many niceties, but the time had not yet come for him to refuse them. The beginnings were too auspicious. It seemed best not to dampen the good Bishop's ardor.

Another foundation was in preparation at Paliano, north of Ceccano. This was the work of Father Thomas, who had once preached a mission there with his usual success. When he entered Father Paul's Congregation, one of his friends, a priest in Paliano, offered him a shrine in honor of the Blessed Virgin about three miles from the town. The shrine was in ruins, but the site was favorably located on a height and the air was good.

Informed of this offer, Paul accepted on condition that the Sovereign Pontiff dispense him from obtaining the Fratri's consent. Like Bishop Oldo, he thought it wisest to give up fighting with them.

Father Thomas' friend went to Rome to handle all the negotiations. Upon his return, the plan was rumored about and the Fratri were alerted. One of the Fratri laid all the blame on the zealous intermediary. The dialogue between the two men is worth recording:

"Dom Isidore [Father Thomas' friend], what notion have you gotten into your head?"

"Why, nothing."

"What do you mean by nothing?"

"Nothing, I tell you."

"You want to found a monastery of the new Institute of the Passion at Our Lady of Paliano."

Dom Isidore confessed this was so.

"Listen," the other man went on. "You have gotten an idea in your head that cannot succeed. You will go to great expense, you will throw a thousand crowns into it, and you will lose the lawsuit."

"If God wills it, I shall spend nothing and win the lawsuit in the bargain."

"Beware. You will have to answer to St. Francis. If he sends you a few whiplashes, you'll feel it."

"I think St. Francis will be on my side, considering his great love for Jesus Crucified. Did he not receive the favor of the stigmata? Was he not marked with the wounds of Our Lord? What have I to fear?"[10]

The conversation ended there, but we can see the climate of feeling that prevailed. It gave promise of bitter squabbles.

A third project was taking shape for a retreat at Falvatera in the diocese of Veroli, this one also through the prestige of Father Thomas, who had just preached a mission there. About a mile from the city was a shrine dedicated to St. Sosius, one of the companions of the popular St. Januarius. This site was offered to Father Thomas for a retreat.

The shrine was under the immediate jurisdiction of the Bishop, who gave his consent without hesitation. Some construction work was needed, and the town council took charge of this.

The Fratri established nearby would inevitably oppose the foundation. Bishop Tartagni had taken precautions, however, and obtained from Rome the permission to be dispensed from their fiat. While this solution cut the difficulties short, it merely fanned the Fratri's enmity for the young Congregation. All the more so, as it seemed that Passionist retreats were becoming a contagious epidemic. Many towns and villages now wanted Passionists to dwell in their midst. And several specific projects were taking shape.

The plan for a retreat at Vico, which never materialized, brought the storm of hatred to a head. The Fratri, threatened in their monopoly, decided to have the foundation at Ceccano abolished and to prevent any new foundations in the province of Campagna Marittima.

First there was an avalanche of memoranda to the Roman congregations, to important personages, even to the Pope.

Bishop Oldo, who was deeply devoted to Father Paul and in favor of his plans for a foundation at Terracina, was impressed. Nonetheless, he thought there were far too many projects pending. He expressed his fears to Father Paul, who agreed.

"The truth of what you say is quite evident," he wrote to Bishop Oldo, "and although I am only a poor blind man, when they wrote me about the foundation at Vico I answered to do nothing about it. But my letter did not arrive in time. I was then at Ceccano, ill. The stone had already been thrown into the well. As for me, I intended to found only at Ceccano and Terracina. But afterward the Most Illustrious and Reverend Bishops, as well as certain cities that wanted to have some of our retreats, wrote several times to Father Thomas and insisted so much that he, with holy intentions, agreed to negotiate. Profoundly convinced of his prudence, I authorized him to do the best for the greater glory of the Lord and the good of the Congregation, especially as I was far away and could not be apprised of everything in letters. . . . God permitted that my letter should arrive too late. I see in this a manifest sign that the Divine Majesty wants to derive the greatest glory from our trials. I am even more confident that it will be to the great advantage of the Congregation. To this end, I encourage Father Thomas as much as I can. I know he is a 'true Israelite' and that he has tried to act with the right intention. I speak to him only of precautions to take for the future."[11]

Paul was obviously worried about the gathering storm, but he proved himself a leader who does not abandon his subordinates when things go badly. Such leaders are rare.

Moreover he had taken all necessary precautions and been assured that all obstacles had been removed.

Amid these anxieties and despite his delicate health, Paul agreed to preach a mission at Viterbo after Easter. An incident occurred there that made a deep impression on him and on his listeners. This was the sudden death of the Bishop of Viterbo at the very moment of Father Paul's sermon on the last ends.

The mission closed as usual, and Paul was preparing to go and preach another one when he was laid low by fever.

Cardinal Simonetti was named to succeed Bishop Abbati of Viterbo. The Cardinal, warned from the start against Paul and his various plans for foundations, showed his mistrust at once by sending a delegate to visit the retreat of Vetralla.

Father Mark Aurelius, the Superior, took refuge behind the papal brief which exempted retreats of more than twelve religious from the jurisdiction of the bishops. The delegate bowed before this refusal, but the Cardinal was deeply offended.

When Paul returned from his missions, he hoped to win over the Cardinal by his personal affability. He asked for an audience, and it was granted. But the Cardinal accused him of being "a proud man and a hypocrite"[12] and requested him not to come back. Paul fell to his knees to receive these insults, and not a muscle in his face betrayed his feelings. Then he rose and went out, as serene as when he had come in.[13]

Once back at the retreat, he simply asked his religious to pray with all their hearts for His Eminence.

When we call to mind the natural ardor of Paul's temperament, we can well admire his self-control on this occasion. It was at least equal to the impassibility of a Talleyrand or a Fouché before Napoleon's fits of anger.

When Cardinal Simonetti became better informed about Paul and his Congregation, his attitude quickly changed. He received Paul graciously several times and even offered to defend him. However, the Cardinal died a few months later.

The storm was not subsiding. During 1748 isolated instances of libel against particular foundations became an orchestrated attack against the whole Congregation of the discalced poor men of Jesus, amid a veritable campaign of disparagement.

How did they dare appropriate the cult of the Passion of Our Lord? St. Francis of Assisi had spread it far and wide long before.

Was it really necessary to display the symbol of the Passion on their tunics? Should it not rather be engraved in a man's heart?

Other complaints were less harmless. And so the war of pamphlets went on, whose tone we can grasp from the following, addressed to the Pope and signed by the superior of one of the Fratri's monasteries:

"The missionary Fathers of the Most Holy Passion of Our Lord think they can get away with anything. They flatter themselves that they succeed in their plans by virtue of their name or rather by virtue of a new motto, a new coat of arms which represents a heart pierced by various instruments of penance. In this manner they want to singularize themselves among all the holy orders and institutes, and their great specialty is to sow tares, to arouse dissensions, to worry and disturb religious and faithful alike. . . . If the spirit of the first founders of the new Congregation of the missionary Fathers of the Passion of Jesus Christ consists in the art of stirring up disputes, stripping the poor laity of their goods, ravishing from the mendicant orders the charitable help of the people, then without any doubt in a short time they will have no other rule than violence."[14]

As the memorandum was signed by a religious from Alatri, the Pope sent it to the ordinary of the town, Bishop Cavallini, for investigation.

It happened that Father Thomas was preaching a retreat in Alatri when the Bishop received the libel. His Excellency transmitted it to the missionary, who informed Father Paul about it, adding: "I had a good laugh over it."[15]

Father Paul took it harder because he was more directly attacked. "We are treated worse than Luther, Mohammed, and Calvin," he wrote to Father Fulgencio. "The Pope has sent it for investigation to a Bishop who is a friend of ours and who will make every effort to refute it. This vicious piece was written in a well-reformed Order. So that you may pray, I will tell you that it is a monastery of Capuchins. I am telling this to your heart and not to anyone else. I have no merit, for my nature is so gross and vulgar that it is not subject to resentment. On the contrary, I feel still more tender affection for this Order."[16]

Paul's attitude, in fact, had more than a little merit, and his affection for the Fratri was not merely a matter of words. If by chance he met one of them, he would go out of his way to be gracious to him.

In the end, the adage "Who wants to prove too much proves nothing" was demonstrated once more. The libel was so extravagant that it convinced no one, and the calumnies boomeranged against their authors.

Paul's enemies decided to use more powerful weapons against him.

In June 1748 twelve monasteries of Fratri concerted to initiate a formal lawsuit against the retreat at Ceccano and the other proposed foundations.

On June 26 Paul learned of it through Father Thomas, who sent him a copy of the citation to appear before the Roman Congregation of Bishops and Regulars. Paul took his old writing kit and alerted all his friends and his religious houses: "Everyone has taken up arms against the poor little flock of these blessed lambs of Christ. . . . Prayers, prayers, I beg of you, so that the Divine Majesty may grant us victory."[17]

He was full of confidence. Secure in his rights and certain that he was accomplishing a divine mission, he predicted success. But the drama of his life was not yet over. Defeat awaited him.

One afternoon Father Thomas, rector of Ceccano, was going out for a walk when the sheriff of Pofi handed him a message. It was a "monitory from the Auditor of the Apostolic Chamber" — in today's parlance, a notification from the Procurator-General — who, before handing down any judgment, explicitly forbade the Passionist religious to continue their construction work at the retreats of Ceccano and Terracina or to undertake any other proposed foundation under pain of a fine of a thousand gold ducats, not to mention other more serious penalties.

As soon as Father Thomas read this stunning monitory he left for Rome. There he saw four cardinals. The monitory was severe but legal. Everything had to remain as it decreed until the tribunal's decision. The Congregation had to obey.

Father Paul did not learn of this new thunderbolt until August 6. He was deeply grieved but did not lose courage. "We shall be the victors, but first we shall suffer great tribulations. . . . We must insist, as usual, that everyone pray. Father Thomas is a pillar. He suffers and works like a hero, ready to give his life for the Congregation. . . ."[18]

Meanwhile the matter ran its course. The monitory was hung up "like a bed sheet" (the expression is Paul's own) on the doors of the churches of Ceccano, Paliano, Terracina, and elsewhere. Thus thrown before the public eye, it had unexpected repercussions. The townspeople and municipal councils reacted violently and, in true Italian fashion, not without an element of comedy.

One day the people of Ceccano saw the Passionists come out of their retreat. The religious were merely going for a walk, but the people thought they were going away for good. Armed with staves and tools, the good men dashed forward to drive the religious back, by force if need be, to the retreat that they did not want them to leave at any cost.[19]

At Paliano things took a different turn. Upon receipt of the monitory, the municipal council asked to see the Rule of the Congregation. They were so edified by the Passionists' strict poverty and austere mode of life that they unanimously voted in favor of the proposed foundation near the town. Dom Isidore, who had assumed responsibility for the repairs and found little co-operation among his compatriots, was now free to go ahead with his work.

At Terracina the Bishop had taken the proposed foundation into his own hands. The Fratri threatened to have him excommunicated. This did not alarm him at all, and the townspeople sided with him.

Moreover, the three cities decided to institute a lawsuit in the Roman courts against the Fratri, who were opposing their right to found a Passionist monastery if they so desired.

Father Paul would have preferred less uproar about his affairs. "We would never have pleaded, for the poor do not institute lawsuits. It is the townships that are facing up to the Fratri. They are all united against them. Oh! How it displeases me.

I have written and written again to prevent this lawsuit. *The servant of the Lord must not quarrel.* [II Tim. 2:24.] It seems that the devil wants to make use of this means to gain ample advantage to our detriment. I have protested that I do not want any retreats by dint of lawsuits. I want them only if they can be had peaceably. . . . We shall have to continue to pray a great deal."[20]

Paul had the distrust of the poor for lawsuits. He thought a papal authorization by legal channels would be much quicker and more dependable. At his request, Bishop Oldo tried to obtain such an authorization.

The people of Ceccano presented a petition asking permission to continue the construction work that could not be left in mid-air without serious damage to the buildings. Rome would not hear of it. The prohibition against construction of any kind was maintained until the case was tried.

For once Paul lost courage. Up to that time he had preserved his beautiful faith. "Let the Capuchin scurry about as much as he wants to," he had written, referring to his enemies' proceedings. "God will give us victory."[21] But now he wrote to Father Fulgencio:

"Barring a miracle, I assure you that the lawsuit is lost and we shall have to give up this retreat [Ceccano]. And if we give it up, then it is good-by to all our new foundations! I still have a little trust in the depths of my heart. But, speaking in natural terms, that is where we are going. We must therefore take our precautions and above all defer the acceptance of new subjects until after the end of the lawsuit. For if they abolish this retreat there will scarcely be enough room for our present number at Monte Argentario, here at Holy Angel, and at St. Eutychius. . . ."

And he closed his letter of disillusionment by saying: "Believe me, to judge things according to their ordinary course, they are trying to destroy the whole Congregation." But at the very end he used his favorite formula, whose meaning we shall see later: "The Will of God be done!"[22]

The letter he wrote to Bishop Oldo at the same time and on the same subject is but a commentary on this acceptance: "May this Divine Will always be my food. . . ."[23]

As the days passed, some bringing favorable news and others unfavorable, Father Paul swung back and forth between optimism and pessimism.

Expert surveyors were assigned to measure the actual distances between the monasteries. Thus it was found that there were more than eight miles between the retreat at Ceccano and the Capuchins of Pofi. That was more than required.[24]

Out of a spirit of solidarity, however, other monasteries of Fratri not directly involved joined forces with the first twelve. On the other side, more towns banded together in the same spirit as that at Ceccano, Paliano, and Terracina. Parishes where the Passionists had preached missions sent laudatory attestations.

Paul approved of his friend's efforts. His trust in God had never led him to neglect human means. For his part, he wrote to cardinals he thought favorable to him. Finally he set out for Rome at the beginning of November. After making the journey almost entirely on foot, he wrote to his habitual confidant, Father Fulgencio: "Yesterday . . . I arrived in Rome, completely soaked by the rain. I have no idea how long I shall remain here. I think at least until the end of November. Believe me, I have never been in so many difficulties. I do now know where to begin.

"The Fratri of Soriano have also forbidden us to beg for grain, wine, etc., which our syndics do everywhere, that is to say, in the diocese. There are the lawsuits of Ceccano and Terracina. I do not know which way to turn. I shall do what I can. I have placed everything in God's hands. This morning I began walking through the city of Rome until noon. . . . I am tempted to do nothing more, but I must bow my head. If the Albani family does not give us strong support, we shall have to abandon the Retreat of St. Eutychius, because how shall we live? For the rest, there are contradictions and tempests on all sides. It does not frighten me. The Will of God be done. . . ."[25]

We can well imagine that the Fratri meanwhile were not inactive. They planned a stroke which, so they thought, would ruin Father Paul and his religious by winning the Pope's decision.

At that time there was a religious missionary in Rome, famous for his oratorical gifts and his virtue, who enjoyed extraordinary favor with Benedict XIV. In fact, this religious was not allowed to leave Rome without the Pope's permission. Every Sunday afternoon the Pope received him, so highly did he esteem his holy conversations.

This man was Father Leonard, a missionary of the reformed Friars Minor, who was to become St. Leonard of Port Maurice. His Superior-General wanted to take advantage of his influence on Benedict XIV to prejudice him against the Passionists.

Reluctantly, but through a spirit of obedience, Father Leonard agreed to counsel the Pope to beware of this new enterprising Congregation, whose new mode of dress and professed love of solitude could well give rise to suspicion.

Benedict XIV listened and then said simply: "Would you want Us to destroy what We ourselves have erected?"[26] Thus the expected effect was lost. True, Father Leonard must not have put much conviction into his argument, for he held Father Paul and his religious in high esteem. It is said that he always regretted what he had been obliged to do under obedience.[27]

Nonetheless, Benedict XIV was troubled by this intervention of a person whose opinion he valued. Feeling the need of further enlightenment on the matter which the plaintiffs had completely confused, he named a commission of cardinals in utmost secrecy to make a study.

The cardinals had the behavior and doctrine of the Founder and of his religious carefully investigated. The results of their study, when communicated to the Pope, placed Paul and his Congregation in a very good light. But the inquiry took some time. Meanwhile Paul, who had no inkling of what was afoot, was perplexed by the gracious yet reticent reception he received in Rome. He wanted to go and throw himself at the Pope's feet. "I have asked advice of His Eminence Cardinal Tanara, as well of His Eminence Cardinal Gentile. After careful reflection they advised me to wait. I think I did well to place the matter in God's hands."[28]

The cardinals' embarrassment is understandable, in view of

Pope Bendict XIV's latest decision. Paul left Rome toward the end of November, partially reassured. But now he learned that the Fratri's attacks were no longer limited to the province of Campagna Marittima. They were now directed against his retreats north of Rome.

As the case was not due to come up for trial until December 20, there was nothing to do but wait. Paul had been obliged to neglect his apostolic work, but he could not refuse to preach three missions in the diocese of Porto at the request of Cardinal Albani. Upon leaving Rome, therefore, he preached missions at Cerveteri and Cerri but was taken ill and could not preach the third one as he had promised.

He wanted to return to Holy Angel Retreat but had to stop halfway at Oriola, where he spent Christmas. It was not until January 4 that he arrived at Vetralla.

Meanwhile the case had not come up on December 20 as scheduled. The commission instituted by the Pope was apparently not ready to give its opinion.

At the start of 1749 the litigation seemed to take a favorable turn. A new petition by Bishop Oldo in favor of the Terracina retreat, addressed directly to the Pope, was referred by His Holiness to Cardinal Gentile for his views. As the Cardinal was Paul's friend, he immediately recommended that the matter be removed from the jurisdiction of the Congregation of Bishops and Regulars and be judged by a special commission.

The Pope accepted the Cardinal's recommendation, and the commission was appointed. Its object was to inquire whether it was possible to grant the Passionists the right to found retreats simply on the favorable judgment of the ordinaries of the place without considering the privileges of the Fratri. This was a clever strategy and made it unnecessary to prove that these privileges were not being violated in the cases under litigation.

The members of the commission seemed favorable. Paul was exultant: "I am leaving for Rome today. I received its decision yesterday. God has worked a miracle. Things are going wonderfully well. God wants to bless His work in a magnificent way and to extend it far and wide. The signs are evident. Help us, as sons of the Congregation, to thank the Lord and continue to pray."[29]

Alas! He arrived in Rome to learn that the commission would not meet until Lent. Leaving a few documents with Cardinal Gentile, he returned to Holy Angel Retreat. He had been given full assurance by the Cardinal, and encouraging news soon reached him, confirming him in his confidence: Bishop Oldo had obtained the right to continue construction of the Terracina retreat.

Early in Lent the meeting of the cardinals' commission was put off until Easter. When Paul went to Rome at Easter, disappointment awaited him. Cardinal Albani, one of the commission's members, on whom he thought he could depend and who had until then been favorable to him, announced he was against him. The pressure of the Fratri had finally had its effect on him.

An unexpected turn of events restored Paul's chances and hopes. Most of the religious houses in league against the Passionists abandoned their plaint at law. The others, caught off guard, asked that the case be adjourned for further consultation. Their request was rejected and the pleading set for April 28, 1749.

Paul breathed more freely. "The devil has unleashed all his efforts to have the case deferred. God in His mercy has done me the favor of obtaining a meeting of the special commission on Monday, the 28th of the month, at two o'clock. The opposing party has no printed brief. They are in disagreement. From what I can see, things are happening that are in the nature of miracles. . . ."[30]

The matter came up for judgment on April 28. According to the instructions of Cardinal Gentile, the lawyer did not defend the rights of each individual retreat, but rather the over-all right of the Passionists to establish retreats. The judges deferred the concession of this general right until a later time. However, they decided that in the case of the three retreats at Ceccano, Terracina, and Paliano, the favorable recommendation of the ordinary of the place would suffice.

This was an initial success. Paul was delighted. "Tomorrow I leave Rome, as satisfied as if I were taking with me a Bull crammed with privileges for all the foundations in the world, for I am most confident that He Who began the work will complete it."[31]

His optimism was to be put to severe tests.

On the advice of Cardinal Gentile, Paul had tried to obtain, together with the general authorization to found retreats, the permission to arrange for the ordination of his own priests with the title of poverty. Both of these authorizations were deferred until a later time.

As prospective candidates for the Congregation were increasing in number, he tried again to obtain the favor of ordinations without limitation as to number. His efforts were fruitless.

And already the worry of lawsuits over Ceccano, Terracina and Paliano was looming again. It was much less simple than he had imagined. He had thought there would be only three requests to present and that everything would be settled in a few months.

The people of these three towns hastened to address a petition to the cardinals' commission. The interested bishops expressed extremely favorable and laudatory opinions. Even the monasteries of the Fratri near the retreats gave their consent.

But the commission was in no hurry to meet in order to issue its decrees. Meanwhile intrigue flared up again, and Paul was once more filled with anxiety. The situation was not improved by the fact that his religious who were so poorly lodged at Ceccano began to fall ill.

Father Paul encouraged his brothers in religion while trying to win over his various opponents. Twice a week as many as twenty letters would pile up on his desk. This correspondence was a heavy burden, added to all the others. "I have been writing all morning, and there are many more letters to write. God help me, for the devil is watching. . . ."[32]

He dreamed of the day when he would have leisure to write the history of his foundations, for love of writing grows through practice. Although he had had very little formal schooling, he had now become a remarkable letter writer. "After the present tempests, I shall strive, during my moments of leisure, to prepare a report on the foundation of our retreats. The account of these great events, most of which are very secret, would require a large volume. When I have prepared the reports, I shall ask one of our religious, a true servant of God and well educated, to set them in order. But for my work I would need several months of holy repose, and it is most improbable that this will be given to me."[33]

At the moment, the storm was reaching a new peak of violence. The Fratri of Soriano, who had kept clear of the lawsuit until then, now started a suit against the Retreat of St. Eutychius. This retreat had been founded six years earlier under the protection of Cardinal Albani, who now announced he no longer had any interest in it.

Paul was crushed. "Like a poor shipwrecked sailor in a raging sea and in the heart of the night, I cling to a tiny plank, expecting to drink the lethal water from one minute to the next."[34]

The months passed by in nerve-racking expectation, and still the commisssion gave no decision. This delay was not surprising during the heat of summer when the cardinals left Rome for the countryside or watering places. But when autumn came, the delay seemed inexplicable.

Paul kept writing, but even his friends seemed weary. "Our ship has run aground on a sand bank. I no longer have anyone's support. I have only the support of God's Providence, from which I hope great things in the measure that I lack the protection of men."[35]

In the face of this abandonment, we can glimpse the desolation of his heart.

The period of waiting was exasperating, but Paul did not spend it idly. During that autumn when Rome kept silent, he resumed his usual campaign of missions, this time going to Caprarola, Fabrica, Corchiano, and finally to Rome, where a retreat was being held in all the churches in preparation for the 1750 Holy Year.

When Father Thomas informed Paul in a letter that the pontifical authorities had invited him to preach the retreat exercises in the Church of St. John of the Florentines near the Farnese Palace, he refused. "I cannot and must not accept. I am a donkey, and the little I have written I have drawn from books, especially from the *Svegliario* [a collection of sermons]. . . . But that would make little difference. The worst is that I am in ill health."[36]

At most he agreed to come as an assistant and take charge of the meditation on the Passion. Yet humble as he was where he himself was concerned, he was surprised that only one church and not two had been offered to his Passionists.

Nevertheless, he went to Rome to assist Father Thomas. In the end, Father Thomas fell sick during the mission, and Father Paul had to preach the sermons and also give the meditations on the Passion. His fervor was so great that he touched all hearts. The chronicle of this mission reports, apparently without any attempt at irony: "His hearers could not hold back their tears. Five cardinals who were present were so moved that they, too, wept."[37]

While Paul was forgetting his worries about the foundations amid his apostolic labors, his benefactor and friend, Bishop Oldo, died. With the disappearance of this prelate from the scene, the plans for a retreat at Terracina almost foundered.

This is not to say that Bishop Oldo's successor, Bishop Palombella of the Servite Order, was hostile, but the estate of the deceased prelate was contested by his heirs and the chapter of the cathedral. The latter put an embargo on materials for the retreat at Terracina that Bishop Oldo had been building at his own expense, until the sum of five hundred crowns was paid. This was more than Paul could afford to pay, and the matter dragged on for a year.

After these many delays which prevented all further expansion of the Congregation, the lawsuit finally came up for judgment on

April 7, 1750. Three lawyers pleaded in favor of the retreats at Ceccano, Terracina, and Paliano. The case was won.

The question of a general authorization to found retreats with or without the consent of the Fratri never came up. In any event, the three proposed retreats were saved, and this was a limited success.

Paul hastened to resume construction work at Ceccano and to take possession officially of Terracina and Paliano. At Ceccano the people were so overjoyed by the outcome of the lawsuit that they eagerly helped with the work. Even the children carried materials to the retreat. Father Thomas in his enthusiasm declared that the retreat at Ceccano deserved to be kissed stone by stone.

Chapter XVI

LIKE A BIRD ON A BRANCH

What do you think of it. Is this not a Bohemian's life, to pack my bag at every moment, and to run now here, now there! ST. PAUL OF THE CROSS

FREED at last from the anxieties of the lawsuit, from alternating hope and fear, Paul longed for rest and solitude. "I hope to retire in order to devote myself to holy exercises, at least for two weeks, and to set aside my habitual duties. . . ."[1]

His health also left much to be desired. But how could he get the rest he needed? He was more and more in demand for missions, and when he offered one of his religious in his place the people protested. Referring to the insistence of the people of Camerino, he wrote in a joking mood: "What do you think? Should we not have a good laugh over it? They do not know me, I can assure you! If they did, they would not speak in this way." But he concluded: "I am leaving for Camerino."[2]

And so he was on his way again, trekking from mission to mission. This was to continue for eight years, and it is no figure of speech to say that he spent those years walking the roads of Italy.

Referring to the Camerino mission, he said: "I made the entire journey on foot. God gives me the strength."[3] The distance from Holy Angel Retreat to Camerino is about seventy-five miles and involves crossing the Apennines from south to north. But his zeal had its reward. The mission did much good. Among those converted was the famous chief of a group of smugglers, Horace, who was so feared that the police did not dare interfere with his lawless activities.

When Horace heard Father Paul preach he experienced some remorse but found an indulgent confessor who was not able to persuade him to change his ways. Father Paul was deeply concerned. Fearing that this partial step toward conversion would lull the man into a sense of false security, he went to see him and obtained a complete conversion. He even secured letters of remission for Horace and all his band, thus protecting them from prosecution for their past misdeeds.

Without waiting for the end of summer, Paul took up his missioner's staff once more, but this time to go into healthful regions.

From Ceccano he wanted to go on to Falvaterra, where Bishop Tartagni had offered him the shrine of St. Sosius through Father Thomas. Having trusted Father Thomas in the case of Ceccano and been so completely disillusioned, Paul decided to see for himself the new site and its facilities.

The site of Falvaterra was healthful but did not offer perfect solitude. A few hundred yards away was a "casino," a word that in those days signified a rustic pavilion where merry company sometimes gathered.

This chagrined Father Paul: "That casino! How it dulls my eagerness for the foundation!" But on the other hand, he needed more retreats. Despite new construction work, the existing foundations were filled to overflowing. When he learned that the undesirable casino was used only to shelter livestock, he finally agreed to accept the site.

His difficulties kept multiplying. Plans for new foundations called for more religious priests. He therefore went from Falvaterra to Rome to ask permission to have a certain number of subjects ordained. After spending only a few days in Rome he went to Monte Argentario. .

How he made the journey — whether on foot or horseback — is not known, but somewhere near Montalto he suffered a fall that must have caused him severe bruises, for he wrote: "My left side suffered most, and I have difficulty coughing."[4] This did not keep him from preaching a retreat at Orbetello however.

After spending Christmas at Monte Argentario he resumed his visitations of the various houses of the Congregation.

Early in 1751 Paul received the permission, requested a few weeks earlier, to have twelve subjects ordained. With this additional personnel he decided to carry out his plans for a foundation at Falvaterra.

Bishop Tartagni had obtained all the necessary authorizations from the Holy Father, and so this project had been invulnerable to attack during the great lawsuit initiated by the Fratri.

Father Paul went to Ceccano, sent for a few religious from the other retreats, and set out with them for Falvaterra, a distance of about seventeen miles. On April 2, 1751, the usual ceremony took place. Considerable property was attached to the shrine of Sosius, but Paul accepted only a small piece of ground, the right to which would later be disputed. He installed his religious on premises devoid of comfort and even indispensable necessities. The temporary cells were separated only by cloth partitions smeared with plaster, and everything else was equally poor. This provisional arrangement was to continue for years.

Paul did not tarry long at Falvaterra. On April 13, 1751, he was off on his spring campaign of missions. The Holy Year had been extended to the entire world, and parishes everywhere were clamoring for missions.

With the coming of summer, he returned to Vetralla. There, in the solitude of the retreat, he began to work once more on a project that had long been close to his heart: obtaining from

Rome the privilege of solemn vows for his religious. This favor seemed necessary to him for the expansion of his Congregation, and it would put an end once and for all to the annoyance of continually requesting permission to ordain small groups of religious.

He had all his religious and the devout souls under his direction pray for this intention. We find no trace of any official request, however, nor do we know if he carried on private negotiations.

In the autumn Paul visited the foundations at Terracina and Paliano, long awaiting completion.

At Terracina the canons had decided to lift their embargo on construction materials in return for a cash payment. Paul hoped to be able to collect the money needed, but he was not given time. The chapter even threatened to take over the buildings under construction as well as the materials. Paul retorted that he had legally taken possession of the retreat. Some good friends, the Angelettis, advanced him the money he had promised to the chapter.

Without waiting for further difficulties to develop, Paul decided to settle his religious at Terracina at once, even though it was still under construction. He went to Holy Angel Retreat to get his men together. "I came back to this retreat exhausted. I am stopping here like a bird on a branch, awaiting my flight. . . ."[5]

He took to his wings again on January 16, 1752. It would be more accurate to say he set out on foot with his companions from Vetralla to Terracina, a distance of about 125 miles. It was freezing, and the ground was covered with snow. When Paul arrived at his destination, his feet were a mass of bloody bruises.

First a mission was given to the people of Terracina and a retreat to the clergy. In the fervent atmosphere thus created, the usual installation ceremony took place on February 6, 1752.

When the crowd had dispersed, Paul and his companions found themselves, as so often before, in a rudimentary structure with neither doors nor windows.

The religious life of the group took shape, nonetheless. Father

Anthony was designated rector. Paul remained at the new foundation for three months, meanwhile preaching missions and retreats in the surrounding towns and villages. Then he resumed his errant life.

Paul went first to his headquarters at Holy Angel Retreat in Vetralla. But he still had to make his visitation at Soriano. "Not the slightest chance to rest for eight full months! Always traveling and on missions!"[6]

He hoped to find calm and solitude during the heat of summer. Instead, he had to drink the bitter waters of tribulation.

Scarcely had he left Terracina when his brother Anthony, now rector of the new retreat, provoked trouble within the house and on the outside by his behavior. We do not know whether it was a matter of imprudence or serious misconduct. The chroniclers chastely veiled the facts, and Paul himself kept silence. At any rate, as soon as he was informed of this turn of affairs Paul withdrew Anthony from his post and sent him as a simple religious to St. Sosius.

Father Anthony's conduct invited new attacks against the young Congregation. Paul admitted that it made him lose his "appetite and the sleep that ordinarily nourishes. I go to sleep trembling like a man who upon awakening will be led to the gallows. I embrace the Will of God as firmly as I can, but on all sides I find only suffering. . . ."[7]

He requested all his religious to pray and asked them to make special mortifications until the Feast of the Assumption. "The Superior may allow more frequent Communions than those prescribed by the Rule, and on the day of the Assumption all priests are to offer up Holy Mass for Father Paul's intention."[8]

That he should have taken these exceptional measures gives us some idea of his anguish. He admits it himself: "Never in my life — although it has been a continual succession of sufferings — never have I been in such tribulation as I have been recently, in consequence of an incident that makes me foresee a heavy trial for the whole Congregation."[9]

We can be betrayed only by those near us, but that does

not lessen the pain of it. Once again Paul yearned for death, "like a bird on a branch" ready for the supreme flight.

The storm "with its high waves" soon calmed down, but it was not without its backwash. For when Paul returned to Terracina that autumn he wrote: "I have nothing to wait for but death, and I think it is closer than my friends believe. But first I shall drink a great chalice of bitterness that will be made sweet by my resignation to the Will of God. This chalice will consist in seeing the work begun dashed to the ground, for that is what everyone is trying to do."[10]

Little by little the difficulties were smoothed out. Paul did not die, but instead took to the road once more.

On January 12, 1753, he was at Toscanella; on the thirteenth, "after a long absence and completely exhausted," he was back at Holy Angel Retreat in Vetralla.

It was at Vetralla that he convoked the general chapter for his eight retreats, which now sheltered more than one hundred religious.

Paul was re-elected Provost General. He kept under his immediate direction the houses north of Rome but delegated a portion of his powers to a provincial who would be in charge of the retreats to the south. Father Thomas was given this new post.

Then, giving the example to the others, Paul began his spring campaign of missions in the province of Campagna Marittima. As a result of his stay in the Pontine Marshes he suffered a severe attack of fever. In June he returned to Holy Angel Retreat to rest. But by August he was off on his fall campaign. Illness forced him to halt so often on his travels that he did not dare venture far from his retreats.

Meanwhile the number of his religious continued to grow. He therefore decided to occupy Paliano, but once again he wanted to go too fast. The retreat was not ready, despite Dom Isidore Galzelli's tenacious efforts.

Dom Isidore had taken charge of the preparations. In the sum-

173

mer he went from farm to farm begging for grain, which he then
resold. But his zeal did not produce the needed results. Besides,
his knowledge of construction work — not to mention his practical sense — left much to be desired.

And so Paul had the surprise, upon visiting the site, to find
a hole in the ground filled with stagnant water meant to serve
as a cistern. Even though he and his religious loved poverty
passionately, they could not occupy the retreat as it then stood.

This was all the more annoying since Paul had just obtained
from the Holy Father, through the intervention of Cardinal
Crescenzi, the faculty of having twelve more subjects ordained.
The novitiate was overcrowded far beyond its capacity.

On the other hand, Paul had the consolation of learning that
the Sovereign Pontiff had praised the great good his missionaries
were doing for souls. This made up for many persecutions. And
so he took up his staff with renewed courage.

The year 1745 was a remarkably active one for Father Paul. His
letters, written now from a rectory and now from a convent of
nuns, show that he was constantly on the move. His spring and
fall campaigns came much closer together than before, barely
allowing him time to recover from an attack of fever. He no
longer had to solicit missions. The people were clamoring for
him. "I have all the missions to preach that I want. I have still
two large dioceses to evangelize."[11]

But he was feeling the effects of illness and age, for he was
now sixty years old. He was so pressed for time that he appointed
Father Thomas to make the visitations of the various houses,
thus enabling him to preach a few more missions.

As soon as these engagements were completed, Paul planned
to retire to a little cell, "without ever speaking to anyone except
to the confessor."[12] The bird on the branch longed for his nest.
But the time had not yet come. The "poor bark" still needed
its pilot.

The foundation at Paliano was approaching completion. To
hasten matters, Paul sent Father Thomas to supervise the work.

The latter asked permission to install a confessional for women, but since the shrine was close to the parish churches of Paliano and Agnani, Paul thought it wiser to refuse. Offended, Thomas left Paliano without telling anyone. This incident had no untoward consequences.

Other difficulties arose, some of them of a serious nature. Cardinal Gentile, Bishop of Paliano, died. His successor, Cardinal Spinelli, having been misinformed, was at first hostile to the foundation. Paul was frightened, for he was still feeling the effects of the Fratri's recent blows. "I see the Congregation dashed to the ground," he wrote.[13]

Dom Isidore Galzelli came to the rescue. He told Cardinal Spinelli of the steps taken by his predecessor to establish the foundation. The Cardinal soon realized that his good faith had been imposed upon and allowed the work to go on.

The storm was over in the south, but another was blowing up in the north. One of the Fratri was spreading a rumor against the retreat at Toscanella, claiming the religious there refused to render the services they could give to the neighboring communities. The calumny miscarried.

A great sorrow now descended upon Paul: the sickness and death of Father Fulgencio. This good priest was not simply one of his beloved sons. He and John Baptist had been his very first companions who remained faithful.

When Father Fulgencio was rector of Monte Argentario, he was the one in whom Paul confided his troubles. Reading the letters Paul wrote when Father Fulgencio began to fail is like hearing St. Bernard's tender accents as he worried over one of his disciples: "Let him omit Matins, let him have bouillon and even donkey's milk, so highly recommended for tuberculosis."

Father Fulgencio died on April 16, 1755, at the age of forty. Paul kept his sorrow over his death to himself, simply saying: "I believe it was precious before the Lord."[14]

Once more Paul threw himself into his apostolic activities. "I am leaving for the missions after Easter. I shall go to La Tolfa, then to Nepi, Ronciglione, and Capranica."[15] But his health gave way. His rheumatic pains became so severe that he was not able to complete even the first of these missions. A cure at the Vicarello baths brought no improvement, nor did the heat of summer. Paul's feet remained swollen and his joints painful. Otherwise his general state of health was good, and he found his forced inactivity the harder to bear, knowing that his missions were awaiting him.

In September he accepted a pony that a benefactor had offered him and set out for Ronciglione and Capranica, where he had been expected since spring. Then he returned in October to Holy Angel to preside over a chapter which was to provide for a successor to Father Fulgencio and settle pending business.

For years Paul had yearned for new recruits, and now he had to refuse applications. "It is not possible for me to accept the postulant of whom you speak. The novitiate is more than full. Next November, about fifteen novices will receive the habit, and then we shall not be able to clothe anyone for three years for lack of room in the retreats."[16]

Great was his joy, therefore, when he learned that the new retreat at Paliano was at last ready for occupancy. As he could not go himself, he sent Father Thomas to preside over the installation. It took place on November 23, 1755, without incident. But what poverty! The cells looked more like prison cells than rooms; and in the church, without vault or ceiling, the dilapidated rafters were visible.

Dom Isidore Galzelli had to admit: "The work was done without any pretensions at architectural skill. I did the best I could, as the inspiration came to me. In so doing, I hewed a very heavy cross for the future rectors by obliging them to do much of the construction work over again. And even so it was a special grace from God to have gotten that far, for I am a builder only in name."[17] Could anyone be more modest about his achievements?

This was the first retreat founded in Paul's absence. He had wanted to take advantage of his improved health to preach a few more missions. After evangelizing the Sisters of Ronciglione, he went to Nepi, Bracciano, and La Manziana. He returned to Holy Angel for Advent, setting out once again three days after Christmas. He was still like "a bird on a branch," or, as he now said, "like a Bohemian."

Paul had made up his mind to retire in 1759. "In the most profound recollection of mental prayer. I shall prepare myself for death." But he still had two dioceses to evangelize, and so many convents were clamoring for him!

Instead of retiring, therefore, he decided to take a water cure or perhaps a cure of herb decoctions. Then, with his vigor restored, he would take up his staff once more. Three years passed in this way, from 1756 to 1759. It would be tedious to enumerate all the localities and convents he visited during this period.

Joyously he declared: "What do you think of it? Is this not a Bohemian's life, constantly to pack my bag at every moment, and to run now here, now there! Patience!"

It was not until 1759 that he gave up his apostolic work. For several more years he was to remain "like a bird on a branch," ready "to fly" to souls in need. Patience!

Chapter XVII

THE DOVES

I did not open the way myself. Such a thing would have seemed folly to me. ST. TERESA OF ÁVILA *Foundations*, II, 16

IF WE dared follow through the metaphor used by Paul himself, we would say that, in the shade of the tree where Paul sometimes stopped, many "Doves" came to rest.

It was not that he sought to attract them, and even less to hold them. "I desire to be rid of the direction of devout women. Indeed, I would like to give them all up, and I hope to succeed in doing so soon. I am ignorant, imperfect, and blind. . . ."[1]

He made this a rule for his religious: "Priests, and especially young ones, are not to take on the ordinary direction of devout women, laywomen or religious. . . ."[2] And he himself followed the rule.

Writing to one of these ladies, he said: "Paul of the Cross has received Mrs. Maria Anna Avolta's letter. He answers that she should make use of the holy teachings received without disturbing him by writing to him. For he will not answer her, in view of the fact that he is not accustomed to correspond with women unless there be a very specific need. He has acted in the same manner with other ladies of quality."[3]

But his ministry demanded that he preach ever more frequently to religious communities where there were many abuses and where souls of good will asked him for help. He could not refuse without failing in his mission.

It was precisely these abuses that had deterred him from entering one of the extant religious orders. And now he felt the need of founding a congregation of women, more austere and fervent than those in existence, for the benefit of chosen souls. How could he refuse to take an interest in the formation and perseverance of those in particular who desired to enter this proposed congregation?

At the same time, it should be clearly understood that even when he used terms of endearment, which are so abundant in the Italian language, Paul never allowed himself any human attachment. "I confess before the Lord that while I love the souls I direct in God just as I love the others, yet I feel profoundly detached from them. Indeed, if I were never again to speak to them, nor hear, see, nor receive any news from them, it would not grieve me at all. I would love the Will of God in this. Thank God, I have already had such experiences. When I have left one or another person whom I was directing, I felt no sorrow. If I had, I would have feared some attachment, even if for a good motive, and this would have been sufficient reason for me never to direct anyone else."[4]

178

So that no one should make any mistake about it, he declared openly: "A sinner I am, but a thief, no! With great effort and delicacy I have always reserved the love of my heart for God. I have helped many souls, but I have never sought to do anything but love God and make others love Him."[5]

With equal energy he discouraged any attachment toward himself. "I did not want others to be thieves on my account, by giving me love that was not a love of pure charity."[6]

"Woe to those who put their trust in their spiritual father or who become attached to him — especially young girls. Above all, woe if this attachment is mutual! From this evil, deliver us, O Lord."[7]

And we can well admire his virtue, when we remember his loving and ardent temperament.

With this necessary preface to avoid any misunderstanding, we can say that Paul was an incomparable director of souls, an awakener of vocations, a prudent guide through the dwellings of the interior castle of the soul, a beloved and loving father.

Beginning with his first mission, preached at Talamone in 1730, he was able to draw one of these chosen souls to Christ. This was Agnes Grazi, of whom we have already spoken. Attracted by the vanity common to her years, she was conquered by the burning faith of the young missionary and remained faithful to him until her death in 1744.

Paul wrote 165 letters to her, which guided her in the path of humility to the heights of mystical union. While she was not able to enter Paul's congregation, which was founded much later, she had the privilege of being laid to rest in the church of the Presentation on Monte Argentario.

In 1733, during his third year as a preacher, Paul gave a retreat at the convent of the Franciscan nuns of Piombino. This was the first time he had addressed cloistered nuns.

One of these nuns, Mother Cherubina Bresciani, had been living a life of spiritual tepidity. Transformed by the retreat, she decided to give herself totally to God. It was Paul who initiated her into the life of fervor, into the struggle against scruples, into pure love of God without attachment to creatures.

She followed his teachings so well that he picked her out in his mind as the future foundress of the women's institute he hoped to establish. As early as 1733, when his efforts to found his own miraculously revealed Congregation were unsuccessful, he thought of founding a congregation of women who would follow the same rule of life.

We should note, however, an essential difference in his procedure and interior attitude with regard to these two congregations.

Where his Congregation of men was concerned, Paul forged right ahead, while accepting the Will of God as manifested by the decisions of his superiors. His repeated defeats, far from deterring him, made up the very fabric of his life. For he was sure of his divine mission.

In the case of the women's institute, he went ahead with infinitely more discretion, and his efforts were more widely spaced. He allowed himself to be governed much more by exterior events than by his own inspirations. "When the time decreed by Divine Providence comes," he wrote concerning this institute, "all paths will be opened."[8]

This is very close to the line of conduct followed by Teresa of Ávila.

And so from year to year he continued to bridle Mother Bresciani's zealous desires: "As for the convent of nuns, we must await fuller illuminations. If God wills it, He will make Himself understood very clearly. For the moment, do not allow your heart to be disturbed by this desire."[9]

In 1737 it seemed as if the paths were going to be opened after the foundation of his first retreat. The spirit of mortification of his penitent delighted him, but the time for the new community of women had not yet come.

When in 1746 Mother Bresciani was elected abbess of her monastery, he urged her to devote her efforts above all to correcting the abuses in her own house. Anyone who has read the *Autobiography* of St. Teresa of Ávila can easily imagine these abuses. The life of the world had invaded too many convents. "Presents were sent to the priests of the town. When a postulant received the habit, comedies were given. The parlor was transformed into a drawing room."

Mother Bresciani died without witnessing the birth of the eagerly awaited congregation. The forty-sixth letter addressed to her by Father Paul was dated December 15, 1761.

It was also the preaching of a mission that brought another luminous soul across his path: Lucia Burlini.

In 1737 Paul and his brother were preaching in the town of Cellere. Drawn by their renown for holiness, Lucia came to hear them, although she lived in a neighboring community. She waited in vain for two whole mornings before Paul's beleaguered confessional. On the third day Paul called her himself. Although she was illiterate, he agreed to be her spiritual director.

When the retreat was founded in Ceccano, Lucia generously came to help the religious, and she had the opportunity to meet Father Paul quite often. In his absence Father John Anthony Luccatini acted as secretary, writing letters to Paul from Lucia and reading Paul's letters to her.

This humble and fervent soul was favored with great graces. Among others, she had a vision of doves representing the souls that Paul was in time to group under a rule analogous to that of the Passionists. "I asked the Lord to let me know in some way if the new convent for women would ever be founded. At the same moment it seemed as if I were on Calvary. There I saw Love crucified, and at the foot of the Cross a multitude of souls weeping like turtledoves for their deceased Spouse. Some of them wiped off the bleeding wounds of Jesus, others embraced the most holy Cross very tightly. . . . Still others, like innocent doves, made their nest in the most holy wounds of the Savior. . . ."

Paul, though little inclined to believe this type of vision, accepted the prediction and the symbol. Writing to Lucy, he said: "Pray for the intentions of this great affair. Otherwise the doves will not come to the nest, and you will remain in your nest at Piansano."[10] For Lucia Burlini also desired to enter the new institute; and, illiterate though she was, Paul had thought of making her its cornerstone.

Without changing his opinion of Lucia's virtue, Paul gave up his plans. The path to such a foundation was not yet open, especially in view of the offensive launched against his own Congregation.

When Father Paul or his companions happened to be passing through Ronciglione, they were always received by the Palozzi family.

In 1755 Paul came to Ronciglione to preach a mission, and as usual stayed at his benefactor's house. There he found Teresa Palozzi, whom he had known as a child, now a young lady of eighteen.

Teresa had received a fine education. Paul noticed her frank and joyous temperament. He soon learned to know her generous soul, for she placed herself under his spiritual direction.

Like St. Teresa of Ávila, Paul believed it was necessary first of all to consider a subject's natural qualities before judging the authenticity of a vocation. He esteemed Teresa Palozzi so highly that he prevailed upon her to remain patiently with her family for fifteen years until the institute was finally founded.

It is true that on several occasions he thought the new congregation was about to come into being. For a long time he expected it to be approved at the same time that the favor of solemn vows was granted to his own religious. For the ancient institutes of women like the Carmelites were attached to similar institutes of men having solemn vows.

And so it was that he tried over and over again, but without success, to obtain the favor of solemn vows for his religious. When "the way was finally opened," Teresa Palozzi was one of the first Passionist nuns, and she became the second superior of the new institute.

Through Paul's correspondence we learn of other women who entrusted their souls to his spiritual direction. Among them was Teresa Maria Cosimelli, a sister of one of his religious, whom he advised to sanctify herself in the state of life in which she then found herself. Also Sister Agnes Nepi, whom he firmly turned away: "I never felt inspired to share her sentiments in her determination to join our poor institute. I feel an ever-growing repugnance against it. . . ."[11] And Maria Aldobrandini, a member of an illustrious patrician family, whom he certainly did not turn away since he asked her to pray for the fulfillment of his plans.

Many others whose names will never be known to us begged Father Paul to found an austere convent. "I advise them to diligently address their supplications to the Lord for this intention."[12]

Only to his intimate friends did Paul reveal his hopes, out of discretion and prudence. Among these friends was the Benedictine Sister, Maria Crocifissa Costantini, who was to become the first Passionist nun.

Faustine Gertrude was born on August 18, 1713, in Corneto, now Tarquinia. She belonged to an excellent family. One day as she sat distractedly in class, her eyes paused on the crucifix hanging on the wall. She had seen it many times without paying particular attention to it. That day she felt a great pity for Jesus Crucified which was to mark her for life, and she offered to suffer in union with Him.

Being a child, she forgot her promises. But when she was thirteen she regained her first fervor. At eighteen she entered the convent of the Benedictines in her native city taking the name of Maria Candida Crocifissa.

Soon afterward, in 1736, Paul gave a retreat at the Benedictine convent, whose property was being administered by Anthony Costantini. From the start he won the esteem of the father and the absolute trust of the daughter.

Like the Palozzis in Ronciglione, the Costantinis received Paul and his religious whenever they passed through Corneto. Although Paul had no inkling of it yet, the Costantinis were to "open the way" for the foundation of his institute for women.

Mrs. Costantini had died when Faustine Gertrude was fifteen, leaving three daughters and two sons. The three daughters entered the Benedictine convent and later wanted to become Passionist nuns. Of the two sons, Dominic married but had no children, and Nicholas became a priest.

In 1753 the two brothers agreed to build a convent for their three sisters and told Paul of their decision. In his joy, Paul referred to the proposed convent as "a nest for the beloved doves of Jesus Christ."[13] A great step forward had been taken, but it was only the first step. Rome's approbation was needed, and Paul knew from experience that it was easier to overcome material difficulties than to obtain this approbation.

As we have already said, Paul hoped to win approval of his women's congregation at the same time as the granting of solemn vows to his religious. But his discreet negotiations failed. In 1756 he advised the Costantinis with rare generosity to present their plans to an already existing congregation. He feared to involve his benefactors in useless expenses. But in his heart he kept hoping.

In 1757 Paul again preached a retreat to the Benedictine nuns of Corneto. As he was staying with the Costantinis, he had the opportunity to take definite steps toward establishing the proposed foundation.

Bishop Gustiniani of Corneto approved the plan and agreed to have it executed in his name to circumvent any intrigue against Paul.

Upon his return to the Retreat of Our Lady of the Oak in Toscanella, Paul thought over the decisions he had made. Remembering the difficulties occasioned by Bishop Oldo's premature death, he feared lest the same thing should happen in Corneto if Bishop Gustiniani should die.

He therefore wrote of his fears to Dominic Costantini and advised him to obtain from the Bishop a secret but explicit declaration that he was only lending his name to the undertaking. "We are mortal, and the undertaking will not be completed in a day."[14]

A week later he wrote another letter to Dominic, specifying the width of the corridors and the dimensions of the cells, as well as a mass of details that reveal his practical turn of mind. He wanted everything to be just right, "for we are preparing a nest for the pure doves of Jesus Crucified, so that they may wear perpetual mourning for His most sacred Passion."[15]

He had no illusions about the speed with which the plans would be executed. In fact, it was not until January 29, 1759, that the cornerstone was laid. And even then his letters called for secrecy and indicated to the impatient "Doves" that the foundation was still a matter of the distant future.

He was deluding himself with regard to his chances of obtaining solemn vows for his own Congregation. He requested them officially in 1760, but they were not granted. This was a hard blow to him. However, he continued to prepare the "Doves." If the congregation was not to be founded in his lifetime, then it would be after his death.

How carefully he watched over the fervor of Mother Maria Crocifissa! She had told him of the humiliations she endured in her convent. "Rejoice, Doña Maria Crocifissa, and be patient in carrying the cross where you are. The time will come to carry it elsewhere. Now, you must suffer and be silent. . . ."[16]

But she had no reason to worry. Paul continued to put all his trust in her. What pure tenderness in these lines: "I remember what St. Jerome did. On a certain occasion evil tongues tried to alienate his holy spiritual daughters, St. Paula, St. Marcella, and other holy Roman ladies. He wrote a letter to a friend, defending himself and asking the friend to greet these holy women on his behalf. And he added that they were his daughters, whether they wanted to be or not. *Velint, nolint, filiae meae sunt.* I dare say as much to Maria Crocifissa. Whether you want to or not, you are still my blessed daughter in Jesus Christ, because I hope someday to see you clothed in this livery of the most sacred Passion of Jesus Christ which I myself wear. It is already many years since God placed your soul in my care."[17]

But now a new difficulty arose which was unexpected to say the least. Dominic Costantini, not content to supervise the construction and planning of the future convent, got the idea into his head of defining its rules. The new nuns were to eat meat, receive visitors in the parlor, and not rise for Matins.

From the time he preached his first retreats in religious communities, Paul had fought against the unfittingness of worldly visits as well as against the two other points. If the new institute was to abolish all austerity, then there was a question as to whether it was really needed. Paul's opposition to Dominic's ideas was expressed very clearly and forcefully in a letter to Mother Maria Crocifissa: "Well! Let Dominic compose the rules and Constitutions, let him get the Pope to approve them, and then let him put into his convent the nuns that he pleases! As for me, I shall never consent to the arrangements he proposes. It would be the destruction of our Institute of the most sacred Passion.

"Parlors are the ruin of convents. I know it from experience. I have been preaching retreats to nuns for quite some time.

"If the new convent is to be a convent of the Institute of the most sacred Passion, just like our monasteries, then the nuns will have to observe the Holy rules approved by the Pope, just as our religious do. *If not, I wash my hands of the whole thing. I shall never consent, for God does not want it.* We want to found a convent of magnanimous and holy souls, souls that are dead to all created things and that become, through their holy virtues, their penance, and their mortification, like Jesus Crucified and Mary the Mother of Sorrows. This Mother must be the abbess of the convent.

"The nuns of Santa Fiora, to whom I have just preached another retreat, fast every day. In the evening they receive only two apples, one cooked and the other raw, and a small piece of bread, etc. They sleep on a straw mat, rise at midnight, walk barefoot in sandals, etc. And yet there are among them girls of delicate constitution, born of fine families. If you want to communicate all this to your brother for his enlightenment, you may."[18]

The following year Dominic Costantini admitted he had been wrong and asked Paul to draft the Constitutions himself. Paul accepted and set to work with the help of two other religious. But this was not the biggest hurdle. He still had to have the

Constitutions approved. Bishop Gustiniani would have liked to mitigate the austerities, just as Dominic had, and above all he insisted that the subsistence of the nuns be assured.

Paul agreed with the prelate and concluded that the hour for the foundation had not yet come. "I do not know when we shall put the finishing touch to the convent," he wrote to Maria Crocifissa. Great are the difficulties. The Bishop does not seem favorably inclined, nor does he show any enthusiasm for it.

"We must therefore implore God to complete His work Himself. If God grants me life, and if I can be present at the foundation, it is absolutely certain that you will be the first to put on the habit of the most sacred Passion. And I hope to give it to you with my own hands, for the glory of Jesus Christ and of the Most Blessed Virgin. But keep this for yourself alone."

Bishop Gustiniani was in no hurry to take the matter in hand. Knowing that without the Bishop nothing could be done, Paul tried to instill patience in his zealous disciple, who wanted to throw herself at the feet of the Holy Father. "The Pope would never grant you this favor without first hearing from the Bishop, to whom he would turn over the whole affair. . . . Dispel these thoughts, therefore. Apply yourself to perfection, to which God has called you where you are, and await with silent and resigned patience God's future dispositions."

This was wise advice, as Clement XIII granted no favors of his own accord. A few weeks later, on February 28, 1769, he died, and Cardinal Ganganelli succeeded him on May 19 under the name of Clement XIV.

With the new Pontiff, "God's ways," which Paul was awaiting, were to open up both for his own Congregation and for the foundation of "the nest of the Doves of Jesus Christ."

Chapter XVIII

IN THE BRINY WATERS

*Pray for a poor man who is being shipwrecked, and who
expects to drink in death at any moment.*

ST. PAUL OF THE CROSS

PAUL had set 1759 as the end of his active life. If he did not
carry out his intention, it was certainly not his fault. The general
chapter, obligatory every six years, was to take place in 1759,
and he was not eligible for re-election. He even advanced the
date a year so that he might retire into solitude sooner.

It is true that he had other more serious and less personal
motives for convening the general chapter. The Congregation,
after its slow and painful beginnings that had tested even the
sturdiest and turned some away, was now flourishing. New retreats had been founded in rapid succession, and candidates
were coming in droves. Out of necessity the novitiate had perhaps
been unduly abbreviated, and fervor does not make up for sound
training. Above all, the Congregation was young, devoid of a
tradition, and obliged to provide local superiors too hastily.
In short, it was experiencing quite normal growing pains. The
time had come to stop and reconnoiter.

Thus the general chapter was called on February 22, 1758, at
Holy Angel Retreat in Vetralla. All the capitularies renounced
their right to the last year of their tenure of office. They then
proceeded to elect new superiors. Paul's hopes were disappointed.
The capitularies had secured a dispensation from Rome in advance and re-elected him their Provost General. "He lowered his
shoulders," as he himself has said, and accepted.

Then the rectors of the retreat were chosen, but with the restriction that the Superior General could revoke the appointments
at the end of a year if he deemed it necessary.

There must have been some exchange of views on the needs for certain reforms, for in his circular to all the religious which preceded the chapter Paul insisted more than usual on the necessity of obedience and renouncement of their own will.

The young Congregation displayed its vitality by establishing a new foundation less than a month after the chapter. This was the retreat at Monte Cavo, which had been offered to Paul many years before.

In 1747 Paul had found the site humid and in ruins. Ten years later, with his consent, Father Thomas took up the project again, obtaining the approbation of the Bishop and of Rome, thus obviating the Fratri's complaints.

Monte Cavo, like Ceccano, was a fief of the Colonna family, which granted the use in perpetuity of the convent and garden, and the right of cutting wood over a portion of the forest. All this was given in return for an annual rent, which had been reduced to the presentation of a bouquet of flowers on Trinity Sunday.

Next Paul made arrangements to have the most urgent repairs taken care of. To this end he sent two brothers and a servant to help Father Thomas. In a state of poverty worthy of the hermits of the Egyptian desert, they set to work.

It was winter and the ground was covered with snow. They were obliged to clear the snow away to find a few herbs to make soup. They went out to beg their bread, and if by chance they obtained more than enough for their barest needs they had to hide their meager provisions lest the ravenous young servant devour them too quickly.

Their begging expeditions were not without unexpected incidents. One day the two brothers met a charitable priest who sent them to his home, saying he himself would be there later. They went trustingly and were received by his shrewish housekeeper, who drove them off with a volley of insults.

Another day Father Thomas accompanied them to Rocca di Papa. He fell into a crevasse hidden by the snow and was pulled out only after much effort. It would be cruel to insinuate that the good priest was too much engrossed by the beauty of the site to watch where he was going, but it must be admitted that Monte Cavo commands a magnificent view.

Monte Cavo, the highest summit of the Alban Mountains, is a wooded volcanic cone rising majestically to a height of thirty-one hundred feet between the Albano and Nemi lakes, some fifteen miles southeast of Rome. From this summit the eye embraces a panorama that is remarkable for its natural beauty and perhaps even more for its historic memories.

To the west the view is unobstructed all the way to the sea but includes the meanders of the Tiber through the plains of Latium down to Rome, where the River is encircled by ancient ramparts and overshadowed by the enormous dome of St. Peter's. To the east the verdant rim of the Alban Mountains is dotted with villas, castles, and the buried ruins of Alba Longa. To the south and north lie the cerulean-blue lakes of Albano and Nemi in their somber setting of lava.

And what legendary and historical memories come to mind in such familiar names as Tivoli, Frascati, Tusculum, Castel Gandolfo.

For Paul, the new retreat at Monte Cavo was simply located "near Rome, at a distance of about fifteen miles on a high and beautiful mountain from which one can see the metropolis of the world."[1] This was already a great deal. But within this magnificent setting the retreat looked very poor indeed despite all the efforts of Father Thomas and his companions.

The solemn installation took place with the usual rites on March 19, 1758, during a violent storm. Father Thomas had been expressly delegated to preside. "For two weeks wind, fog, and rain kept the religious indoors, without the respite of a single ray of sunshine. Hell seemed to be unleashed. When the weather became a little calmer a benefactor from Rocca di Papa came up to see if the religious were still there. He feared they had departed, driven away by this squall the like of which had never been seen."[2]

We can easily imagine the plight of the unfortunate religious, crowded together in a few dilapidated rooms and with few provisions. The rector of the new retreat sent Paul an account of the incident and received this answer: "The troubles Your Reverence and your devout community are experiencing because of want and the rest are precious jewels."

With his usual practical sense Paul pointed out that a wing should be built that would be less exposed to the elements, "protected against the sirocco and less humid." Meanwhile he advised them to overcome present difficulties by burning a good fire and to fear nothing.[3]

The advice was sound, but the wing was not to be built for sixteen years.

While this foundation was taking root, Paul did not remain idle. For a moment he thought illness would keep him from his spring campaign of missions. He even wrote to the pastor of Ischia di Castro, who was expecting him.[4] But two days later he changed his mind and so advised the pastor in a delightful style: "Scarcely had my preceding letter been sent when I felt a merciful battery of powerful impulses in my heart (*ho avuto una misericordiosa batteria al cuore di gagliardi impulsi*) that made me resolve to come and console your beloved people. . . ."[5]

The mission exhausted him. However, he completed the campaign as originally planned and accepted to evangelize the diocese of Montefiascone in November.

For his spiritual sons, Paul aspired to more remote apostolic fields among the pagans. This was one of the primary aims of his Congregation, and he thought the time had come to fulfill it.

With this in mind he offered a few of his missionaries to the Congregation of Propaganda, which alone had the power to assign missionaries and to grant faculties to them. After various negotiations, the project failed. There was no place for the young Congregation.

Paul took this refusal hard, for it was a new proof that he had not completely overcome opposition. But as was his custom, he resigned himself: "I adore and bless Divine Providence and I conceive all the more hope for a more glorious success when the Congregation will have taken to its wings. . . ."[6]

An event had just occurred which might favor this "upward flight." On July 6, 1758, Cardinal Rezzonico became Pope, under the name of Clement XIII, following the death of Pope Benedict XIV in May.

We know how precious the Cardinal's help had been to the newly founded Congregation. Paul hoped that his elevation to the pontificate would make possible the obtaining of a favor hitherto refused: solemn vows for his religious.

In fact, Paul considered this favor so important that he promised to make a pilgrimage to Loretto if he obtained it. He even delayed certain end-of-the-year missions he was scheduled to preach in order to be free to go to Rome.

The Sovereign Pontiff received him most graciously and even indicated what requests he should prepare.

Paul set to work, had the memoranda prepared, ordered his "little army" to pray, and waited confidently for an early solution. He did not know that the new Pontiff had made it a rule never to grant any personal favors but to let everything go through administrative channels, a procedure not noted for bringing quick results.

Disappointed once again, Paul went to preach his missions in the diocese of Montefiascone as originally planned.

Early in 1759 he went to Corneto. His health suffered so badly from this journey that he was obliged to remain in bed for a month afterward at the retreat in Toscanella.

In addition to the spiritual good he accomplished by his mission in Corneto, as in other towns, he obtained two other results. For one thing, the people of Corneto offered him a piece of property on the outskirts of the town on which to found a Passionist retreat. Negotiations were begun, which culminated in 1765. In addition, the cornerstone of the convent for Passionist nuns was laid. As we know, Paul had long wanted to found an institute of women analogous to his own Congregation.

As soon as he was well enough he began his spring campaign, after which he returned to Holy Angel Retreat, "exhausted and disabled."

Meanwhile the matter of the solemn vows, still pending in the courts of Rome, required his attention once more. This time he did not go to Rome himself but sent Father Thomas in his place. The Pope planned to name a commission of cardinals to study the question. Paul wrote to one of his friends, Bishop de Angelis, asking him to urge the Holy Father to hasten the appointment of the commission. Our Saint was not yet in step with the Roman rhythm of activity.

During 1759 Paul suffered another disappointment. Once again he made efforts to send two of his religious into mission lands, but after several aleatory answers the matter was dropped.

Also during 1759 Father Thomas' departure for Corsica was, if not a disappointment, at least a great sorrow for Paul. Bishop de Angelis, newly appointed Visitor Apostolic of Corsica, asked for Father Thomas as his companion, in the capacity of consulting theologian. This was an honor for the humble Congregation, and it was to prove a still greater honor when Father Thomas became the Bishop of Corsica a few years later. But Paul lost the services of an eminent religious.

Paul did have the consolation of seeing the new Bishop remain faithful to the spirit of the Congregation. When Corsica was ceded to France in 1770, the prelate had to abandon his see and return to Rome. Paul then had the pleasure of telling him: "I congratulate you on the fact that you are coming back from Corsica a poor man, just as you went there a poor man."

The year 1760 was still less kind, and Paul wrote that he was in extremely deep "briny waters," that he had "a foot in the grave."[7]

As was his custom, he began the year by preaching missions, and continued to preach in the spring in order to complete his evangelization of Montefiascone. In May he came back to Holy Angel Retreat, more exhausted than usual, "to patch up his poor humanity so that he might be able to devote himself for a few more days to the service of this minim Congregation."[8]

On August 15 he was still confined to his bed and unable to

celebrate Mass. Meanwhile the "minim Congregation" was once more being subjected to "the persecutions of men and demons."[9]

Clement XIII had at last created the commission of cardinals to study the question of solemn vows. However, such powerful opposition to the plan arose that Paul thought he saw "his whole work crumble or go up in smoke."[10]

He accepted the worst: "God gives me the grace not to want anything but His good pleasure."[11] But he faced up to his difficulties.

In October he ordered the canonical visitation of all the retreats, in preparation for eventual inspections. He himself visited the houses north of Rome and delegated another Father to visit those to the south.

In November he left for Rome, in order to deal directly with the commission about the matter of vows. He expected objections, but not the one that was made from the start: the cardinals asked whether his religious really desired the favor of solemn vows.

"Why, certainly, and with all their hearts," he answered without a moment's hesitation.

The cardinals then took sly pleasure in showing him the protests of certain of his religious who declared they did not intend to be bound by solemn vows.[12]

Paul's heart was broken. But something even more serious if not as painful came up. As solemn vows would make the Congregation a religious order, a new study of the Rule was required. And the cardinals wanted to mitigate the Rule.[13] This can easily be explained. Since solemn vows were practically indissoluble, a religious who pronounced them could leave the Congregation only with great difficulty. Too often one of two things happened: either a lax subject remained in an order under solemn vows, or else he left and went astray. The cardinals' commission wisely wanted to make life in the monastery endurable to tepid religious.

Paul could not enter into these views of human prudence. Had he not received the divine mission to found an institute destined to recall the sorrowful Passion of Christ? In consequence, "he refused to agree to the proposed mitigations."[14]

There was another point under discussion. The cardinals wanted the houses of study at least to have the right to own property. Paul wanted above all to maintain poverty.

Under these conditions there could be little doubt as to the cardinals' decision. On November 23 "the cardinals, in view of the strictness of the Institute, judged it more opportune to leave it under simple vows, so that a way out might remain open."[15]

While the blow was not unexpected, it was a bitter disappointment to Paul. He wrote to his religious, saying: "After all my efforts and my sweat, and after all imaginable diligence on my part, for I have spared no pains or labors in my travels and in my sojourn in Rome, finally on the last Sunday after Pentecost, the 23rd instant, the special Congregation of the Cardinals met. They asked me to come in twice, and decided that for the present we would not adopt solemn vows. . . . And note well the words *pro nunc*, for the present."

Attributing the defeat to the tepidity of his religious, he went on: "When our initial fervor is restored, our Congregation will immediately be raised to the rank of veritable religious orders with solemn vows. I assure you of this before the Lord."[16]

To his intimates he admitted that he preferred poverty and abjection to solemn vows.

Later he learned to appreciate the cardinals' prudence. When it would have been easy for him to obtain the favor without any concessions on his part, he did not request it.

Simultaneously with his request for the favor of solemn vows, Paul had besought of Clement XIII the right to have his own religious ordained.

The two matters were entrusted to the commission of cardinals. It was decided to consider the latter request when the eighteen ordinations authorized by Benedict XIV were completed. Three years later the same favor, limited to eighteen more ordinations, was renewed, but no blanket authorization was granted.

On the other hand, at Paul's own request, a few slight changes in the Rule were approved by the cardinals' commission. The superiors of retreats were allowed to refuse to place religious at the service of their bishops for the parochial ministry. They were no longer obliged to entrust the money of the community to a layman. The religious assigned to the missions were to be given a special examination. Finally, every religious was to make an eight-day retreat at the close of each of his apostolic campaigns.

While these were interesting changes, they altered nothing of the spirit of the Rule. No doubt Paul had been induced to ask for them as the result of certain abuses to be remedied.

It is in the same spirit that he requested the faculty to dispense his religious from their simple vows — obviously, only for a just cause. At the present time this faculty is granted to the superiors general of orders, whereas the Pope alone can dispense from solemn vows.

The spontaneous measures taken by a few of his companions who had protested against the solemn vows had no doubt opened his eyes. There were malcontents. Indeed, where are there not? It was better to open the doors and let the scabby sheep out.

The cardinals' commission did not hesitate to grant Paul this faculty. He in turn informed his religious of it without delay: "We exhort those who desire this dispensation to come to us on the occasion of the next provincial chapter."[17]

Clement XIII sanctioned the four decisions of the cardinals' commission, and no more. This attitude was a far cry from what Paul had hoped for at the time of the new Pope's enthronement. We should not, however, conclude that the Pope was hostile to the Passionists in principle. A few months later he sent his apostolic blessing to Paul and to his religious, but he remained parsimonious with his favors.

The year 1760 had brought heavy crosses to Paul, and the following year brought others.

Illness caused Paul severe suffering. He did not want to renounce his missions, but cold brought on an acute attack of rheumatism. As a result he was obliged to remain in bed three months, most of the time too ill even to celebrate Mass.

Meanwhile a grave difficulty arose at the retreat at Falvaterra which caused Paul much concern.

One of the great benefactors of the retreat, Deodato Amati,

took the notion to build a casino very close to the retreat
and with a very clear view of it. Besides, he claimed the right
to cross the property of the religious to reach the casino. As
mentioned earlier, casinos as then understood were rural pavilions
where country folk enjoyed dancing and merrymaking.

Neither prayers nor entreaties had any effect. The religious
had to appeal to the diocesan authority and even to the Papal
Court. The matter dragged on for years and ended with the con-
tinuation of the status quo.

Paul did not await the decision to declare solemnly once
again the need of absolute solitude for his retreats.

Years later he was to write: "Our Congregation, according to
the light that it has pleased the Divine Majesty to give me, is
based entirely *in oratione* and *jejunio* and on solitude according
to the infinitely holy counsels of our Divine Savior. He wanted
His Apostles to retire into solitude after their holy missions.
Requiescite pusillum in solitudine. And the Master gave the example, since He withdrew on the mountain after His divine and
admirable sermons *solus orare.* Our Congregation is established
on this foundation. If the foundation is dashed to the ground,
the structure will be totally destroyed because we shall be outside
the vocation that God has given us. . . . Believe me, an evangelical
worker who is a man of prayer, a friend of solitude, and detached from all created things accomplishes by himself more
than a thousand others who are not such men. . . . Let each
one throw all his zeal into preserving the spirit of the Institute,
and in this way Holy Church will have workers who are always
vigorous and holy, *aliter nihil.*"[18]

Brother Bartholomew, who was Father Paul's infirmarian, re-
ported that he often heard him say: "If we love solitude, our
Institute will grow; but once solitude is destroyed the whole
Congregation will fall into ruin."[19]

He was equally intransigent in demanding that his religious
remain within the retreats except for the needs of the ministry.
During 1761 he decided to send his brother Anthony away a
second time, and for good, precisely because he did not observe
this rule.

The separation caused Paul great suffering. When Anthony asked to be readmitted several years later, Paul answered: "I can assure you that I shall die more peacefully if I see you in the Congregation." While Paul was not to have this consolation, his brother Anthony lived up to his obligations as a secular priest until death.

For many years Paul had been deeply concerned with the problems resulting from the fact that the novitiate was located at the Retreat of the Presentation on Monte Argentario. The obligatory contacts between young novices and embittered or merely disenchanted religious had very real drawbacks.

Paul had been obliged to reprove his brother Anthony on this point, and his was not the only case. Speaking of another religious whose influence left much to be desired, the Founder wrote: "This is something that touches me to the quick."[20]

Moreover, the Retreat of the Presentation, despite its high elevation, was subjected to the unhealthy vapors of Lake Orbetello during the summer. This was truer then than it is today, for the lake now empties into the sea and no longer dries up.

Using the second reason rather than the first in his official request to the King of Naples, Paul asked for the concession of a few acres of land on a more favorably located site. He knew that the Neapolitan court, violently hostile to religious orders under the influence of its minister Tanneci, would have paid no attention to the first reason.

More fortunate than St. Alphonsus Liguori, who was met with refusals on similar requests, Paul obtained what he wanted through the support of the King's representative in Orbetello. Paul had already carefully chosen a site located about a mile from the Retreat of the Presentation, toward San Stefano. Being 230 feet higher than the retreat, it boasted an even more beautiful view. The flat tableland made possible necessary construction and a small garden.

Paul fell on his knees and took "possession" of the property while reciting the hymn *Te Joseph celebrent*. He had decided to dedicate the house to St. Joseph. The next day he led the whole community of the Presentation up to the new site. After they sang the hymn to St. Joseph, Paul traced the plan of the church and retreat on the ground. Construction began at once.

All this had transpired in 1754. Soon afterward progress was slowed down for lack of resources. By 1761, however, the major construction work was completed. In June of that year the church was blessed and the novices moved in. Happy as he was over this successful undertaking which made up for so many disappointments, he did not have the joy of attending the installation. He was preaching a mission at the time.

It was not until 1762 that he went to visit the new novitiate. His purpose was above all to establish special regulations "so that it might be for the whole Congregation a nursery of holy men." He took care to discourage all visits that were not indispensable. When a personage could not be dismissed because of his dignity or his benefactions, the religious were to accompany him with a watch in one hand and a bell in the other, for the visit was not to last over a half hour; and the novices were to be warned to remain in their cells.[21]

The Rule has become less rigid. Nowadays guests are received at Monte Argentario without a watch and bell and with perfect graciousness. From the little esplanade that leads to the retreat one can admire the fairyland beauty of the sunrise, and the panorama is magnificent at any hour.

Paul's visit to the novitiate was the outstanding event of 1762 for him. His declining health had forced him to renounce the active ministry. In his picturesque way he described himself as follows: "I am reduced to the state of a dried-up tree trunk, abandoned in the forest because it is rotten and cannot even be used as firewood; an uprooted tree trunk moreover, carried away by the storm and cast into the sea. But I am not saying enough. I do not know how to express the state to which I am reduced. Pray for a poor man who is being shipwrecked, and who expects to drink in death at any moment."[22]

Death was not as near as he thought, and he was not yet out of the "briny waters."

When he lay on his poor bed, tormented by rheumatic pains, he would resign himself to give up the missions. Then a pressing invitation would arrive, and he would get up and be off.

The time came in 1763, however, when he was unable to finish a mission he was giving at Caprarola. He laid down his arms on the battlefield. After that he gave only a few spiritual exercises in convents.

He was so tired that he had to delegate the canonical visitation of his retreats to one of his religious, Father John Mary. For in addition to his usual suffering, he had had a severe fall from a mule on his way home from Caprarola.

This did not keep him from keeping a watchful eye on the activities of Father John Mary. Between two visitations the latter felt he could preach a retreat at Fondi. "I sent him to make visitations and not to preach missions. Patience! I must swallow each pill and digest it in the heat of the Divine Will."[23]

Paul was experiencing the annoyance of the man of action who must sit by while others carry on his work. It was not that he wanted to keep his post as Provost General. At the chapter of 1764 he thought he would be freed from this heavy responsibility. But Father Mark Aurelius, the provincial of the retreat at Campagna Marittima, played the same trick on him that he had planned to play on Father Mark.

Both men, unbeknown to the other, had obtained a dispensation making possible the other's re-election. "Thus, each hoping to lay aside his burden, he nailed the other to the cross."[24]

Father Paul accepted his re-election from his sickbed, but he summoned enough strength to concern himself with the unfortunate folk who were then besieging the door of the convent. As it happened, 1764 was a year of terrible famine in Italy. It is claimed that more than 300,000 persons died of hunger throughout the country.[25]

Paul ordered the distribution of half the meager provisions of Holy Angel Retreat, where he was residing. At each meal he successfully exhorted his religious to deprive themselves in order to help the poor who were waiting at the gate.

Indeed, he went much farther than that. A whole system of regulations was set up through his efforts for the sifting of flour. Only the coarse bran was to be removed from the flour, and the size of the loaves of bread was reduced by half. Rations of food and oil were reduced one third.

It goes without saying that Paul gave the example and demanded much greater privations of himself than of the others, meanwhile "weeping hot tears of compassion for the poor."

Summer brought an improvement in the food situation of Italy. It also brought Paul some relief from his rheumatic pains. But he had become quite deaf. He concluded sadly: "My indispositions are constantly increasing — I have almost completely lost my hearing — and will end in the grave, which I do not believe to be far."[26]

He still had a few more "pills" to swallow. For one, plans for the foundation of the institute of nuns were not progressing. Once more, in 1764, the question of a retreat on the island of Elba came up. It had been pending for thirty years.

"If only these Islanders are not fooling me with fine words like the other time," he wrote skeptically, "for retreats are not founded with idle words, but by acts."[27] And acts were not forthcoming.

On the other hand, the project at Corneto was given a fresh start as the result of a new mission preached by Passionists in January 1765. But this time the site offered was down in a valley. Paul was very displeased. "It would be a cemetery for my religious. . . . It is such a low place that one never feels the wind blowing there. We would be eaten alive by gadflies, flies, mosquitoes, and other insects. In summer, the air would be unbreathable. . . . How could the religious live there? . . . How could anyone pray with a heavy head?"

He demanded a higher site. "It is ventilation that purifies the air. As for the sirocco, that can be remedied by placing the church on the south side."[28]

Efforts were made to find a desirable site. As Paul could not go himself, he sent his brother John Baptist to Corneto with very precise instructions: "Observe . . . if there is room to have a nice garden, and water near at hand. . . ."[29] John Baptist's report was favorable, and Paul gave his approval.

The foundation of new retreats was not the essential. Before "drinking in death," Paul wanted to assure the future of his work by obtaining the favor of ordinations without conditions or limitations.

Crippled with rheumatism and scarcely able to get up from his straw mat, he thought the best thing he could do was to appeal directly to the Pope: "I would not want to pass through the channels of these Congregations, which are in less of a hurry than my decrepit old age, which is advancing rapidly toward the grave. And yet I should like if possible to see things well taken care of. . . ."[30]

He had planned to go and throw himself at the feet of Clement XIII. An accident kept him from carrying out his intention. The carriage in which he was traveling overturned, and he suffered a bad fall. "I still feel the pain of it when I cough or even breathe."[31]

Obliged to entrust his petition to a protector, Bishop Garampi, he asked him to transmit it personally to the Holy Father "without going through the Congregations. By this latter way, which takes up a great deal of time, one does not attain the goal. They see only difficulties. Expenses and documents are necessary. I have already had the experience. . . . I would gladly have come to Rome, but I am unable to. I have no strength left, and I celebrate Mass only with great difficulty."[32]

The petition, drawn up in the names of Paul and of his brother John Baptist as co-founders, set forth the needs of the Congregation. Although it was sent to Bishop Garampi on May 18, 1765, he had not yet transmitted it to the Pope in November. Paul then sent two of his religious to Rome to hasten matters. He directed them to Cardinal Antonelli, who brought the petition to the Holy Father's attention.

As was his custom, Clement XIII sent the petition to the

Congregation of Bishops and Regulars for study. Paul had to wait for God to open "other ways" to him. He was thinking no doubt that there were two long and costly roads to follow in Rome: the Via della Lungara and the Via Giulia.[33] Without mincing words, he wrote to Bishop de Angelis: "I do not have the health and vigor of former years to move about Rome and push the matter by dint of expenses and exhausting efforts. . . . Let us rather bury the whole thing in a profound silence and wait until the Lord provides for our needs and those of Holy Church."[34]

That year brought Paul another trial that was more personal and no less painful: the death of Father John Baptist. This man had been not only his brother but his first companion, always faithful, even if sometimes ill-tempered. He had been the sharer of his first enthusiasms, of his hours of solitude, prayer, and penance, his companion on his first missions, the confidant of his hopes to found a religious congregation and establish new retreats. He had shared the long years of disappointment and the ultimate fulfillment. It was with him that Paul had drafted the last petition to complete the organization of the Congregation.

Now John Baptist was leaving him to shoulder his troubles alone. One morning in July 1765, Paul had a presentiment that tribulation awaited him. He refused to entertain the idea. A few days later Father John Baptist fell seriously ill. He seemed at first to improve, but by the end of the month his condition worsened.

Paul often dragged himself to his brother's cell, leaning on his crutches. Their conversation was filled with trust in God's mercy. "All told, we have served God well."

John Baptist died on August 30. Paul wept and had to repel the strange temptation to believe that his brother was damned. He waked him and insisted on singing the funeral Mass himself. His voice broke with emotion during the service.

Shortly afterward, writing to a benefactor who had sent his condolences, he said: "I have been left an orphan."[35] And he added: "I shall say no more." He had indeed said a great deal.

Paul still had his Congregation. The retreats to the north had received rather frequent visitations from him, but he had not been in the southern province for almost fifteen years. He determined to go to these provinces as soon as his infirmities allowed, "to say farewell for the last time." He was able to set out on November 11, 1767, and his first stop was Rome.

The Eternal City was along his way, but he had a special reason for stopping there. He had long wanted to have a house in the center of Catholicism, not as a matter of vanity, but in order to spur the growth of his Congregation. As his efforts to establish a retreat in Rome had failed, he worked toward establishing a pied-à-terre, an *ospizio*, or hospice, and this had been recently installed.

Paul had already gone to Rome in the spring of 1766 for the specific purpose of obtaining the Pope's permission for such a foundation. Clement XIII, as was his habit, received him graciously but turned his request over to administrative bureaus. It was decided that the permission would be granted as soon as the site and the conditions of the foundation were determined upon.

Paul had asked Father John Mary to find a suitable site for the house, but this was no easy matter. It was then that the fiery Founder used the play on words about the Via della Lungara and the Via Giulia, to symbolize Roman dilatoriness and the high cost of all services.

The house was finally chosen and bought for 550 crowns through the generosity of Anthony Frattini, who was acting as a behind-the-scenes intermediary. The Pope's authorization still had to be obtained. Clement XIII hesitated, saying: "We must think twice before allowing a new religious order to settle in Rome." And he left the final decision up to the Cardinal-Vicar. The latter, Cardinal Colonna, was more categorical. Knowing the Passionists of Monte Cavo, he at once agreed to grant the authorization.

The simple residence was called the "Hospice of the Holy Crucifix," and the installation took place without pomp or fanfare. Paul sent Father John Mary and a lay brother to take it over during October 1767.

Paul arrived on November 12. He found Father John Mary studying and Brother Sebastian working in the garden. Some workmen were making the more urgent repairs. Paul was delighted with the little house, surrounded with its small enclosure, on St. John Lateran Street. This was his twelfth foundation, "the perfect number," he said.

The hospice could never be transformed into a retreat for lack of space and solitude. But Paul felt it was a temporary pied-à-terre. With this thought in mind he authorized only indispensable repairs.

Two days later he set out for Monte Cavo to begin his visitations of the retreats in the province of Campagna Marittima.

The journey of this deaf old man, crippled with rheumatism, was a surprising one. He who had suffered so many contradictions and been received at times with jeers was now welcomed as a father and a saint.

As soon as the religious of Monte Cavo saw him approaching, they hastened to meet him, kneeling joyfully at his feet. He raised each one to his feet and gave him a warm embrace.

Paul remained about ten days at this retreat, amid the indescribable beauty of its landscape. On November 24 he started out for Terracina, where he received the same enthusiastic welcome.

As winter had set in, he decided to prolong his stay in this gentle climate. And so the people of the region had the opportunity to become acquainted with him and to manifest their veneration. Despite the mildness of the sea air, he suffered another rheumatic attack in February which kept him in bed for a month.

At the end of March he set out for Ceccano in the carriage of a benefactor. Now he encountered not merely isolated marks of veneration but the enthusiasm of crowds rushing up to greet him. Some tried to snip off pieces of his coat, others brought him their sick to bless. He had become *il Santo*, the Saint.

At St. Sosius he was welcomed as he had been at the other

retreats, and visitors flocked to see him. When he left for Ceccano, there was a delirium of excitement. Wherever he passed, the streets were filled with people imploring his blessing. When he stopped in a town for the night, the local religious communities begged him to visit them.

It was amid the same noisy demonstrations that he reached Paliano. Even the church bells rang out in his honor, and his slashed coat had to be replaced.

The prestige of his holiness was recognized not only by the people but also by the clergy. The Bishop of Anagni, following the example of the Bishop of Gaeta, asked the privilege of a private interview with him. Even the religious orders, so long his rivals, showed their veneration for him. Among these were the Augustinian Fathers in charge of the Shrine of Our Lady of Good Counsel, where Paul stopped to venerate the famous Madonna.

At Frascati, the Cardinal Duke of York, brother of the last pretender to the Stuart throne, received him with utmost graciousness. And when he arrived in Rome, he received a kind welcome from the Church's dignitaries.

The Holy Father expressed his satisfaction over the Congregation's progress. In a gesture of exquisite kindness Clement XIII held out his ring to be kissed by Paul, so that the old man would not have to bend down to his feet.

Paul had become *il Santo*, the Saint, but how humble he was, and how embarrassed by all these manifestations which he tried to avoid.

Great was his joy at finding his retreats prosperous and fervent. And yet he wrote: "As for me, thank God, I find consolation in nothing whatever. I am always afflicted by interior and exterior anguish, and I am very crippled."[36]

His health continued to deteriorate rapidly. When he returned to Holy Angel Retreat in Vetralla on May 15, he had to be carried in an armchair. Obliged to remain in bed, he distracted himself from his acute sufferings by singing the Litany of the Blessed Virgin as loud as he could. This had long been his custom in time of sickness.

For the remainder of 1767, Paul was bedridden. He showed little improvement during the following year, except at rare intervals.

Although the hostility of men had given way to veneration, the devil did not give him any respite in his lamentable state. Strange interior sufferings continually assailed him. "Of my very serious anxieties and calamities, I say nothing. To my mind, they cannot be explained. I let everything die in the divine 'good pleasure.'"[37]

Triumph at last, but what a painful one!

Chapter XIX

GOD'S WILL BE DONE

The Founder of the Passionists is obsessed by the will of God at least as much as the Founder of the Jesuits. M. VILLER [1]

Now THAT we have reached this human summit in the life of Paul of the Cross, the time has come to interrupt our account for a moment to try to grasp the driving force behind his remarkable spiritual ascent. While a complete exposition of Paul's spirituality would require a volume in itself, we shall try to set forth briefly the dominant idea that governed his life.

Everyone knows the primary place that Jesus gives to the fulfillment of the Will of God, first of all in His own life: "My food is to do the most holy will of my Father in all things." (John 4:34.) "Not my will but thine be done." (Luke 22:42.) But He is equally explicit about it for His disciples: "Not everyone who says to me, 'Lord, Lord,' shall enter the kingdom of heaven; but he who does the will of my Father." (Matt. 7:21.) And their daily prayer must ask that "His will be done on earth as it is in heaven!"

However, two attitudes are possible with respect to the Will of God:

To desire to know it in order to conform to it fully and to accomplish in one's life the commands and desires of God. That is the attitude of St. Ignatius of Loyola, the fiery officer always ready to obey, always at attention: "Lord, what will You have me do?" This is the acceptance of the Will of God as signified to us.

To accept that God's Will be fulfilled within us and outside of us in a spirit of submission to the divine good pleasure, whatever it may be. This is the attitude of St. Paul of the Cross, the obedient lover who can only say: "Thy Will be done!" It is the acceptance of the Will of good pleasure.

The first attitude is more active and the second more passive. The fact remains that Ignatius accepts and Paul knows how to act.

This passive conformity to the Will of God shines forth on every page of Paul's life, from the time of his submission to the strange confessor of his adolescence and his acceptance of his miraculously revealed mission as Founder, which was to be the drama of his life.

The burning lines written during his forty-day retreat at Castellazzo reveal this conformity to us: "I know that everything comes from my God. To Him be honor and glory eternally . . . may the most sweet Giver of all good be blessed in all things. . . . I would like to be able to say that everyone feels the effects of the great grace that God gives through His mercy when He sends suffering to anyone. . . ."[2]

Each trial, each contradiction, was accepted in this spirit of submission. The account of defeats and illnesses always closes with the formula of Gethsemani, which became his favorite ejaculatory prayer: "The Will of God be done!"

Such has been the tenor of our narrative so far. Let no one be mistaken about Paul's attitude. It is in no sense a kind of lethargic fatalism. When the hour comes for him no longer merely to accept suffering but to act, he finds he is as zealous as ever.

For all his trust in God, he does not neglect any human means. His motto might well be: "Do everything as if you depended on yourself alone, and hope for all things as if you counted only on God."

Once he has adopted this attitude, he is not obstinate, he does not get discouraged, he does not do violence to the Will of God. He waits with resignation until "the ways are opened."

This abandonment to the Will of God which he practiced to a heroic degree is the central idea that dominates his entire spirituality. It is the keynote of his letters of guidance to laymen, to priests, as well as to the "future Doves of Christ."

It is his favorite definition of perfection: "True perfection consists in the fulfillment of the Will of God and in scorn of self."[3] And he explained what he meant: "Practice the holy virtues: humility, obedience, both interior and exterior mortification, which are the foundation stones. Love to scorn yourself. Above all, form a great habit of abandonment to the Will of God."[4]

Let us note the word "abandonment," which for Paul of the Cross is synonymous with resignation and union to the Will of God. In this, as he sees it, consists the whole of perfection and the shortest road to attain to it.

He never confused abandonment with absolute passivity, any more than he ever thought himself dispensed from action in his own life even while accepting the Will of God in success, failure, and suffering. "St. Paul of the Cross understands very well that while God does His part, man must also do his."[5]

And to Paul, man's part consists in the practice of the fundamental virtues; in overcoming all obstacles to mental prayer that would hinder the ineffable action of God.

He revealed his thought on the matter to the master of novices at Monte Argentario when he reminded him how a soul prepares itself for infused prayer: "It [infused prayer] being a gratuitous gift of God, we must not seek to drive a person to it by strong-arm methods, as they say. But the Master's great concern must be to raise them to it by a great habit of virtue and of true humility of heart, knowledge of their own nothingness, scorn for themselves, true, blind obedience — which virtue they must learn to have great love for, and above all true and perfect abnegation of their own will in all things, the personal mortification of their inclinations, sympathies, and antipathies. These are the fundamental virtues for the spiritual edifice and to obtain the gift of holy prayer and union with God. Otherwise we are building on sand."[6]

Once this is done, let God do what He pleases, "let Him accomplish His work," let Him "play His games of love."[7]

Elsewhere he specifies the necessary virtues in a clearer and more succinct manner: above all, humility in the awareness of one's own nothingness and concern with the present moment.

"Believe me, my daughter, I am never happier than when I live my wretched life in particles, that is to say, in the present moment as if it were the last moment of my life. Here and now I want to suffer joyously, without thinking of the future. O my soul, do the Will of God perfectly in this instant, as if it were the last of your life; and you will continue in the same way. Vive Jesus! Amen. And so, be very careful not to feed these mad desires to go there, or come here, and other similar desires."[8]

After the personal examen, he gave this general counsel, which is, after all, but the paraphrase of the Gospel: "Sufficient for the day is its own trouble." (Matt. 6:34.)

"Happy is the soul that rests in the bosom of God, without thinking of the future, but strives to live in the present moment, without any other worry than that of doing well His most holy Will on every occasion, accomplishing it faithfully in the duties of its state."[9]

The fruits of abandonment to the Will of God, thus conceived and practiced, are wonderful.

This is the shortest path toward perfection, as we have already noted. Writing to a religious, he said: "In such circumstances, let Your Reverence hide in the inexpugnable fortress of the Will of God. You are then certain that neither winds nor storms can ever destroy your peace and tranquillity of spirit, so necessary to do all things well. . . ."[10]

This is also the way to solve every interior and exterior difficulty: "The misfortunes which happen in this world, when accepted from the living hand of God with submission to His most holy Will, enable us to run in the path of the divine commandments. Besides, resignation to these events serves as a very efficacious means of obtaining favors, even temporal favors."[11]

It seems almost improper to insist on the advantages of abandonment to the Will of God. Paul, who addressed himself more often than not to souls already advanced in spiritual ways, pointed to this abandonment more as the means of pleasing God Himself and of conforming perfectly to His Will, after the example given by Jesus Crucified.

Had he not written at the time of his forty-day retreat: "Through the mercy of our dear God, I do not want to experience anything . . . or enjoy any consolation except that of being crucified with Jesus."[12]

The Passion of Jesus! This was the food of his soul, the constant subject of his meditations, the raison d'être of his foundations, and the explanation for the fruitfulness of his apostolate. As he himself used to say: "The most efficacious means for converting the most hardened sinners is the Passion of Jesus Christ."

But, above all, the Passion is the explanation of the spirituality of St. Paul of the Cross: *it is the center toward which everything converges, and from which everything flows.*

The suffering Christ, "obedient to death, even to death on the Cross" is the unique example of abandonment to the good pleasure of His Father. Meditation on the Passion thus sets before the Christian's eyes a living lesson of total acceptance of the Will of God.

Christ said *"Fiat"* to the agony in the garden of Gethsemani. The Christian must also say *"Fiat"* to each day's suffering, even the most severe. And so we can easily see the very simple and logical relationship between the way of abandonment, the Passion, and suffering.

Father Paul has left us a multitude of texts on this subject: "Just as the most beloved Jesus willed that His most holy life here on earth . . . should be spent amid . . . continual sorrows, trials, exhausting labors, hardships, anguish, scorn, calumny, pain, whips, nails, thorns, and the most bitter death of the Cross, so He made me understand that in dedicating myself to Him, I was to lead the same life, amid every suffering. With what jubilation my poor soul embraced all kinds of sufferings. . . ."[13]

This confidence, made to Agnes Grazi, is all the more precious inasmuch as Paul was very niggardly with revelations of his interior life. In this case he had made an exception in order to encourage his spiritual daughter to follow the way of the Cross. In writing to Thomas Fossi, he even set down explicit rules: "Whoever wants to be a saint loves to follow faithfully in the footsteps of Jesus Christ, to become the opprobrium of men, the abjection of the people, because he acknowledges he is guilty of lese majesty against God by his sins. He who wants to be a saint loves to be hidden from the eyes of the world. He considers the sweet bitter, and the bitter sweet. *My food is to do in all things the most holy Will of the Father.* And since this is accomplished more in suffering than in pleasure, because self-will always clings to pleasure, that is why the true servant of God loves naked suffering, receiving it without any intermediary from the pure Will of the Lord."[14]

It could not be expressed more cogently. And we understand why Paul wrote to the same correspondent: "The Passion contains everything. That is where the science of the saints is learned."[15] For souls in love with perfection, this is self-evident. And for all souls, the simple meditation of the Passion brings graces of light, strength, and conversion.

Here indeed lies the secret of the life, the apostolate, and the spirituality of St. Paul of the Cross.

Where had he discovered this secret? This question is not an idle one, for the answer to it contains the key to the originality of the greatest mystic of the eighteenth century.

Let us first of all point out a difference between Paul and other mystics. The thought of others progresses rather slowly by a gradual evolution. With Paul, the doctrine of abandonment to the Will of God and imitation of the Passion emerges full-blown from the start, without undergoing any significant variations later. In short, we find his doctrine presented integrally in his *Retreat Journal*; that is to say, in 1720, when he was twenty-six years old.

We must therefore look into Paul's life before that date to discover any outside influences on his thought, if any there were.

Even in his adolescent years Paul was familiar with St. Francis de Sales, and perhaps already with St. John of the Cross and St. Teresa of Avila. But their practice does not explain the astonishing depth of Paul Danei's doctrine of abandonment even at that early age.

There is another mystic, however, who sets forth at length the necessity of renunciation of one's own will, acceptance of trials and even of the temptation to despair "without consenting to it." This acceptance withal is joyful, for the soul seeks to console Jesus by constantly remembering the abandonment He suffered on the Cross.[16] This mystic is Tauler.

We know that the famous German Dominican whom Luther relished so much was Paul's favorite author. In fact, he "spoke of him [Tauler] with so much unction that his face lighted up at the very mention of Tauler's name."[17]

When Paul was a youth the only extant edition of Tauler was the Latin one of Surius, which included works attributed to Tauler in rather indiscriminate fashion. And Paul was not sufficiently conversant with Latin to familiarize himself with Tauler through this Latin text. It was only later, when Surius' work was translated, that Tauler became one of Paul's bedside books. This translation is still preserved at Holy Angel Retreat in Vetralla.

The problem of St. Paul of the Cross' originality still remains unsolved. However, we are inclined to attribute to the famous Rhenish mystic at least an indirect influence on Paul.

Tauler fell into disrepute because Luther had been influenced by his works. In Spain he was placed on the Index by the Inquisition. In Belgium, Capuchins were forbidden to read his writings. In France, Bossuet first admired him but later judged him harshly because the quietists looked to him for their inspiration.

In Italy there is no indication of an anti-Tauler trend. The enthusiasm of Paul of the Cross for Tauler would seem to prove it. It is therefore quite probable that Father Columban of Genoa, who was well versed in mysticism, or perhaps the devout Canon Cerrutti nourished their young disciple with Tauler's doctrine.

Even granting this, it is safer to think that Paul, once he had been directed to the path of abandonment, found the secret of his spirituality by himself, with God's grace, through his assiduous meditation on the Passion.

On several occasions Paul made known the extraordinary lights he had received during mental prayer. This would indicate that God may have chosen to inspire him directly in the path of abandonment.

At any rate, we find Paul in 1769 burdened with infirmities but rich in merits, a director who was obeyed, a revered founder. He was living his own doctrine of abandonment to the Will of God to the hilt, and in order to complete his work before "drinking in death," he waited with resignation for "God to open the ways."

Part Three

APPEASEMENT AND DEATH

(1769–1775, October 18)

Chapter XX

THE WAYS ARE OPENED

When the time decreed by Providence has come, all the way will be opened.   st. paul of the cross, L. III, 812

PAUL had kept on working until he reached the utmost limit of his strength. His work had not attained the success he had dreamed of. He still did not have the pure and simple approbation of the Rule which would place his Congregation in the ranks of regular institutes. Nor had he founded the institute of Passionist nuns which would harmoniously complement the institute of men.

At any rate, the tiny seed sowed on Monte Argentario had firmly taken root and become a beautiful tree where choice vocations came to rest. Among them was young Vincent Strambi, whom Paul had been obliged to win away from his father. The words he had used were simply these: "The Lord has chosen your son to make a great saint of him."[1] His prophecy was to be fulfilled a century later.

Paul was now utterly exhausted from his life of effort. He even asked himself whether his own unworthiness did not hinder the development of his work. In the intervals of activity permitted by his infirmities he kept working without thought of self for the establishment of the new foundation in Corneto.

Meanwhile he continued to look forward to his retirement from office. He fully expected to be relieved of his functions at the general chapter of 1769. "Once the new General was elected, he would remain in the solitude of Argentario, to make his novitiate. He would put a sign on the door of his cell: 'Paul is dead.' "[2]

The chapter opened on May 9. Paul solemnly gave up his responsibilities. He was unanimously re-elected. For all his protests, supplications, and written renunciations, he had to bow and take up the yoke once more.

Paul's re-election was the outstanding event of the chapter, which also officially approved of the division of the twelve retreats into two Provinces: the province to the north of Rome, or the patrimony of St. Peter, and the province to the south, or of Campagna Marittima. The regimen of the students and even of the religious was somewhat mitigated.

While Paul kicked at the goad, God was opening the ways. Precisely at the same time as the general chapter, a conclave was being held in Rome to elect a successor to Clement XIII, who had died on February 28, 1769.

On May 19, Cardinal Ganganelli was elected Pope and took the name of Clement XIV. As it happened, he was a great admirer and friend of Paul's. The meeting of the two men had taken place several years before, at the home of the Angelettis, who were among Paul's great benefactors. From the start they had esteemed each other. The Cardinal had admired the Founder's holiness, and the latter had admired the prelate's eminent qualities. Paul had even told the Cardinal he would one day be Pope. In fact, Paul alluded several times to the future elevation of Cardinal Ganganelli and to the advantages this would bring to the young Congregation.

After the death of Clement XIII, when several other names were being talked about as papal possibilities, Paul was more convinced than ever who the next Pope would be. He began making preparations during the conclave to go to Rome without delay in order to greet the newly elected Pontiff.

Such assurance might well seem astonishing. However, according to Paul's confessor, Paul once declared that, "aside from the lights that God had communicated to him regarding the foundation of the Congregation, he had never received a more explicit revelation."[3]

On May 25, 1769, Paul left Vetralla for Rome to cast himself at the feet of Pope Clement XIV. Referring to this journey to Rome, he wrote: "If God blesses this undertaking, as I hope He will, I shall leave a solidly established Congregation before I die."[4]

The Pope, for his part, was waiting for him. Indeed, he was surprised that Paul had not come sooner. Paul had been delayed in the preparation of a petition that he wanted to present to the Sovereign Pontiff.

As soon as the Holy Father learned of Paul's arrival he wanted to receive him. He even sent a coach to the Passionists' Hospice of the Holy Crucifix to take Paul to the Vatican.

As Paul rode through the streets of Rome in this lordly vehicle, he could not help taking a quick glance at the past. "Oh! How many times I have been through these streets barefoot! What sufferings I have had to endure in this city to advance the holy work of the Congregation!" Father John Mary, his confessor, who accompanied him, answered: "And now at last your labors are bearing fruit."[5]

When he arrived at the Vatican, the "vagabond" of former days was immediately introduced into the private quarters of Clement XIV, who showered him with attentions, made him sit down and try on his zucchetto, embraced him several times, and offered him a cup of hot chocolate with his own hands.

Paul, embarrassed and touched, wept.

As the Holy Father was about to grant a public audience, he took Paul with him and had him sit near the pontifical throne. Turning to him, the Pope pointed him out to some of his visitors, saying, "That one is Father Paul."

After an hour the audience came to an end. Paul was then able to hand his petition to the Sovereign Pontiff, requesting the approbation of his Institute with simple vows but with the privileges of regular orders.

The Pope read the petition and promised to grant it.[6] Remembering his past expenses in Rome, Paul dared to say: "Holy Father, I don't have a single *baiocco*" — that is, not a cent. And he emphasized his words with a telling gesture.

Clement XIV laughed and answered: "We know very well that you do not have a single *baiocco*."

Paul went away, radiant. To one of his confidantes he wrote: "The Pope received me with extraordinary cordiality and charity, to the point that I would be ashamed to tell the details of it, in view of my lowliness and the majesty of the Vicar of Jesus Christ."[7]

The Pope had accepted the petition. However he lost it a few days later, on his way from the Vatican to the Quirinal. He kept it in mind and asked Paul to send him another. The loss of the first petition proved to Paul's advantage, as he had forgotten to include in it a request for the confirmation of the Rule. Two other omissions in the first petition were intentional. Paul had deliberately refrained from asking the privilege of ordinations and the right to beg.

As soon as the new petition was ready, it was transmitted to the Sovereign Pontiff, who asked two prelates to examine it and give him their opinion.

One of the prelates proposed a few mitigations, but Clement XIV sent him to see Father Paul. The latter, touched by this delicate attention and also more indulgent with age, willingly accepted the prelate's suggestions. They easily agreed to improve the food and to allow a little more time for sleep.

The Pope wanted this to be an enduring work and preferred not to trust too much to the initial fervor of the Founder. Paul was eager to put the seal on his work and asked the Sovereign Pontiff to grant him the favor of promulgating the bull of approbation on August 15, saying: "Holy Father, on Assumption Day I should like to go to St. Mary Major and thank God and His Holy Mother for the favor obtained, for it was before this picture that I vowed for the first time, about fifty years ago, to promote devotion to the most sacred Passion and to gather together companions to this end."

Clement XIV, who was to pontificate on that day at St. Mary Major, agreed, with the words: "And We from Our Throne shall give you Our apostolic benediction."

The apostolic bureaus could not get the bull ready by the date requested, but the Pope sent word to Paul that the favor was granted. The Founder went to St. Mary Major to give thanks.

Three more months were to pass before he received the bull. Writing to one of his religious, he said; "As everyone knows, to complete one's business in Rome takes a thousand carats of patience, 280 carats of prudence, and two thousand carats of painful waiting. The Pope's favor to us is assured, his bull will be delivered. But the employee responsible for transcribing it has fallen ill, so that we must add a few more carats of patience."[8]

The Via della Lungara was still there. But now Paul no longer traveled it on foot and on the brink of discouragement.

The wait was cut short for Paul by the preaching of the Extraordinary Jubilee granted by Clement XIV on the occasion of his election.

Cardinal Colonna, the Vicar of Rome, invited Father Paul to participate. At first he refused, saying he was too old and infirm. However, the invitation was so pressing that he finally accepted, choosing the Church of St. Mary of Consolation in a working-class neighborhood. But Cardinal Colonna assigned him to the basilica of St. Mary in the Trastevere.

Paul took the mission entrusted to him seriously and wanted to prepare himself. As his sermons were all in Vetralla, he wrote to one of his religious: "I need to call upon your charity. I beg of you to send me my writings with the book which is near them. They are in the archives closet. The key [to the closet] is in the drawer of my table, and as I cannot send you the key to the drawer in this letter, try to open the drawer any way you can. I think that with your ingenuity you will easily succeed. Close the drawer again by means of a wooden peg, to be placed between the table and the drawer, so that you alone will be able to open it.

"Send me the manuscripts carefully sewn into an old cloth, and attach a ticket to it with my address. . . . If you can do me this service for the Feast of the Assumption, I shall be most grateful to you, for I must prepare myself. You know that it is five years, and perhaps longer, since I have done any preaching."[9]

This concern on Father Paul's part does him honor, but it was totally unnecessary. The crowds of the faithful were not coming to hear a preacher, to pass judgment on his knowledge or his eloquence. They were coming to hear the Saint, who no longer needed human means.

And this is the way things turned out. Paul, laid low by an attack of fever, was not able to participate in the Jubilee exercises until the seventh day. But the moment he came, there was a crowd. The clergy and the laity, noblemen and prelates thronged the basilica. "The very presence of the man of God was eloquent. Here was an old man of seventy-five, convalescent and weak, hardly able to stand up. Several persons had to help him mount the steps of the platform. Some held him by the hand, others supported him under the arms. The servant of God stood before his audience, leaning on his staff, barefoot and head uncovered. The very sight of him already moved the audience profoundly. Then he preached with as much fire, energy, and power as if he were suffering no indisposition. . . . After each sermon a crowd gathered around him to kiss his hand and his garment, or to receive his blessing."[10]

On the last day there was such an overflow of people that the square in front of the church was filled. The enthusiasm was so delirious that a company of soldiers had to be summoned to maintain order and to protect the preacher, who was almost caught in the crush.

This was his swan song, the apotheosis of fifty years of apostolic ministry.

Paul admitted it in all simplicity: "At every sermon there was a crowd of people of every condition, canons, prelates, noblemen and common folk, also a large number of priests and religious. Meanwhile, this poor 'rotting' and ignorant old man was found pleasing. Everyone gladly listened to him and with fruit. Blessed be God for it!"[11]

By September the vacation period of the bureaus was not yet over. Paul decided he wanted to pay a last visit to the seven basilicas of Rome while he awaited the promised bull. A benefactor placed a carriage at his disposal.

To avoid all display, Paul started his pilgrimage secretly and early in the morning, accompanied by three religious. He tarried longest at St. Paul outside the Walls and at Tre Fontane, to venerate his illustrious patron.

His movements were not so secret that a great Roman lady could not manage to learn of them. She arranged to be on his path and invited him to her country house under the pretext of giving the horses a rest.

Paul accepted the refreshment offered him. During his visit, still filled with the sentiments of devotion that the sight of the places sanctified by the martyrdom of St. Paul had rekindled in him, he let his heart's feelings overflow into words. "It was wonderful to hear him."[12]

The only thing Paul had yet to do was to pay his respects to the Holy Father. On September 29 he was received in a private audience with much deference. The Pope made him sit down while he himself stood up, telling him of his great satisfaction over the success of his recent sermons and expressing the desire that he remain permanently in Rome. "I know what you would do in your Retreat of the Holy Angel," the Pope said to him. "You would pray, you would meditate for yourself, for Us, and for the whole Church. Well! You can do it here in Rome, and you can do even more."[13]

Paul accepted by simply bowing his head, and Clement XIV admired his humility and obedience.

In November the bull was ready at last. The Pope received Paul once more, this time in his bedchamber, which was furnished like a cell. "It is the room of a simple religious," Paul wrote, "with a poor bed, two seats, a crucifix, a picture of the Blessed Virgin, as well as one of St. Francis, and another of St. Joseph Cupertino. The bare walls are completely devoid of ornaments, nothing but the partitions. The Pope is a man of holy life. The delicate marks of charity that he gave me as usual are beyond description. He handed me the bull with his own hands. . . . It is rich with privileges."[14]

The bull approved the Institute, whereas the Rule was approved separately by a simple brief. The whole thing, which should have cost two thousand francs, was given gratuitously.

Henceforth the Congregation enjoyed autonomy with respect

to the ordinaries and received the privileges of the regular orders, without being held to solemn vows.

Paul was able to write: "All our business is finished. I have in my hands the bull and the brief, rich with privileges and favors. Thus, before dying I leave the Congregation well established and strengthened forever in the Church of God."[15]

The end of the year was to bring the Founder new joy and hope.

On December 21 he went to offer his Christmas wishes to the Sovereign Pontiff. The latter granted the Passionists permission to celebrate Midnight Mass in their private oratory in Rome and promised to provide a house and a church for the young Congregation.

This went far beyond the desires of the Founder, which had until then been denied.

Chapter XXI

THE NEST OF THE DOVES

I sincerely desire to see you become saints.
ST. PAUL OF THE CROSS
TO MOTHER MARIA CROCIFISSA

PAUL rightly considered his Congregation the great work of his life and rejoiced in its definitive recognition by the Church. However, he had yet to found the corresponding institute of women, which he considered the necessary complement to his institute for men.

But the time was over when he had to take the initiative. Now the "ways" were opened. He had only to wait. Besides, his increasing infirmities no longer allowed him to make long-range plans. He was often nailed to his straw mat by attacks of sciatica. Even writing was a great effort for him. He was convinced that his death was near.

With regard to his own Congregation, he had but one desire. Now that he had visited the province to the south of Rome, he wanted to go and embrace for the last time his religious in the northern retreats.

On December 21 he went to offer his Christmas wishes to the Holy Father to ask his permission to leave Rome for a few weeks. The Pope granted this request, while referring Paul to the Cardinal-Vicar. At the same time, the Holy Father gently complained that Paul was not asking some favor of him.

Paul saw in this genial reproach an unexpected invitation to talk to Clement XIV about his project to found the institute of Passionist nuns and about the beginnings already made in Corneto. The Pope listened with interest and promised his benevolent protection.

Paul's predictions to Mother Maria Crocifissa were about to be fulfilled. God's hour would soon ring. They had only to wait "in calm and patient silence."

According to the Sovereign Pontiff's instructions, Paul went to see the Cardinal-Vicar, who gladly granted him permission to leave Rome, although he advised him to return no later than the Feast of St. John the Baptist.

On March 27, Paul set out to visit his retreats to the north. Winter was not yet over, and he suffered from the cold. His companion, Father John Mary, called to mind the even greater hardships he had suffered on the same road from Rome to Civitavecchia in the past. Paul agreed: "I used to go from Monte Argentario to Rome and back, barefoot and without provisions."[1]

They stopped at Monterone to spend the night at an inn. As soon as Paul was a bit rested and warmed, he addressed a pious exhortation to his hosts and to the other travelers. Early the next morning the two priests resumed their journey to Corneto.

Paul's first concern was to visit the convent destined to shelter the first Passionist nuns. It was almost completed, but he was not altogether pleased with it. He demanded that certain apertures and grilles be closed, for he intended to have the rules of enclosure strictly observed.

Next he made his canonical visitation of the retreat of his own religious in Corneto, edifying them by his words and acts. During his stay with them he wrote to Pope Clement XIV to report to him on his journey, on the progress of construction of the convent, and on the spirit of his own religious.

On Easter Sunday, Paul set out by sea for Monte Argentario. A violent storm cast the boat up on the coast at Montalto. As he could not find a carriage in which to continue his journey, he took the risk of going on horseback. Despite his infirmities, he arrived in Orbetello with no more serious annoyance than the cold and the rain. Forced by the bad weather to spend the day in the town where he had so often exercised his ministry, he was surrounded by the inhabitants, who came to manifest their veneration.

The next day, as he climbed the paths on the flanks of Monte Argentario, his eyes filled with tears. "How many memories these mountains bring to my mind!" he said. Their wild ruggedness, amid a magificent landscape bathed in light, reminded him of his difficult beginnings, his conquering enthusiasms, and his cruel disappointments. The thought made him weep quiet tears. The moment of calm had come.

When he addressed his religious, and above all the novices, he did so with great tenderness.

However, his humility was subjected to a severe trial. Clement XIV's answer to his letter reached him as he was reliving his memories on Monte Argentario. It was a brief, honoring him and his Congregation. Paul was overwhelmed. He had done so little good, he thought, and he was already being rewarded for it here on earth.

The provincial found him in this state of anxiety and succeeded in calming him by making him see the Pope's brief as an encouragement to do better rather than as a reward.

Actually Clement XIV expressed his admiration for the work accomplished, his trust in the prayers of the servant of God, and his benevolence for his future undertakings.

Paul did not have an opportunity to remain at Monte Argentario very long. He was wanted in Rome. With his usual simplicity he asked a benefactor for the use of a carriage, saying: "I come to urgently implore your great charity, that your coachman may take me to Corneto on Saturday, May 5, for he knows the way well. I would like him to get me there without accident, for I am scarcely more than a corpse." and with his practical sense he added: "And may Your Most Illustrious Lordship deign, if you will, to give the necessary and opportune orders to this person and have some food brought, without forgetting the horses, so that we may take some refreshment at Tuffone."[2]

The usual scenes of popular enthusiasm occurred at Montalto and all along the way. Paul lost his coat, which was slashed to pieces by the people. "Woe is me," he exclaimed. "I shall have to look myself up. The world is wrong. People think I am what I really am not."[3]

The journey ended without further annoyance, except for fatigue resulting from traveling on a road cut off by heavy rains and overflowing torrents.

Paul's return to Rome had been hastened by the confidant of a cardinal, in view of great events that were in preparation. All we know about it is that as soon as Paul arrived in Rome he was received by the Pope and by Cardinal Colonna. Did the question of the savage attacks the Society of Jesus was undergoing come up? We do not know.

The following days the aged Founder was laid low by illness and obliged to remain in bed. It was not until a month later that he was able once again to celebrate Mass and write a few letters.

On May 23 he managed to drag himself to an audience with the Holy Father but did not have the opportunity to talk to the busy Pontiff about his plans for the foundation of Passionist nuns.

The important thing was to have the Rule for this new institute ready when the moment came. Paul had already outlined them. Now that he was merely adapting the Constitutions of his own Congregation to one for women, he no longer dared trust his own inspirations. Each morning his three consultors met with him in his cell and discussed his project chapter by chapter before deciding on the final text.

On July 1, Paul was able to present this text to the Sovereign Pontiff, who had it examined at once by two eminent theologians: Father Pastrovitch and Bishop Zelada. Their reaction was most favorable. The former considered the Rule "prudent, discreet." The latter proposed a few additions, without sparing his praise.

As early as July 26, Clement XIV received Paul and returned the proposed Rule to him, saying that he wanted to approve them in a brief. Paul, the wiser for his past experiences, asked for a less solemn approbation in the form of a simple rescript. Thus, after the Rule had been tried out in practice, it could more easily be amended.

The Holy Father accepted Paul's point of view, dictated as it was by prudence. The audience then continued on an intimate, friendly tone and turned to the needs of the Church as a whole. Paul, emboldened by his success, dared to broach the delicate question of the laxity of certain religious orders. He said it would be opportune if superiors made discreet efforts to promote reforms by spiritual exercises that need not be known on the outside. Clement XIV expressed high praise for this approach, as well as for Paul's recommendation that priests and bishops practice mental prayer.

Times had changed, and God's way had now been opened. Thus Paul was able to write about this time: "The negotiations for the new convent of nuns are progressing very well. In a few months you will receive news that will amaze you."[4]

On September 3 the papal rescript appeared, as promised, approving the Rule of the nuns of the Passion.

It was time to think of the foundation and of all the practical details. Paul took charge of everything himself, even to specifying the length of the veils and the kind of material to be used. "Toward the end of February I shall go and put everything in order, and be present at the foundation. Pray to God to give me the health and moral strength necessary for this great work. For

He has made me its mainstay — me, a frail and wretched reed."[5]

God did not grant his wish, but sent him sickness instead. He was not able to preside at the inauguration of the convent. In fact, his condition was so serious that the end was feared. Although tormented by the devil and by interior desolation, he prepared for death with his usual resignation to the Will of God. His only concern was to make sure he would have a simple burial in the event that he did die. Actually he did not believe this was his last illness.

"If I die," he said to his confessor, "my last request is that I be given the alms of a private funeral in the hospice chapel. Very late at night, let two servants from St. John's Hospital carry my body to the Church of Sts. Peter and Marcellinus . . . and have me buried without any honors. When my flesh has disintegrated, have my bones placed in a bag and carried on a donkey to Holy Angel Retreat, there to deposit them next to my brother John Baptist."[6]

His confessor was obliged to admit that the Pope had declared he would take care of his burial. Paul was silent at first, then announced that he would have preferred to die without honors. He was silent again, however, when the confessor added that Jesus Christ allowed Himself to be buried by His loved ones in the place of their own choosing.

Meanwhile his premonitions proved right. He did not die of this illness but gradually regained strength. At Christmas, however, he was allowed only to receive Holy Communion as a matter of prudence and by command of Clement XIV. In January he had a serious relapse that brought him to death's door several times and kept him in bed the entire year. Nonetheless, he was able to make a few steps once in a while with the help of two crutches.

It was during this period that the foundation of the Passionist nuns was established in Corneto. From his bed of suffering Paul took a keen interest in all that transpired.

Although he had thought about the institute of nuns for years, he had recommended extreme discretion to others in talking about it. Now that the approbation had been obtained, news of it inevitably spread. Among those who learned of the new convent was a great Roman lady, Princess Anna Colonna Barberini, the widow of Duke Sforza.

Somewhat of a fanatic, the Princess became enthusiastic over the new Institute and dreamed of performing dazzling mortifications. She declared that "even though the monastery were situated in a cellar and she were sure to die the day after her arrival, she wanted to follow the Will of God which was calling her to this place of refuge." In fact, she said, she would be its foundress.

In the face of objections to her desires, she consented to submit her case in writing to Clement XIV. The latter temporized and finally agreed to her request in order to assure the new convent sufficient income.

The delighted Princess went to Father Paul and threw herself at his feet. He, for his part, received her with his usual charity and gave her advice.

After the interview, however, Paul did not seem very pleased. A few days later, warned by his interior visions or by precise reports, he allowed himself to voice some of his fears in confidence to his infirmarian: "Her sentiments have changed."[7] He said no more, and events continued their course.

The three Costantini sisters had asked permission to enter the new institute. This favor was granted only to Mother Maria Crocifissa, and then only after the foundation. Finally it was advanced to the very day the convent opened.

The date was set for March 22, Feast of Our Lady of Sorrows. But the Princess was not ready and asked that it be delayed until April 7.

As Paul lay helpless on his sickbed, he delegated Father John Mary to attend the ceremony and put the finishing touches to the foundation. The latter went to Corneto and on March 29 received a letter from the Princess, asking another delay as her health was bad and the roads impassable. What was he to do? The postulants had already arrived or would soon arrive. Father John Mary decided to go ahead as planned on April 7, and so advised Princess Barberini.

On April 6 the church was blessed and the postulants attended Mass and received Holy Communion. Everyone was waiting for the "foundress" to arrive. April 7 was a day of anxiety and disappointment for both postulants and benefactors. Meanwhile enemies and skeptics scoffed.

The next day Paul declared that to his mind the foundation had not taken place. This statement would seem strange if we did not know of his supernatural intuitions on the matter. For obviously he had no way of knowing the facts through natural means.

On April 9, Father John Mary received a letter from the Princess, telling him he could go ahead with the foundation if he so pleased. As for her, she had to spend two months at Narni before going to Corneto. Distressed, Father John Mary rushed to Rome to ask Paul's advice. The latter was grieved by this disappointment, but, being a man of decision, he immediately sent his delegate to the Holy Father to inform him of the situation and ask permission to clothe the nuns in their habits.

Clement XIV was disagreeably surprised and asked Paul to prepare a memorandum for him. Paul then narrated the genesis of the foundation through the generosity of the Costantini family. Now that the Pope saw the situation clearly, he himself set the date for the ceremony as the following May 3.

Meanwhile the whimsical Princess had written to the Pope, telling him that she now doubted she had a vocation and placing the matter in his hands. Clement XIV commanded her to persevere in her original plan and go to Corneto. And so the Princess went to the new Convent on May 18 and was welcomed as the superior. She herself declared, however: "I come simply as Anna Barberini."

Another letter from the Pope encouraged her to persevere. For a while she seemed to be happy at the retreat, but she soon sent a messenger to Rome, saying she had found neither health nor peace of heart at Corneto. Clement XIV answered simply: "We have never intended to kill anyone. Let her do what she wants."

When the Princess received the Pope's message on June 4, she decided then and there to prepare to leave on the sixth. She kept her word and left with dignity, after kissing each of the nuns and giving an alms for the chapel.

On May 3 the clothing ceremony had taken place according to the Pope's wishes. It was carried out with all possible solemnity under the presidency of Bishop Paluzzi, the Vicar Capitular of the clergy of Corneto, and a member of the Costantini family.

Maria Crocifissa carried the crucifix, and it was she who received the keys of the convent. She was also made mistress of novices and temporary superior.

A few days later she felt it her duty to thank the Holy Father in the name of her companions for all his favors to them. Clement XIV was greatly touched by this attention and always maintained his interest in the foundation afterward, even in the matter of financial help.

Things followed their normal course. After a year's novitiate the eleven postulants were professed and chose Mother Maria Crocifissa as their superior. Paul, kept informed of developments, was thoroughly pleased. He sent his encouragement to the nuns and his advice to his spiritual daughter. He continued to watch over the nest of the Doves of Christ until his dying day.

Chapter XXII

THE ROYAL GIFT

"A beautiful property, a monastery already built, a venerable basilica, Christian memories of inestimable value."

PAUL's long illness, from which he was never to recover, did not keep him from concerning himself with the serious interests of his Congregation.

Thus during the summer of 1771 an incident took place that obliged the Founder to have recourse to Pope Clement XIV.

Through the brief approving the Rule in 1746 and more explicitly by a bull of the reigning Pope, the retreats of the Passionists were exempt from canonical visitations by diocesan authorities. Nonetheless, Cardinal Stoppani, Bishop of Palestrina, claimed the right to have the retreat at Paliano visited by his Vicar General. He declared that this exemption had not been specified by the Holy See.

In an effort to safeguard the rights of his Congregation, Paul brought the matter to the attention of Clement XIV. As a matter of discretion, his memorandum mentioned neither the place nor the persons involved.

The Pope appreciated Paul's charity but learned through other sources what had happened at Paliano. When he reproached Cardinal Stoppani, the latter put the blame on his Vicar General.

"But you're the one who are the Bishop," Clement XIV answered. And to obviate any further difficulties, the Pope declared that all retreats having at least twelve religious were to be exempt.

Paul, confined to his bed was unable to thank the Pope personally. Meanwhile the Holy Father kept himself informed as to Paul's condition. When in 1773 he learned that Paul had taken a turn for the worse that might prove fatal, he declared in his benevolence that Paul must not die. "Tell him that I grant him a reprieve. He must obey!"

In his devotion to Clement XIV, the sick man found enough faith to ask Christ to improve his health. And he did get better. On the Feast of Corpus Christi he was well enough to celebrate Mass. He continued to celebrate it afterward, although not without great effort.

About this time a sad event in the history of the Church took place which was to have important consequences for the new Congregation: the suppression of the Society of Jesus.

During the violent attacks to which the Jesuits had been subjected for several years and which had caused them to be expelled from most of the nations of the West, Paul had not spared his praises for the famous Society. When Clement XIV consented to the suppression of the Jesuits in August 1773, it is most improbable that Paul was among those who counseled him to take this measure.

Once the thing was done, the matter of transferring the property of the Society of Jesus in the Papal States, and especially in Rome, had to be settled.

Paul carefully refrained from joining the ranks of those seeking Jesuit property and forbade his religious to say a word about his desire to establish a retreat in Rome. Actually he had long hoped to obtain some thing more significant than the temporary quarters of the Hospice of the Holy Crucifix. And the Pope had promised him a retreat.

As it happened, Clement XIV remembered his promise without any prompting and offered Paul the Jesuit Fathers' Novitiate of St. Andrew of the Quirinal, opposite the Vatican. His Holiness said that this proximity pleased him. Paul had no objections to this nearness, but there were drawbacks from the point of view of the requirements for a retreat.

When a prelate came to Paul to tell him of the Pope's intentions, adding that he himself thought the monastery of Sts. John and Paul would be more suitable, Paul readily agreed. At that time the monastery was situated amid vines and open fields, although it is now in a heavily built-up area.

When apprised of Paul's preferences, the Pope gave orders to settle the matter without delay. The Lazarist Fathers, who then occupied Sts. John and Paul, were to receive in exchange St. Andrew of the Quirinal, which offered a better income.

It looked as if the transfer would be effected without difficulties. However, several powerful religious orders had their eyes on St. Andrew and in addition thought the Passionists were getting too big a share of the spoils. After all, these poor religious "barely out of the woods" would be "incapable of maintaining this church [Sts. John and Paul] in good condition."[1]

Resigned to the Will of God as always but also accustomed not to neglect human precautions, Paul submitted these difficulties to Clement XIV. The Holy Father was extremely surprised to learn that the matter was still pending. He repeated his orders, and despite new obstacles the act of cession was signed on December 6, 1773.

This was indeed a royal gift: "a beautiful property, a monastery already built, a venerable basilica, Christian memories of inestimable value."

In the eighteenth century these memories were known only through tradition. John and Paul were brothers, Christian officers attached to the court of Constantine and in particular to his daughter, St. Constance. When Julian the Apostate became Caesar, they renounced their posts as officers of the palace. Angered, Julian gave them a few days to choose between the worship of Jupiter and death. The two brothers distributed their goods to the poor and prepared themselves for martyrdom. Meanwhile the Emperor ordered the prefect of the Praetorian Cohort to execute his threat. The latter had John and Paul decapitated and buried in their own house.

While this event has many counterparts in the history of the early Church, it took a special significance because until A.D. 751, when Pope Paul I had the bodies of the martyrs transported from the catacombs to the Roman basilicas, Sts. John and Paul were the only martyrs whose remains rested within the city.

As early as the fourth century a shrine had been built over the house and tomb of the two martyrs by Pamachius, a friend of St. Jerome. In the twelfth century the church was rebuilt, and pilgrims to Rome never failed to venerate the tomb of the Martyrs John and Paul. Then for centuries the memory of these saints seemed to be lost.

In the eighteenth century the church was completely remodeled before it was entrusted to the Passionists. They in turn erected a lateral chapel to hold the body of their Founder.

It was not until 1887 that a religious of the Congregation, Father Germano, sought to verify ancient claims by making excavations under the foundations. The results were magnificent. Under the present basilica, the foundations of the twelfth-century church and the fourth-century shrine were discovered. Better still, the very house of the martyrs John and Paul was recovered and even more ancient structures, including a Christian oratory, the most ancient known to exist in the city of Rome itself. The walls of tuff are adorned with frescoes both pagan and Christian, including the Orant, a familiar figure of the catacombs.

Thus from the bowels of the earth came confirmation of oral traditions and written documents.

The present church has preserved the façade with its Lombard portico, its portal flanked by two ancient lions, its apse and Romanic campanile, which has just been restored by Francis Cardinal Spellman, whose titular church Sts. John and Paul happens to be.

In the center of the main nave, a little to the right, a stone surrounded by a grille indicates the spot where the two martyrs were decapitated. Their bodies, which were rediscovered under the reign of St. Pius V, are enclosed in a beautiful urn of porphyry under the main altar.

The ceiling in compartments, richly decorated in Renaissance style, masks the great antiquity of the structure, especially as the two rows of columns which formed three basilica-type naves have been replaced by pilasters.

In more recent years the monastery has been enlarged by the Passionists. The ocher of its present walls contrasts harmoniously with the patina-covered bricks of the campanile and the grisaille of the façade.

The visitor who is permitted to enter the enclosure comes first into an inner court resplendent with marble-bordered flower beds filled with masses of brilliant dahlias and petunias. Beyond is a large vegetable garden, whose paths are bordered with amphoras adorned with graceful garlands. These ancient vases were uncovered in the process of cultivating the land, for the property is on the site of the Temple of Claudius, whose enormous substructure can be seen on the slope of Mount Coelius. Along the broad avenues lined with fig trees, one gets a splendid view of the Colosseum and a panoramic vista of most of Rome.

Such was the magnificent gift Paul received from Clement XIV. In time, after various additions and changes, it became the mother house of the Passionists.

The servant of God did not allow himself to be dazzled by all this grandeur but chose for himself the poorest room on the ground floor. He also saw to it that his religious did not relax their observance. While asking all his retreats to offer up prayers of thanksgiving for the favor of a house in Rome, he forbade his religious to consider Sts. John and Paul as a kind of inn and an excuse for unnecessary trips to Rome. They were to come to Rome only with his written authorization or that of his successors.

Paul feared lest this royal gift make his religious lose their taste for simplicity and solitude. On the other hand, he realized how much young religious could benefit by pursuing their studies in Rome, the center of Catholicism. With this in mind he sent for nine students and gave them Father Vincent Mary Strambi (later to be canonized) as their teacher and director. This gave Father Strambi the unexpected opportunity of living in intimate contact with the servant of God and enabled him to become the postulant of his cause and also his first biographer.

Paul did not have a chance to remain very long in the poor little room he had chosen for himself. Cardinal Pallota came to visit him and considered the room too damp and stuffy. In obedience, the old man moved to a well-ventilated room on the second floor. But visitors began to pour in to see him in such numbers that the tranquillity of the monastery suffered. Paul begged to return to the ground floor, where he occupied two adjoining rooms until his death. One of the rooms was transformed into a chapel, where he celebrated Mass early every morning when his failing health permitted.

The two rooms have been reverently preserved as well as the familiar objects he used: his writing kit, his traveling bag, his staff, even a snuffbox, his watch, and other more precious mementoes, such as his chalice, his breviary, his favorite books, some autographed letters, and of course his instruments of mortification.

It was here that he used to gather his religious together to give them pious exhortations and called in the students one by one to give them personal advice.

When he was well enough to do so, he liked to go to the basilica and preside over the ceremonies for great feasts of the Church. This was the sum of his movements, and even then he had to be carried in an armchair.

On the last day of 1773 he wanted to go to the Vatican to thank Clement XIV for his generosity. For fear of being retained at the last moment because of illness, he had not asked for an audience. But when the Pope was informed of his presence he received him at once and conversed with him almost two hours. As Paul returned to his carriage, the Holy Father kept watching after him from a balcony.

From time to time the Holy Father sent a coach to bring Paul to visit him. On such occasions he manifested not only kindness but actual veneration for the aged man. The day came when Paul in his infirmity could not even get into a carriage any more. Clement XIV decided to pay him a visit. On June 26, 1774, the Pope went to Sts. John and Paul, where the holy Founder received him, sitting in his armchair, at the entrance of the basilica. The Holy Father's mark of attention had moved Paul to tears.

While the Holy Father and his retinue prayed for a few moments in the church, Paul was carried to the reception hall, where a throne had been erected. The Pope then came in and granted an audience to all the religious as well as to a few benefactors and close friends. Then he and Paul retired to an adjoining room, where they talked in private for a long time.

This was to be their last meeting. Soon afterward Clement XIV was taken ill and died in September 1774. It was said that his last days were saddened by remorse over his suppression of the Society of Jesus. Be this as it may, it must be said that he had agreed to settle this disturbing affair "for the sake of peace."[2] As for his death, it is on record that he was miraculously assisted in his last hour by St. Alphonsus Liguori.

St. Paul of the Cross sincerely mourned his passing and commanded all his retreats to celebrate a solemn requiem for the deceased Pontiff.

At Sts. John and Paul the Founder asked to be carried to the foot of the catafalque. There he prayed throughout the service, weeping many tears "for the soul of the great Pontiff who had done so much good to the Congregation."[3]

The marble bust of Clement XIV can still be seen near the sacristy of Sts. John and Paul. Paul had it carved to perpetuate the memory of his great benefactor, whom he considerd as his father even as the Holy Father had looked to him with filial affection.

Chapter XXIII

A HOLY FRIENDSHIP

". . . as if the physiognomy of a saint did not take on its full luster unless reflected in a woman's face."

WE HAVE seen that the interior life of Paul of the Cross, like his active life, could be divided into three periods:

After twelve years of consolations, mingled with trials and notable for extraordinary visions, came forty-five years of interior desolation, strange temptations, tribulations and discouragement, softened by mystical favors.

During the last years of his life, from 1770 to 1775, although trials did not entirely disappear, consolations dominated. Many astonishing mystical phenomena took place. This was the period of appeasement, illumined by the friendship of Rosa Calabresi.

Theirs was a wholly spiritual friendship, analogous to that of St. Clare and Francis of Assisi, of St. Jane de Chantal and Francis de Sales, as if the physiognomy of a saint could not take on its full luster unless reflected in a woman's face.

Rosa Calabresi was such an intimate confidante of Paul of the Cross that she alone knew of many of the mystical favors with which the servant of God was favored. On several occasions she alone witnessed some of the extraordinary phenomena of his last years. In consequence, her deposition at the canonization process is of capital importance.

Before discussing the final stages of Paul of the Cross' interior life, it is therefore necessary to give a brief sketch of Rosa Calabresi and examine her moral life, in order to evaluate rightly the worth of testimony.

Rosa was born in Cerveteri, in the diocese of Porto, about 1746. Her family was rather well off financially. As a small child she lost both her parents but remained in her father's home with her brothers. One of her brothers later became secretary to Cardinal Zelada and received Rosa in his home when she went to Rome.

In 1748 Paul preached a mission in Cerveteri. As Rosa was then only two years old, she was unable to benefit from his sermons. Her mother, however, deeply moved by the missionary's holiness, often spoke of him afterward. Her words made a profound impression on her daughter.

When Rosa was twenty, she was filled with a desire to attain perfection and sought an enlightened director. Remembering her mother's words, she wrote to Father Paul.

The answer came immediately, providing the needed advice. A correspondence was begun, which continued for ten years before they met in person.

This correspondence would be precious to us, enabling us to measure the ascent in the mystical ways of this privileged soul and to appreciate the wisdom of her director, but it has been destroyed. As a matter of discretion, Paul did not keep the letters of persons under his spiritual direction. Rosa Calabresi, for her part, burned Paul's letters to her during an illness, out of a similar sentiment and at his command.

We do know, nonetheless, that Rosa received extraordinary graces, that she crossed the threshold of all the dwellings of the "Interior Castle" of the soul, and was favored with heavenly visions and apparitions.

It was precisely to put her at ease and help her to know herself and make herself known that Paul was induced to tell her of analogous graces he himself had received. And so Rosa Calabresi was able to bring extremely precious testimony to the canonization process on the interior life of her director.

In 1775, on the occasion of the Jubilee, Rosa went to Rome and met Father Paul in person for the first time. She was about thirty, and he was in his eighty-second year. Their spiritual joy in meeting, in conversing on the realities of grace and the wonders of the divine life, led them to have frequent conferences in the sacristy of the Basilica of Sts. John and Paul, where the aged invalid was carried almost every day.

It is through Rosa Calabresi that we know, for instance, that during the last years and especially the last months of his life Paul received favors just as extraordinary as those of his adolescence, and even more numerous.

The Blessed Virgin had once come to confirm his mission as Founder by presenting him the habit adorned with the sign of the Passion. She reappeared to him toward the end of his life in the attitude of the Pietà. This happened on Good Friday, 1768. There was such desolation on the face of the bereaved Mother as she received her inanimate Son upon her knees that Paul could not eat his usual food that day. "You want me to eat when I think of such things!"[1]

This was not the only time Mary appeared to him. One day the painting of Our Lady of Sorrows, above the altar where he celebrated Mass, came to life. The Blessed Mother's eyes filled with tears as she told him that her greatest suffering during the Passion had been to hear her Son treated as a seducer and herself upbraided for bringing Him up badly.

The Gospel tells us all we need to know. And yet is there not a human resonance in this private revelation that allows us to picture more realistically the cruel comments Mary had to listen to? A few weeks earlier, when Jesus was going through Palestine as a popular miracle worker, she had been the object of envy. But on Calvary she was the butt of derision.

During 1775 Paul received an unusual number of extraordinary favors during his conversations with Rosa. Or do they seem numerous because we have a witness to them? Here is a portion of Rosa's testimony:

"On only two occasions did I see the servant of God raised above the ground and suspended in the air. Much more frequent were the sweet ecstasies during which his spirit was elevated and immersed in God. These ecstasies usually lasted somewhere between a quarter of an hour and a half hour. For as soon as our conversation on God or on the sublime mysteries turned to the deeper aspects of the subject, he could no longer contain his fervor and became absorbed in God in spirit."[2]

At such times his face sometimes became radiant, as if all the infirmities that kept him a prisoner in his chair had disappeared. Without any help, he would get on his knees before the heavenly apparition. It was under such circumstances that the Blessed Virgin, the Child Jesus, St. Michael, and another angel appeared to him.

But rather than distort the facts by trying to summarize them, it is better to quote from Rosa Calabresi's own account of one of these apparitions:

"During one of our spiritual conferences in the sacristy of Sts. John and Paul, a doubt arose in the mind of the servant of God regarding what I was telling him. In order to obtain the necessary light and to give me appropriate advice, he commanded me to pray inwardly, and this I did. He was doing the same on his part. While I was thus kneeling in prayer and the venerable servant of God was seated in his armchair facing the painting of the Blessed Virgin hanging on the wall above the clock, as I have described elsewhere, this most loving Lord appeared unexpectedly before Father Paul in the form of a little child, joyful, beautiful, and gracious. It delighted one's heart just to see Him. He gave forth brilliant, blinding rays of light. In the presence of this vision, which was real and not imaginary, Father Paul not only got up under the impulse of respect and love as if he did not feel his very painful infirmities that confined him to his armchair, but he even prostrated himself on his knees, his face against the ground, to adore the Holy Infant Who was making Himself visible to him.

"I did the same. While we were both prostrate on our knees, we raised our heads ever so little to ask the most loving Lord to give us His benediction. He deigned to grant it to both of us. While I silently admired God's work and made interior acts of love, the venerable Father Paul, overcome by astonishment and delight, cried out: 'O goodness, O benignity, O love! The great Son of God deigns to allow Himself to be seen by a most vile worm!'

"At the same time, he asked forgiveness for his unbelief; and he wept abundant tears of tenderness. In a voice shaken by sobs, he continued: 'Lord, I ask Your forgiveness for my countless sins committed during so many years of preaching, in so many sacraments received and administered, for so many irreverences, for so much ingratitude.'

"He was given the consolation of hearing the Holy Infant answer that everything he had done was well done. Word for word, this is what Jesus said: 'Everything was well done and according to My divine Will.'

"Father Paul showed his desire to have the divine Infant in his arms and to be able to press Him against his heart. In this also, the most loving Lord was pleased to satisfy him. As I saw it, He went to Paul, and the latter threw his arms lovingly around the neck of the divine Child.

"At the same time, I felt a great consolation, such as it is impossible to imagine.

"Holding the Holy Infant in his arms, the servant of God asked Him for the salvation of his soul, amid many tears. The Holy Child also answered this request with a certain benignity in the following words, which I heard clearly: 'Your salvation is as certain as that you are holding Me in your arms.'

"After these words, the vision disappeared. Meanwhile, Father Paul remained on his knees on the floor. Although he had gotten up from his chair in the twinkling of an eye when the Child Jesus appeared, he was once again overcome by his extreme corporeal weakness now that the vision had disappeared. He was unable to return to his armchair unaided. But in this matter too, I witnessed the wonders of divine goodness and mercy: the glorious Archangel St. Michael and another angel appeared visibly, replaced him in the armchair, and then disappeared.

"Once back in his chair, Father Paul remained for some time deprived of the use of his senses and, as it were, absorbed in God. When he regained consciousness, he spoke very few words to me on the subject of the vision that had just disappeared. He told me that in former years these visits of the Child Jesus had been frequent and that he had received other heavenly favors very often, but that later on, after he entered the sorrowful period of dryness and interior abandonment, these visits from heaven had come more rarely. That was all he told me, and after giving me his blessing he brought the conference to an end."[3]

Such testimony cannot be summed up in a few words. It cannot be challenged without proof or without temerity. It introduces us into the supernatural aura that enveloped the early days of Paul Danei's life, seemed to fade away during the long periods of his painful ascent, and finally shone forth at the end of his life and illumined his last years, and especially the last few months before his death.

It is like a torrent that races joyously at its source, seems to be lost in the sand, and then becomes a calm and peaceful river before flowing into the great briny waters of the sea.

Actually, after Rosa Calabresi left Rome the old man wrote to her, declaring that he had found appeasement; and he concluded: "It makes me think that I am close to death."[4]

But death was not to be bitter for him. He was to "drink it," according to his own picturesque expression, in an upsurge of love toward the One he had loved so much.

He was not even destined to be lost in the innumerable and anonymous throng of the departed, but, like the great saints, to emerge gradually and shine forth with the glory of the elect.

Chapter XXIV

THE SWAN SONG – DEATH

"This is my last work," he said. "Once it is completed, I shall have put everything in order that concerns the Congregation and then I can die."

CLEMENT XIV died in September 1774, and his successor, Pius VI, was not elected until February 15, 1775.

A few weeks after his election the new Pope came to visit Father Paul of the Cross, which gives us some idea of the Pope's high esteem for him.

It was during the Forty Hours' Devotion. The Sovereign Pontiff went to the basilica of Sts. John and Paul and adored the Blessed Sacrament solemnly exposed. At the time, Paul was obliged to remain in bed because of illness, and the Pope went to his room. In his humility Paul was so embarrassed at this attention that he said: "How can it be, Holy Father, that Your Holiness deigns to come to the lowliest creature in Holy Mother Church, to a mere rag of a man such as I, to a great sinner!"

The Pope placed his zucchetto upon him twice, asked for his prayers, and assured him of his good will for the Congregation. Before leaving, he kissed Father Paul on the forehead.

Paul was of course delighted to have found a protector for his Congregation which was mourning the death of Clement XIV. "I have a Father once more, and what a Father!" he exclaimed.

It seems that Paul had premonitions of the persecutions the Sovereign Pontiff was to endure later during the French Revolution. "Poor Church, poor Catholic religion! Lord, strengthen Your Vicar. Give him the necessary courage and light to accomplish Your most holy Will in all things and for all things!" These words escaped him one day after he had meditated for a long time, his eyes fixed on the crucifix.

Meditation before the crucifix was to be his principal occupation from that time on, whether sickness kept him in bed or whether he was able to sit up at his little table. "That was the book he studied."[1]

But for all that, he kept a lively interest in everything that went on around him and in his Congregation.

One of his companions, Father Mark Aurelius, was dying. He asked to be carried to Father Mark's cell, to beg his forgiveness for having so often tried his patience. Then with touching simplicity he gave him his recommendations: "When you arrive in Paradise, do me the charity of adoring the Blessed Trinity for me, offer my respects to the Most Blessed Virgin Mary, greet Father John Baptist for me, as well as Father Fulgencio, Father John Thomas, Father Francis Anthony, and all the religious who lived with us and who now enjoy eternal beatitude. Tell them to pray for me, so that I, too, may possess the Supreme Good."[2] And he wept as he spoke these words.

As Father Paul had often turned to Father Mark Aurelius for advice through the years, he now asked him to designate his successor. "In May the general chapter is to meet. I have been thinking of not being Provost General any more. I am old and I cannot go and visit the retreats. But tell me, whom could we nominate?"

Father Mark Aurelius did not answer; but Paul insisted, mentioning two names.

"Neither of them," the dying man whispered.

As Paul was deaf, he could only see Father Mark's lips moving. "What did he say?" he asked one of his assistants.

No one answered, not wanting to test his humility. Besides, they now knew what to expect at the next elections.

Father Paul was re-elected Provost General despite his protests and was forced to accept despite his refusals. "He used to say he had never known how to govern the Congregation and that he had merited to be driven out of it as unworthy of wearing the holy habit."

Finally he had to bow before the unanimous will of his religious — a unanimity that was quite remarkable in view of the tribulations of other founders, such as Jeanne de Lestonnac, Anne-Marie Javouhey, St. John Baptist de la Salle, and St. Alphonsus Liguori in their respective congregations. Paul's first words of acceptance were: "My very dear Brothers, I deplore your misfortune."[3]

Once Paul had accepted the office, he insisted on exercising its functions despite his age and his infirmities. He presided over the provincial chapters.

There was still one matter on which he had set his heart: a final revision of the Rule. Experience had taught him that certain articles lacked clarity, others needed some mitigation so as not to leave any point of contention or excuse for laxity.

"This is my last work," he used to say. "Once it is completed, I shall have put everything in order that concerns the Congregation and then I can die."[4]

He embarked on this task with the help of the Procurator-General of the Institute, Father Joseph Hyacinth. Their efforts progressed so well that he was soon in a position to submit proposed changes for the approbation of all the Fathers gathered together in the general chapter. He asked the opinion of each one so that everything might be done fairly and openly and to obviate future disputes.

This was the course of wisdom and prudence.

The text thus revised was presented to Pius VI for his approval. He in turn entrusted the examination of the Rule to two cardinals, who declared that the revised Rule was "wise, prudent, and holy." The Sovereign Pontiff confirmed them soon afterward in his bull of September 15, 1775, *Praeclara virtutum exempla*. This was Paul's swan song.

The old man's strength ebbed from day to day, like a lamp that gradually goes out for lack of oil.

On June 26, 1775, the Feast of Sts. John and Paul, he was unable to rise in the morning, and he remained in bed until his death. His stomach could no longer assimilate solid food, and he could keep liquids down only with difficulty. On one occasion, after the example of St. Francis of Assisi, he expressed a desire for some fish soup. When it was hastily brought to him, he could not even swallow it.

On August 29 the doctor advised him that he thought the moment had come to receive Holy Viaticum. Paul agreed but wanted the whole community to be present, so that he could make his final recommendations, ask forgiveness, and make his profession of faith.

The ceremony took place the next day. By the light of candles the Blessed Sacrament was solemnly carried to his room while all the religious followed, singing. Paul welcomed the Eucharist with outstretched arms. "Ah! My good Jesus!" he cried out. He then made his profession of faith and gave his supreme recommendations as Founder:

"Above all, I urgently recommend the observance of the most holy command of Our Lord Jesus Christ to His Apostles: 'By this will all men know that you are My disciples, if you have love for one another. . . .' Next, I urge all of you, and especially the Superiors, to nurture the spirit of prayer in the Congregation, the spirit of solitude, and the spirit of poverty. You can be certain that if these three points are maintained, the Congregation 'will shine like the sun in the presence of God and of men.'

"I recommend with particular insistence a filial affection for our Holy Mother Church, and total submission to her visible head, the Roman Pontiff. . . .

"You must promote in all hearts devotion to the Passion of Jesus Christ and to the Sorrows of the Blessed Virgin. You are not to preach Lenten sermons. . . .

"I ask forgiveness, my face against the ground and with all the tears of my heart, of all the members of the Congregation, both absent and present, for all my failures in carrying out my obligations as Superior-General, which post I held for so many years. Wretched man that I am! In departing from you to enter eternity, I leave you only my bad examples. I must acknowledge, however, that I have never wanted to scandalize you. On the contrary, I have sought your holiness and your perfection. I therefore beg your forgiveness once again, and I ask you to pray for my poor soul, so that the Lord may receive it into the bosom of His mercy. . . .

"I am leaving you, and I shall wait for all of you in holy Paradise. . . ."

Then followed a few specific recommendations concerning his physician, the brother infirmarian who was taking care of him, and the translation of the Rule into Italian for the convenience of the Brothers.

He was exhausted when he closed this long discourse, and said: "I cannot go on any more."[5]

He then received Holy Viaticum and made a fervent thanksgiving in solitude after the others had left his room.

From that moment on Paul desired to concern himself only with his God and his soul.

He used to have the shutters closed so that he could meditate without distractions. His thought and imagination were focused on a single object: the crucifix. He had had a large crucifix in bright colors hung on the white wall of his room, and a tiny crucifix rested near him, within reach of his hand. He would look at the one and kiss the other. His eyes were red from weeping.

However, when he needed some service, he rang a little bell and the brother infirmarian came quickly. His religious took advantage of the infirmarian's visit to come in and see Father Paul too. In talking with them he would sometimes express the desire to die stretched out on a straw mat, clothed in a worn habit. Or again he might give some advice, such as recommending the foundation of a retreat in the Piedmont.

Then he would have the shutters closed again and resume his solitary meditation.

A few visitors were allowed to visit him on rare occasions. They came out edified by his patience and his resignation. "The earth calls the earth," he would say.

The weeks slipped by, bringing no hope of improvement. On

October 8 Paul asked to receive Extreme Unction while he was fully in possession of his senses, and declared he yearned for solitude more than ever.

On October 16 he asked for his writing kit. He wanted to bid farewell to the most beautiful soul he had met upon earth: Rosa Calabresi. Although the handwriting was shaky, the thoughts he expressed were strong. He gave her his last counsels and told her they would meet again in heaven.[6]

On October 18 he received Holy Communion with his usual devotion. Then he asked to be left alone. Visitors came, however, and he agreed to receive them. They wanted to see "the Saint."

Bishop Struzzieri, who had arrived in Rome, had a conversation with him. Everything seemed normal.

About two o'clock in the afternoon chills and fever awakened the patient and he in turn called his infirmarian.

"I am about to die," said Paul. "Call Father John Mary so that he may recite the prayers for the dying."[7]

The religious were at Vespers. When Brother Bartholomew pointed this out to him, he agreed at once to wait until they were finished.

Soon afterward the whole community gathered around the dying man. The doctor arrived and offered no hope. There was no agony in the strict sense of the word. While the prayers for the dying were being said, Paul kept his eyes fixed on his crucifix.

At one moment he made a gesture of greeting, as if to someone seen by him alone. Then, as he had requested, a heavy rope was placed around his neck, and the religious habit which he had not been able to wear during his illness was given back to him. After that, life quietly ebbed away. Paul breathed out his ardent, pacified soul serenely, like a lamp that goes out from having burned too long. But now the light of his holiness was to shine out more brightly than ever before.

It was four-thirty in the afternoon of October 18, 1776. Paul Danei, born on January 3, 1694, was in his eighty-third year.

The Passionists had lost their father. They wept for themselves, if we may say so, more than for him whom they venerated as a saint. Almost as soon as he had breathed his last, some of his religious removed the insignia of the Passion from their habits to lay them upon the heart of the servant of God, thus making them, in their opinion, precious relics.

This sentiment of veneration was shared by all. Pope Pius VI, who was immediately informed of Paul's death, expressed his compassion and declared that he wanted the body to be enclosed in two caskets, one of lead and the other of wood, and then deposited in a separate sepulcher. He himself would take care of all the expenses.

When the death knell was rung, a crowd gathered on the square in front of the basilica, asking to see the deceased. Only a few privileged ones were allowed to enter.

As soon as the burial preparations were completed the body was placed on a plank on the floor, clothed in the religious habit, with a purple stole around the neck and a crucifix in the hands. The head rested upon a few bricks. Four candles burned around the plank. Paul's spiritual sons took turns throughout the evening and night watching and praying.

At dawn the body, still lying on the plank, was transported from the monastery to the basilica, where it was placed in the middle of the nave. The minute the doors were opened, the eager crowd pushed their way in to see "the Saint" for the last time and to obtain relics if possible. Some were content to have devotional objects touch the body. Others, less discreet, did not hesitate to snip off a piece of the habit or even a tuft of hair. Someone went so far as to steal the rosary from the belt on the habit.

Popular devotion would have known no limits if care had not been taken. A barrier made of benches had to be placed around the body, and permission was given only to touch rosaries or pieces of cloth to it.

While the crowd, thus channeled, kept filing by, a solemn Mass was celebrated and the Office of the Dead recited by all the religious. Visitors continued to come in throngs through the day. It was decided to wait until evening to place the body in the temporary bier, which would be replaced by the lead coffin.

At nightfall, when the crowd had been dispersed and the doors of the basilica were closed, the body was moved to a lateral chapel of the basilica in the presence of only sixty persons. The painter John Dominic Porta made a plaster mold of the face.

"The body and the plank on which it rested were transported into a room called the sepulcher, situated in the back of the church. . . . There in the presence of His Excellency the Vice Regent, of the persons mentioned above, and of the religious community, the notary read the act of recognition of the body. After that, the body was unclothed, and parcels of the clothing were distributed to all present. In order to have a few relics of this holy body, the locks of hair remaining on the head were cut off.

"The body was perfectly flexible, as if it were still alive. . . . It was easy to see the Holy Name of Jesus that the servant of God had impressed on his heart with a red-hot iron. . . .

"The face seemed more beautiful and venerable, and reflected rays of light, as it were. Indeed the cry was heard from all sides: How handsome he is! It is a pity to bury him so soon! Even His Excellency the Vice Regent could not refrain from expressing his admiration: 'How handsome he is!'

"After being reclothed, the body was put in the casket. A few bricks were placed under the head, a brass crucifix on the breast, and on the side a glass tube with a Latin inscription containing a short summary of his life. The coffin was closed, nailed down and sealed with six seals, four of them by the Regent, and two by the Congregation. After this, everyone left the room, the door was locked, and the key placed in the hands of the Vice Regent."[8]

These details by an eyewitness are precious. Indeed, the precautions proved to be very wise. For the following days the disappointed crowd almost broke down the door of the chapel, and in their indiscreet devotion they would probably not have respected the integrity of the body of the servant of God.

On October 21 the lead coffin was ready, and it was possible to proceed with the final burial in the presence of qualified witnesses and a few persons of note.

The seals were verified, the wooden casket was placed inside the lead coffin, and this in turn enclosed by wood. The coffin was thus deposited in a standing position in a vault in the nave of the basilica. As the coffin came above the level of the floor, masons at once surrounded this portion of the coffin with a tumulus in the form of an urn, on which were engraved the name, age, and date of death of the deceased.

Sic transit gloria mundi — so passes the glory of the world: this is the thought that comes to mind at the tombs of the great of this world.

But for the saints, the day of their death is a beginning.

Chapter XXV

THE PERSONALITY
OF ST. PAUL OF THE CROSS

Neither do men light a lamp and put it under the measure, but upon the lampstand, so as to give light to all in the house. MATT. 5.15

ST. PAUL of the Cross is certainly not one of the compelling personalities who have influenced the course of the temporal history of the Church, like St. Augustine, St. Francis of Assisi, St. Teresa, and St. Ignatius of Loyola.

While admitting his personal prestige with the crowds and his dearly won renown for holiness, we cannot deny that outside a very restricted geographical area his own century knew nothing about him. His literary legacy consists only of his letters. His sermons were borrowed, and his foundations were relatively few in number.

And yet anyone who has followed the stages of his long life of eighty-two years will see in him a vigorous personality whose appeal constantly grows.

Paul *the man* does not reveal himself at first glance. He is not one of those saints known for their stormy youth, whose lives can be painted in vivid colors. His were not violent passions which, once purified by grace and penance, were directed with equal fire to love of God and love of neighbor.

His very pure adolescence and his extremely mortified life tend at first to astonish rather than attract us. The fact remains, however, that although his human qualities are less apparent than those of some of the other saints, they are no less real.

His excesses of penance as a young man may indeed surprise us. Later, as the drama of his life unfolds, when obstacles arise on all sides to his divine mission and he humbly declares himself unworthy of this mission, he moves us profoundly.

Very early in his life he proved himself a remarkable letter writer, beginning with the scribbled notes of his *Retreat Journal*. His letters show him to be a zealous missionary, but an enemy of undue pageantry, a prudent spiritual director, and above all a clearheaded organizer.

We were expecting to find in him an idealist of sorts, lost in his supernatural visions, without concern for contingencies. And instead we discover in him a poised and practical mind, concerned with climatic conditions, the quality of the water supply, and material details.

Though enamored of austerity and solitude, Paul Danei remained sociable. Better still, he radiated sympathy, knew how to win others to devoted sacrifice and to find protectors for his undertakings. This is the human explanation of his ultimate success.

Moreover, as he advanced in age, his tolerance increased. At his first contact with sin he had exclaimed in astonishment: "I did not believe men were so evil." At the end of his life he mitigated the rigors of his Rule as much as possible, to allow for human weakness.

His early portraits radiated intelligence, his last ones revealed his physical weakness and still more his great goodness.

The Saint in Paul of the Cross shone forth from the start, and if we were to go only by exterior manifestations we might wrongly imagine that his light grew dimmer with time.

The fact is that he had a dazzling adolescence. From his twentieth year Paul Danei was favored with the most extraordinary visions. But these revelations were less a sign of his virtues than a direct call to holiness. It is because he heard this call and strove with all his heart and all his strength to answer it, while accepting apparent defeat with humility and submission to the Will of God, that he became the Saint of heroic virtue whom the Church has canonized.

Before him, Francis of Assisi had reminded the world of the love of Christ crucified, and he had so loved this Christ that the stigmata had been impressed upon his wounded body. But even though the "Poverello" had made of this love a rule of life to be followed by countless disciples, it was Paul of the Cross who established the cult of the Passion as a system of perfection.

It was in the garden of Gethsemani that Jesus most clearly manifested His total submission to the Will of His Father, and it is by the acceptance of suffering that the Christian submits most perfectly to the Will of God. In this submission rests the whole of sanctity and the shortest road to attain it.

If we follow the life of St. Paul of the Cross step by step, we see how his acceptance of the Will of God increased through the years, and hence how he grew in holiness. After the impatient ardor of his conquering youth, after the temptations to discouragement of his mature years, came the peaceful waiting of his old age until "the ways were opened."

The secret of the sanctity of St. Paul of the Cross does not lie primarily in his fasts and vigils, in his scourgings and mortifications. It lies above all in his perfect acceptance of suffering and his total union with the Will of God. The path he opens to his disciples is the "way of abandonment." At the end of his life he repeated what he had said so often before: "I rejoice that the Will of God be done in me and to me,"[1] just as he had said over fifty years before: "In all things the Will of our dear God be done."[2]

Paul of the Cross, *the man and the Saint*, is perfectly one. Both aspects of his personality grew simultaneously and complemented each other. The outpouring of his sympathy helped him to fulfill successfully his supernaturally revealed mission. Likewise his holiness enabled him to remain humble with regard to his human qualities and never to compromise. His burning love for souls preserved him from sentimental weakness. "A sinner, that I am, but a thief never. . . . I have always reserved all the love of my heart for my God."

In this love he drew light and strength and allowed none of the talents he had received as apostle, director, and founder, to lie fallow.

This harmonious equilibrium between the human and the divine, between natural qualities and supernatural virtues, is the very mark of the great mystics.

St. Paul of the Cross was one of these great mystics, the greatest of his time.

THE GLORY OF BERNINI

"For the Saints, the day of their death is the beginning."

ALMOST as soon as the coffin containing the mortal remains of Paul Danei, who became Paul of the Cross, was sealed and deposited in the mausoleum erected in his honor in the basilica of Sts. John and Paul, it became a center of attraction and a source of brilliant miracles.

Cures and conversions attributed to the intervention of the servant of God became so numerous as to hasten the official introduction of his cause. Such a development had been expected. For even during his life Paul had aroused the admiration of important personages as well as popular veneration.

In ordering the specific mode of Paul's burial, the Holy Father seemed to want to assure the safekeeping of the body. Paul's spiritual sons had carefully preserved all the objects he had used. Immediately after his death they began collecting the most varied testimonies concerning his virtues.

Two years later the process and the investigations began, with a view to his future canonization, in all places where he had resided.

In 1784, Pope Pius VI gave the Founder of the Passionists the title of *Venerable.*

In 1792, by a decree of the Holy See, the cause for the beatification was introduced; but the French Revolution and the tribulations of the Papacy brought everything to a standstill.

On February 18, 1821, Pope Pius VII proclaimed the heroicity of the virtues of the Venerable Paul of the Cross.

On October 1, 1852, Pope Pius IX declared Paul *Blessed,* and on June 29, 1867, the same Pope canonized him.

In less than a century the "Poor of Jesus" had passed through all the stages in the triumphal hierarchy of sainthood. On the same day and in the same painting by the glorious painter Bernini, Leonard of Port Maurice and Paul of the Cross were unveiled side by side. Thus the two popular apostles of the eighteenth century, who had once been rivals in holiness and even for a moment involuntarily opposed to each other, ranked among the Church's canonized saints.

Simultaneously with his personal rise to popular favor, the Congregations founded by St. Paul of the Cross grew apace.

Paul had always wanted to see his retreats spread out over the whole world. The drama of the separation of the Church of England from Rome had caused him deep suffering, and he had prayed for England all his life. On his deathbed he urged his sons to found a retreat in the Piedmont, thus showing his concern to the very end for the future of his Congregation.

His hopes have been fulfilled in great measure. Before the French Revolution, which laid his Institute low for a while, five new retreats were founded. Shortly afterward the Congregation began to spread out over the world.

Retreats were founded in Belgium (1840), England (1850), America (1853), France (1863), Spain (1880), Argentina (1884), Australia (1890), Holland (1905), and Brazil (1924).

It is worthy of note that a Passionist, Father Dominic, deeply imbued with the spirit of St. Paul of the Cross, had close contacts with the Oxford Movement. It was he who received the abjuration of the future Cardinal Newman.

Several missions among the infidels have been entrusted to the Passionists: in Peru, China, the Congo, Tanganyika, Japan, and the Philippines.

At the present time there are almost thirty-five hundred religious divided into eighteen provinces and two vice-provinces in thirty-five nations,* living by the spirit of their glorious Founder, "resounding trumpets announcing to the whole world the terrible sufferings of Our Lord and thus destroying sin."

The institute of Passionist Nuns, founded in Corneto in 1771,

---

* As of December 1959, there were 3,870 Passionists divided into 20 provinces. (Tr.)

has also been growing. In 1872 it branched out to France, in 1910 to the United States, and in 1918 to Spain.

In all, there are twenty-three cloistered monasteries† of Passionist nuns living the contemplative life and offering themselves up for the fruitfulness of their Passionist Brothers' apostolate.

In accordance with the spirit of St. Paul of the Cross, who had chosen for himself and his spiritual sons a life at once contemplative and active, several congregations of Passionist Sisters, dedicated to teaching, nursing, and evangelizing women in mission lands, have come into being.

These congregations are:

The Sisters of the Most Holy Cross and Passion of Our Lord Jesus Christ, founded in England in 1850, where they have twenty-eight houses, and now also established in Ireland, Scotland, and America.

The Sisters of St. Paul of the Cross, founded in 1872 in Italy.

The Daughters of the Passion of Our Lord Jesus Christ, founded in 1892 in Mexico and Cuba.

The Missionary Sisters of the Most Holy Cross and Passion of Our Lord Jesus Christ, founded in 1927 under the impulsion of Cardinal van Roey, Primate of Belgium.

The Missionary Religious of St. Gemma, founded in Holland in 1948.

The seed that sprang up painfully on the slopes of Monte Argentario has become a great tree with vigorous branches, in which the same sap flows, producing the same fruit.

These congregations of Passionists draw their deep interior life in solitude, recollection, and inexhaustible meditation upon the Passion, and they pour forth this life for the good of souls, like "reconciled" Marthas and Marys.

This was the mission that Paul Danei miraculously foresaw during his adolescence. This was the very life of Paul of the Cross, and it is the message our Saint has brought to a world that has lost its soul and is drying up in its rage for "activism."

Le Boy, Good Friday, 1952

† Including the foundation in Japan in 1957, there are now 24. (Tr.)

SOURCES AND ABBREVIATIONS

The sources for a biography of St. Paul of the Cross are not numerous, but they are reliable:

1. The canonization processes, including 22 volumes of 800 pages each, with two summaries.

2. The letters of St. Paul of the Cross in four volumes in 8vo, Rome, Scuola tipographica Pio X, 1924. A few others, discovered subsequently, have appeared in *Bolletino*, the periodical of the Passionists.

3. Certain extra-judiciary testimonies preparatory to the processes.

5. The first biography by St. Vincent Strambi, disciple of St. Paul, postulator of his cause, whose work is precious because the author has added his personal recollections to the extensive excerpts from the processes.

These sources may be consulted by anyone who cares to. They have been studied lovingly, and diligently commented upon in the various works of Father Gaëtan du Saint-Nom-de-Marie, who devoted his life to the memory of the Founder of his Congregation.

While today's reader may find them a little heavy from the point of view of style, they are the work of a conscientious scholar and the present biographer is deeply indebted to this reliable guide.

It is well known that a canonization procedure involves investigations entrusted to the bishops or ordinaries of the places where the saint lived, and then investigations by the Roman Curia or the Apostolic Processes.

PA   Process of Alessandria
PC   Process of Gaeta

SOURCES AND ABBREVIATIONS

PO	Process of Orbetello
POR	Ordinary Process of Rome
PAR	Apostolic Process of Rome
POV	Ordinary Process of Vetralla
PAV	Apostolic Process of Viterbo
POC	Ordinary Process of Corneto
PAC	Apostolic Process of Corneto
S. 1	Summary of the Ordinary Processes
S. 2	Summary of the Apostolic Processes
L	Letters of the Saint
AR	Archives of the Monastery of Sts. John and Paul in Rome

N O T E S

Introduction

[1] *Vie du B. Paul de la Croix,* by St. Vincent-Marie Strambi (H. Casterman, 1861), Vol. II, p. 71. This unexcelled witness thereupon gave a remarkable example of this maxim in practice: "He was firmly convinced that much meekness was needed in the exhortations of superiors to their communities. Writing to one of these superiors, he said: 'I am informed that in the examens and chapters Your Reverence makes extensive use of exclamations as if you were preaching a mission to mustachioed gentlemen. But, my dear Father Rector, what good can you accomplish by acting in this way? I praise your zeal, I know that it proceeds from your great love for the observance. However the truth is that our religious are very good men. It is therefore not necessary to make such strenuous efforts. . . . Act with meekness, speak in a collected manner, do not raise your voice, and believe that you will make a greater impression and accomplish more good, and the religious will be happier.' "

Strambi's own meekness is brought out in the charming brochure by Maria Winowska, *Saint Vincent-Marie Strambi* (Editions Passionistes, 1951). There is another biography of the Founder, written by Father Louis-Th. de Jésus Agonisant, *Histoire de saint Paul de la Croix* (Poitiers, Oudin, 1869).

Three outstanding masters have devoted four monographs more to the doctrine than to the person of St. Paul of the Cross. And each of the monographs is a masterpiece of its kind. First of all, Father Joseph de Guibert published, together with a short commentary, in the *Revue d'ascétique et de mystique* (Vol. VI, 1925, pp. 26–48), the French translation of a retreat journal by St. Paul of the Cross, originally published in Rome in 1920–1922 by Father Stanislaus dell'Addolorata, and then republished in Turin in 1926, the *Diario di S. Paolo della Croce con introduzione e commenti.*

In 1948, Father Jules Lebreton, in a particularly fervent chapter of his *Tu solus Sanctus,* presented St. Paul of the Cross as an eminent model and doctor of the mysticism of reparation (Book III, "L'union au Christ souffrant," Chapter 2, pp. 215–36).

In 1951, again in the *Revue d'ascétique et de mystique,* which has done well by the Founder of the Passionists, Father Marcel Viller devoted forty-three remarkably informative and penetrating pages to the study of "La volonté de Dieu dans les lettres de saint Paul de la Croix" (Vol. XXVII, 1951, pp. 132–74).

In 1952, in the *Mélanges Jules Lebreton* (Vol. II, pp. 426–45), the same Father Viller set forth a brief synthesis of the texts already cited and of the essential trends that they express, in his article "La mystique de la Passion chez saint Paul de la Croix." This was sufficient to give an accurate picture of rare spiritual greatness, but it was not sufficient to draw the attention of the general public to the person of the Founder.

As I speak only of France, I can do no more than point out the fundamental works of Father Gaëtan du Saint-Nom-de-Marie, C.P., all published in Belgium: *Oraison et ascension mystique de saint Paul de la Croix* (Louvain, 1930); *Doctrine de saint Paul de la Croix sur l'oraison et la mystique* (Louvain, 1932); *Saint Paul de la Croix apôtre et missionnaire* (Tirlemont, 1933); and the posthumous synthesis edited by Father Thomas, *Esprit et vertus de Saint Paul de la Croix* (Tirlemont, 1950). However, two chapters have appeared in France in the form of articles in the *Revue d'ascétique et de mystique*: the one cited above, by Fr. Viller, and "Saint Paul de la Croix, maître de la vie spirituelle: sa doctrine et sa pratique touchant les visions, revelations et extases (Vol. VIII, 1927, pp. 361–92). Despite their merits, it is quite clear that these technical works are likewise without power to captivate the general public.

[2] Rev. Gaëtan du Saint-Nom-de-Marie, has already attacked such a misconception in his study, "Saint Paul de la Croix, directeur des âmes: Magnanimité, confiance et dilatation de coeur au service de Dieu," in the *Revue d'ascétique et de mystique* (Vol. IX, 1928, pp. 25–54).

[3] Cf. p. 207.

[4] To be absolutely fair, it must be said that Tauler was named by Father Viller in "La mystique de la Passion . . . ," p. 431, following Father Gaëtan. But it was with reference to another problem; namely, the thought of the humanity of Christ in contemplation.

[5] I am in full accord with Father Viller ("La mystique de la Passion . . . ," p. 426, footnote 1), when he firmly parts company with Father Gaëtan, whose explicit intent was to "make the doctrine of St. Paul of the Cross homogeneous with that of the great mystics who inspired him." Such a method, which stresses only similarities, conceals the most original and in many respects the most important aspects of his doctrine.

[6] To do the subject justice, we would have to cite Father Viller's entire article, "La mystique de la Passion . . ." Let us at least single out this very expressive formula on p. 432: "The Passion is the door to contemplation."

[7] Cf. p. 211.

[8] In a series of articles which promise to give us precious insights, "L'Amour sauveur dans la vie saint Thérèse de Lisieux" (*Revue*

d'ascétique et de mystique, Vol. XXXII, 1956), Father Charles A. Bernard, S.J., refuses to consider St. Thérèse, as I do, as "the contemporary of the Crucified" from the time of her vision of July 1887 (cf. p. 312). However, he does not hesitate (cf. p. 323) to use the same expression to designate in the most exact way the state of Thérèse in January 1889. This agreement pleases me, but I do not think the delay is justified. I shall give my reasons elsewhere.

[9] Cf. p. 123.

Chapter I

[1] Marcel Brion, *Laurent le Magnifique* (Paris: Albin Michel, 1941), p. 16. Cf. also Auguste Bailly, *La Florence des Médicis* (Paris: Hachette, 1942).

[2] Cf. S. 2, p. 57, par. 4.

[3] Cf. POV, p. 691.

[4] Cf. S. 1, 46, 10.

[5] Ibid., 58, 12.

[6] Ibid., 47, 21.

[7] Cf. Rev. Stanislaus dell'Addolorata, *Il più bel fiore di Ovada*, p. 65.

[8] Cf. S. 1, 47, 22.

[9] Ibid., 56, 66.

[10] Cf. PAR, 2637 verso.

Chapter II

[1] Cf. PO, 414, v.

[2] Cf. S. 1, 382, 4.

[3] Ibid., 69, 65.

[4] Ibid.

[5] Ibid., 46, 81.

[6] Ibid., 46, 8.

[7] Cf. PA, 132, v., and L. 1. Letter to His Excellency Bishop di Gattinara, p. 17.

[8] Cf. S. 1, 308, 12.

[9] Cf. PO, 74.

[10] Cf. S. 1, 636, 1.

[11] Ibid., 70.

[12] Ibid., 71, 72.

[13] Ibid., 636.

[14] Ibid., 772, 84.

[15] Cf. François Mauriac, *Saint Margaret of Cortona* (New York: Philosophical Library, 1948).

[16] Cf. PO, 392.
[17] Cf. S. 1, 737, 27.
[18] Ibid., 734, 173.
[19] Ibid., 45.
[20] Cf. L. IV, 127. Letter to Bishop di Gattinara.
[21] Cf. S. 1, 50, 41.
[22] Ibid., 51, 46.
[23] Cf. L. II, 274. Letter to Canon Cerrutti, Aug. 2, 1741.
[24] Cf. S. 1, 72, 74.
[25] Ibid., 51, 43.
[26] Cf. L. II, 660. Letter to Bishop Oldo of Terracina, July 9, 1748.
[27] Cf. S. 1, 358, 250.
[28] Ibid., 69, 65.
[29] Cf. PAR, 2323, v.
[30] Cf. S. 1, 47, 48.
[31] Ibid., 47, 18.
[32] Ibid., 46, 12.
[33] Ibid., 46, 13, and 48, 30.
[34] Ibid., 46, 14.
[35] Ibid., 69, 65.
[36] Cf. POV, 126.
[37] Cf. L. I, 410–11. Letter to Anthony Appiani, Mar. 28, 1737.

Chapter III

[1] Cf. S. 1, 46, 7.
[2] Cf. Strambi, *La vie du B. Paul de la Croix* (Paris: Casterman, 1861), p. 26.
[3] Ibid., pp. 26 ff.
[4] Cf. POR, 2734.
[5] Believers who read these lines will probably not be surprised, and unbelievers will kindly remember Bergson's view that mysticism "places the human soul in direct contact with God"; also the history of the great mystics, Joan of Arc, St. Teresa of Ávila, and the others. "The wonderful common sense that Joan manifests . . . as does St. Teresa of Ávila on subjects that are directly accessible to us and verifiable by us, was, for Bergson, the guarantee of the credence that these great mystics deserve when they speak to us of things that are beyond common experience and that we are incapable of understanding and verifying by ourselves." Cf. Jacques Chevalier, *Revue des Deux Mondes*, October 15, 1951, p. 606.
[6] Cf. PAR, 2301.

Chapter IV

[1] Cf. L. IV, 219. Letter to Bishop di Gattinara transmitting his retreat journal to him.

[2] Cf. B.N. 8 H. 8719 (5). Dom L. Gongaud, *Ermites et Reclus. Les Annales franciscaines*, April 1823, "Un prédécesseur," St. Benedict Joseph Labre. H. Brémond, *Hist. du Sentiment Religieux*, Vol. I, p. 336. *Revue des Questions historiques*, C. I, pp. 134–51.

[3] Cf. S. 1, 48, 28. Testimony of Teresa Danei.

[4] Ibid., 904, and 58, 11.

[5] Cf. S. 1, 68, 64.

[6] Ibid., 152, 3.

[7] Cf. Joseph de Guibert, S.J., *Le Journal de Retraite de saint Paul de la Croix*. Excerpt in *Revue d'ascétique et de mystique*, Vol. VI, January 1925. The original is no longer extant, but an authentic copy of it was published in Volume I of his Letters, p. 1, 18. [Translator's note: An English translation of the diary, with an introduction by the Rev. Columban Browning, C.P., has been published in *Cross and Crown*, Vol. VI, March 1954, pp. 127–46.]

[8] Cf. L. IV, 221. Letter to Bishop di Gattinara.

[9] Cf. PAR, 266.

[10] The original was lost at the episcopal curia of Alessandria, and a copy sent to Monte Argentario was burned by the Saint himself. There was time only to transcribe the diary, the preamble, and a passage on discipline.

[11] Cf. "Diary of St. Paul of the Cross," *Cross and Crown*, Vol. VI, March 1954, pp. 127–46.

[12] Cf. "Diary . . . ," *Cross and Crown*, op. cit.

[13] Ibid.

Chapter V

[1] Cf. PAR, 266.

[2] Cf. S. 1, 292.

[3] Ibid., 79, 15.

[4] Ibid.

[5] Cf. PA, 154.

[6] Cf. S. 1, 136, 13.

[7] Cf. PA, 181, v, and 268, v.

[8] Cf. PO, 349.

[9] Cf. POR, 848.

[10] Cf. L. I, 19, *Retreat Journal*, op. cit.

[11] Ibid., 21.

[12] Cf. POR, 816.

[13] Ibid., 815, and PO, 429.
[14] Cf. S. 2, 70, 48, and 67, 24.
[15] Cf. L. I, 18–19, *Retreat Journal*, op. cit.
[16] Ibid., 31. Letter to the Marchesa del Pozzo, Jan. 1, 1722.
[17] Cf. L. III, 754. Letter to Mrs. Marianna Girelli, May 24, 1768.

Chapter VI

[1] Cf. L. I, 22. Letter to Bishop di Gattinara, Mar. 11, 1721.
[2] Ibid.
[3] Cf. S. 1, 54, 58.
[4] Cf. PO, 435.
[5] Cf. Annali, anno 1721.
[6] Cf. POV, 135, v.
[7] Cf. PAR, 399.
[8] Cf. Strambi, op. cit., p. 52.
[9] Cf. St. Gregory, *Dialogues*, Book II, Chap. 17.
[10] Cf. L. I, 52. Letter to his brother John Baptist, Sept. 9, 1721.
[11] Cf. POR, 2428, v.
[12] Cf. PO, 489, v.
[13] Cf. S. 1, 169, 84.
[14] Cf. Strambi, op. cit., Chap. 10, p. 40.
[15] Cf. S. 1, 81, 21.
[16] Cf. S. 1, 82.
[17] Cf. L. I, 30. Letter to the Marchesa del Pozzo, Dec. 31, 1721.

Chapter VII

[1] Luke 17:21. "The kingdom of God is within you."
[2] Cf. PO, 488, v.
[3] Cf. S. 1, 85, v.
[4] Cf. S. 1, 85. In the mosaic of principalities and republics which made up the Italy of the eighteenth century, Monte Argentario, situated on the flank of the peninsula with its three fortresses or *praesidii*, played the role of a citadel and lookout. It is easy to see why the Spaniards and Austrians wrangled over its control.
[5] This is a delicate undertaking. It is not easy to grasp, dissect, and classify life in rigid categories. And the mystical life is life in the strongest sense of the word. To seek the mark of God, to see Him at work in a soul, is a difficult but captivating task. Beneath the apparent variety of mystical experiences, theologians gradually discovered an identical foundation, and they marked the path with unfailing beacons. Then one day Teresa of Ávila appeared, a great

mystic and a woman of genius. Under obedience she transcribed her experience. We owe to her—and to John of the Cross in parallel measure—an analysis of the mystical life that has always remained a classic. The Church honors her with the title of "Mother of Spiritual Souls."

God helped her beyond doubt. The plan of her major work, *The Interior Castle*, was revealed to her in an instant, and many pages were written under the influence of a supernatural grace. In the company of this reliable guide it will be less perilous and a greater joy to follow Paul step by step on the path of Divine Love.

[6] Cf. St. Teresa of Ávila, *The Interior Castle*, Complete Works (Sheed & Ward).

[7] Cf. PAR, 2323, v.

[8] Cf. PAR, 2321.

[9] Cf. POR, 2067, v.

[10] Cf. *The Ascent of Mount Carmel* (The Newman Press), Chaps. 26, 31, 32.

[11] Cf. POR, 2415, v.

[12] Cf. L. I, 435. Letter to Anthony Appiani, Mar. 27, 1759.

[13] Ibid., 198. Letter to Agnes Grazi, Nov. 15, 1737.

[14] Ibid., 819. Letter to Thomas Fossi, Sept. 1, 1773.

[15] Ibid., Letter to Agnes Grazi, April 26, 1736.

[16] Cf. *St. Teresa*, abridged edition of Father Silverio (Sheed & Ward), Chap. II, p. 7.

[17] Ibid., Chap. IV, p. 6.

[18] Ibid.

[19] The Very Reverend Marie-Eugène, O.C.D., in his work *I Am the Daughter of the Church* (Fides, 1955), studies this divergence of orientation in the two great mystics of Carmel. Under the influence of the Holy Spirit, the soul is docile, it accomplishes faithfully the plans of God. And it is John of the Cross who, in the second stanza of *Living Flame*, describes the graces of the apostolate in terms that echo the words of St. Teresa and that seem to apply to Paul Danei to the letter: ". . . there are few souls that arrive at this degree [ablaze with love of God]. . . . A few have reached it. . . . They are above all the souls of persons whose virtue and spirit were to be transmitted through the succession of their disciples. In giving the first fruits of His spirit to these heads of families, God has conferred upon them treasures and greatness in proportion to the large or small succession of children who were to embrace their rule and their spirit."

Chapter VIII

[1] Cf. AR. Bollett., 1929, p. 150.

[2] Cf. S. 1, 646, 1.

[3] "I will visit you with a rod of iron, and I will give you the Holy Spirit."

[4] Cf. AR.

[5] Cf. PAR, 433.

[6] Cf. S. 1, 88, a.

Chapter IX

[1] Cf. L. I. Letter to Father Erasmus Tuccinardi, Sept. 21, 1726.

[2] Cf. AR.

[3] Cf. POR, 1233, v.

[4] Cf. L. I. Letter to Erasmus Tuccinardi, June 11, 1727.

[5] Cf. Strambi, op. cit., p. 85.

[6] Cf. L. I, 76. Letter to Erasmus Tuccinardi, Dec. 20, 1727.

[7] It was still the practice before the advent of recent X-ray treatments.

[8] Cf. official report of the episcopal delegates in the archives of the episcopal curia of Pitigliano.

[9] Cf. L. I, 83. Letter to Erasmus Tuccinardi, June 14, 1730.

[10] Cf. AR. Letter from Bishop Crescenzi, Oct. 11, 1730.

[11] Cf. L. I, 86. Letter to Erasmus Tuccinardi, Nov. 27, 1730.

[12] Cf. S. 1, 73, 1.

[13] Cf. Rev. Gaëtan, C.P., *Oraison et ascension mystique de saint Paul de la Croix*, passim.

[14] Cf. L. I. Letter to Agnes Grazi, July 23, 1739.

[15] Ibid., April 19, 1736.

[16] Cf. S. 1, 603, 74.

[17] Ibid.

[18] Cf. S. 1, 638, 251.

[19] Cf. S. 1, 617, 146.

[20] Cf. St. Teresa of Ávila, *Autobiography*, Chap. 30.

[21] Cf. L. I. Letter to Agnes Grazi, Sept. 27, 1736.

[22] Ibid., 233, July 18, 1739.

[23] Cf. 76.

[24] Cf. S. 1, 294, 147.

[25] Cf. PAR, 2283, v.

[26] These terrible trials plunge the soul into the "purifying night" prior to the spiritual marriage. They have no purpose after this supreme grace. Hence the case of St. Paul of the Cross is almost unique. Father Garrigou-Lagrange sees in it a "redemptive and apostolic" night, the extremely fruitful suffering of a soul in which Christ literally lives and prolongs His Passion "for His body which is the Church . . . ."

Chapter X

[1] Cf. Is. 61:1.

[2] The Dominican motto: *Contemplata aliis tradere.*

[3] Cf. letters to Agnes Grazi, passim.

[4] Cf. Bishop D. Joseph de Barcia y Zambrana, Bishop of Cadiz and Algeciras, *Le Réveil Chrétien,* translated from Castilian into Italian in 1719.

[5] Cf. POC, 367.

[6] Cf. S. 1, 124, 38.

[7] Ibid., 52, 120, 83.

[8] Cf. AR, Tes. extra.

[9] Cf. POV, 926.

[10] Cf. S. 1, 109, 110.

[11] Ibid., 520, 183.

[12] Cf. S. 2, 123, 104.

[13] Cf. Father Berthe, *Vie de Saint Alphonse de Liguori,* passim. *Le P. Léonard de Port-Maurice.* Also Abbé Carron, *Le P. Bridaine.*

[14] Cf. S. 1, 158, 35.

[15] Ibid., 943, 329.

Chapter XI

[1] Cf. L. I. Letter to Rosa of Gaeta, Mar. 19, 1733. *St. Fond. Boll.,* 1922, pp. 343–44.

[2] Cf. PAR, 480, v.

[3] Ibid., 886, v.

[4] Cf. POR, 854, v.

[5] Cf. *St. Fond. Boll.,* 1922, p. 346.

[6] Cf. L. I, 129. San Antonino, Feb. 8, 1736.

[7] Ibid. Letter to Agnes Grazi, Feb. 18, 1736.

[8] Ibid., 540. Letter to Thomas Fossi, Oct. 10, 1736.

[9] Cf. S. 1, 217, and POR, 876, v.

[10] Cf. S. 1, 29, Aug. 22, 1736; 32, Oct. 3, 1736.

[11] Cf. L. I, 35. Letter to Agnes Grazi, Dec. 13, 1736.

[12] Ibid., 36. Dec. 28, 1736.

[13] Ibid., 375. Letter to Cardinal Altieri, Aug. 29, 1737.

[14] Cf. *Acta Congregationis,* 1932, p. 399.

[15] Cf. L. I. Letter to Sister Maria Cherubina Bresciani, Nov. 20, 1737.

Chapter XII

[1] Cf. L. I, 270. Letter to Maria Cherubina Bresciani, Feb. 10, 1738.

[2] Ibid., 109. Letter to Agnes Grazi, June 13, 1738.

[3] Ibid. July 9, 1739.

[4] Ibid. Oct. 15, 1739.

[5] Ibid., 135. Nov. 16, 1739.

[6] Ibid., 136. Nov. 30, 1739.

[7] Cf. *Boll.*, 1928, p. 93

[8] Cf. L. I, 22. Letter to Bishop di Gattinara, op. cit.

[9] Ibid., 265. Letter to Agnes Grazi, Oct. 22, 1740.

[10] Cf. S. 2, 95, 5.

[11] Cf. POR, 479.

[12] Cf. L. I, 280. Letter to Maria Cherubina Bresciani, Jan. 7, 1741.

[13] Cf. L. II. Letter to Father (Count) Garagni, Dec. 28, 1740.

[14] Cf. PAR, 1753.

[15] Cf. AR, *Acta Congr.*, 1931, pp. 156–57.

[16] Cf. L. II, 217. Letter to Father Garagni, May 18, 1741.

[17] Cf. Ibid., 272. Letter to Canon Cerrutti, Aug. 2, 1741.

[18] Cf. L. I, 309. Letter to Agnes Grazi, June 16, 1741.

[19] Ibid., 481. Letter to Maria Cherubina Bresciani, Aug. 22, 1741.

Chapter XIII

[1] Cf. L. II, 275. Letter to Canon Cerrutti, Aug. 2, 1741.

[2] Ibid., 276.

[3] Ibid., 290. Letter to Mother Maria Crocifissa Costantini, Aug. 10, 1741.

[4] Ibid., 222. Letter to Father Garagni, 1742.

[5] Ibid., 227. May 17, 1742.

[6] POV, 991.

[7] Cf. L. II, 227. Letter to Father Garagni, May 17, 1742.

[8] Cf. L. I, 281. Letter to Agnes Grazi, May 16, 1742.

[9] Ibid., 284. June 11, 1742.

[10] Cf. L. II, 337. Letter to the Bishop of Viterbo, Sept. 6, 1742.

[11] Cf. L. I, 486. Letter to Francis Appiani, June 26, 1742.

[12] Cf. L. II, 234. Letter to Father Garagni.

[13] Ibid., 278. Letter to Canon Cerrutti, June 12, 1743.

[14] Ibid., 280. July 18, 1743.

Chapter XIV

[1] Cf. L. II, 43. Letter to Canon Blaise Pieri, July 19, 1743.

[2] Ibid., 237. Letter to Father Garagni, Oct. 17, 1743.

[3] Cf. the privileges of the Fratri, p. 129 above.

[4] Cf. L. II, 350. Letter to the Bishop of Viterbo, Mar. 7, 1744.

[5] Cf. L. I, 494. Letter to Maria Cherubina Bresciani, Feb. 26, 1744.
[6] Ibid. Feb. 22, 1744.
[7] Cf. S. 1, 37, xiv.
[8] Ibid., 661, 115.
[9] Cf. L. II, 70. Letter to Father Fulgencio, Mar. 31, 1746.
[10] Ibid.
[11] Cf. Father Berthe, *Vie de Saint Alphonse de Liguori*, 2d ed., p. 380.
[12] Cf. L. II, 287. Letter to Canon Cerrutti, Aug. 13, 1746.
[13] Ibid., 103. Letter to Father Fulgencio, Sept. 10, 1748.
[14] Cf. p. 129 above, on the privileges of the Fratri.
[15] Cf. L. II, 98. Letter to Father Fulgencio, Sept. 3, 1746.
[16] Cf. Ibid., 107. Sept. 10, 1746.
[17] Ibid., 349. Letter to Joseph Danei, Sept. 30, 1746.

Chapter XV

[1] Cf. L. II, 560. Letter to Canon Andrea Pagliaricci, Vicar-General of Toscanella, Aug. 1, 1747.
[2] Ibid., 127. Letter to Father Fulgencio, Dec. 16, 1747.
[3] Cf. *Storia dei Passionisti della provincia di Sanctissima Addolorata*, pp. 12 ff.
[4] Cf. L. II, 172. Letter to Father Fulgencio, Oct. 26, 1748.
[5] Ibid., 132. Feb. 8, 1748.
[6] Ibid., 134. Feb. 22, 1748.
[7] Cf. *Storia fond. Boll.*, 1924, pp. 177–80.
[8] Cf. L. II, 136. Letter to Father Fulgencio, Mar. 28, 1748.
[9] Cf. *Storia Addol.*, p. 99.
[10] Cf. *Storia fond. Boll.*, 1925, p. 45.
[11] Cf. L. II, 667. Letter to Bishop Oldo, Sept. 3, 1748.
[12] Cf. S. 1, 438.
[13] Ibid., 14.
[14] Cf. Strambi, op. cit., p. 180.
[15] Cf. *Storia Addol.*, p. 30.
[16] Cf. L. II, 143. Letter to Father Fulgencio, May 18, 1748.
[17] Ibid., 148. June 26, 1748.
[18] Ibid., 154. Aug. 6, 1748.
[19] Cf. *Storia Addol.*, p. 22.
[20] Cf. L. II, 157–58. Letter to Father Fulgencio, Aug. 22, 1748.
[21] Ibid., 669. Letter to Bishop Oldo, Sept. 22, 1748.
[22] Ibid., 169. Letter to Father Fulgencio, Sept. 26, 1748.
[23] Ibid., 670. Letter to Bishop Oldo, Sept. 24, 1748.
[24] The required distance was four miles.

[25] Cf. L. II, 174. Letter to Father Fulgencio, Rome, Nov. 9, 1748.

[26] Cf. POR, 1075, and S. 1, 642, 272.

[27] Cf. *Storia Addol.*, p. 32.

[28] Cf. L. II, 674. Letter to Bishop Oldo, Nov. 16, 1748.

[29] Ibid., 768. Letter to Father Francis of Jesus and Mary, Jan. 14, 1749.

[30] Ibid., 184. Letter to Father Fulgencio, April 26, 1749.

[31] Ibid., 186. May 3, 1749.

[32] Ibid., 198. July 4, 1749.

[33] Ibid., 699. Letter to Bishop Oldo, July 15, 1749.

[34] Cf. L. I, 586. Letter to Thomas Fossi, Aug. 6, 1749.

[35] Ibid., 688. Dec. 5, 1749.

[36] Cf. L. II, 754. Letter to Father Thomas, Mar. 25, 1749.

[37] Cf. S. 2, 520, 151.

Chapter XVI

[1] Cf. L. II, 685. Letter to Mrs. Geronima Ercolani, Feb. 22, 1750.

[2] Cf. L. I, 590. Letter to Thomas Fossi, May 16, 1750.

[3] Cf. L. II, 587. Letter to Dr. Ercolani, June 30, 1750.

[4] Ibid., 749. Dec. 2, 1750.

[5] Cf. L. I, 609. Letter to Thomas Fossi, Dec. 6, 1751.

[6] Cf. L. III, 110. Letter to Mother Maria Francesca Forlani, June 4, 1752.

[7] Cf. L. II, 821. Letter to Father John Anthony Lucattini, July 1, 1752.

[8] Cf. L. IV, 232. July 25, 1752.

[9] Cf. L. II, 824. Letter to Father Lucattini, Aug. 8, 1752.

[10] Cf. L. I, 620. Letter to Thomas Fossi, Nov. 29, 1752.

[11] Ibid., 647. Dec. 15, 1754.

[12] Ibid., 646. Aug. 31, 1754.

[13] Cf. L. II, 464. Letter to Sister Columba, July 30, 1754.

[14] Cf. L. I, 655. Letter to Thomas Fossi, May 24, 1755.

[15] Cf. L. II, 607. Letter to Dr. Ercolani, Mar. 22, 1755.

[16] Ibid., 359. Letter to Mrs. Francesca Zelli, Oct. 21, 1755.

[17] Cf. *Storia fond. Boll.*, 1925, p. 80.

Chapter XVII

[1] Cf. L. I, 130. Letter to Agnes Grazi, Feb. 18, 1736.

[2] Cf. AR.

[3] Cf. L. III, 428. Letter to Mrs. Avolta, July 6, 1758.

273

[4] Cf. L. I, 312. Letter to Agnes Grazi, n.d.

[5] Cf. S. 1, 317 ff.

[6] Ibid.

[7] Cf. L. I, 613. Letter to Thomas Fossi, Mar. 15, 1752.

[8] Cf. L. III, 813. Letter to Mrs. Anna Maria Calcagnini, Aug. 20, 1768.

[9] Cf. L. I, 440. Letter to Mother Bresciani, July 12, 1735.

[10] Cf. L. II, 817. Letter to Lucia Burlini, Aug. 28, 1751.

[11] Cf. L. III, 87. Letter to Father Mugnani, O.P., June 24, 1751.

[12] Cf. L. I, 507. Letter to Mother Bresciani, Oct. 2, 1750.

[13] Ibid., 511. Jan. 19, 1753.

[14] Cf. L. II. Letter to Dominic Costantini, Mar. 27, 1757.

[15] Ibid. April 4, 1757.

[16] Ibid., 295. Letter to Mother Maria Crocifissa, Dec. 2, 1762.

[17] Ibid., 299. Dec. 24, 1764.

[18] Ibid., 304. Feb. 15, 1765.

Chapter XVIII

[1] Cf. L. II, 394. Letter to M. J., Fr. Sancez, July 2, 1757.

[2] Cf. *Storia fond. Boll.*, 1925, p. 242.

[3] Cf. L. III, 510–11. Letter to Fr. Thomas, March 25, 1758.

[4] Ibid., 491. April 4, 1758.

[5] Ibid., 492–93. April 6, 1758.

[6] Ibid., 165. Letter to Father John Mary, Aug. 10, 1758.

[7] Cf. L. I, 715. Letter to Thomas Fossi, Mar. 3, 1760.

[8] Cf. L. III, 97. Letter to the Mother Prioress of the Carmel of Vetralla, June 14, 1760.

[9] Cf. L. I, 715. Letter to Thomas Fossi, Mar. 3, 1760.

[10] Ibid., 718. June 13, 1760.

[11] Cf. L. III, 122. Letter to Canon Sardi, Aug. 28, 1760.

[12] Cf. S. 1, 613, 1925.

[13] Ibid., 643.

[14] Cf. POR, 2543.

[15] Cf. PAR, 513.

[16] Cf. L. IV, 267–68. Letter to his religious, Nov. 30, 1760.

[17] Ibid., 272. Jan. 3, 1761.

[18] Cf. L. III. Feb. 13, 1768.

[19] Cf. S. 1, 582, 271.

[20] Cf. L. II, 95. Letter to Father Fulgencio, Aug. 25, 1746.

[21] Cf. Archives of St. Joseph, Mar. 2, 1762.

[22] Cf. L. II, 510. Letter to Sister Columba, June 26, 1762.

[23] Cf. L. III, 253. Letter to Father Joseph Andrew della Concezione, April 30, 1763.

[24] Cf. *Storia fond. Boll.*, 1933, p. 303.

[25] Cf. Father Berthe, op. cit., Vol. II, pp. 93–94.

[26] Cf. L. III, 699. Letter to a nun, Oct. 10, 1764.

[27] Cf. L. I, 750. Letter to Thomas Fossi, July 21, 1764.

[28] Cf. L. III, 705. Letter to Father J.B. of St. Vincent Ferrer, Mar. 15, 1765.

[29] Ibid., 708. Mar. 16, 1765.

[30] Cf. L. III, 564. Letter to Bishop de Angelis, April 18, 1765.

[31] Ibid., 565. Letter to Bishop Garampi, May 18, 1765.

[32] Ibid., 568. Letter to Bishop de Angelis, June 4, 1765.

[33] To understand Paul's disillusioned play on words, we must know that the *giulio* is a coin. The Via della Lungara (the Long Street) is in the Trastevere, and the Via Giulia (the Street of Money) goes from the Farnese Palace to St. John of the Florentines.

[34] Cf. L. III, 571. Letter to Bishop de Angelis, n.d.

[35] Cf. L. II, 636. Letter to Bishop Giuliano Sparziani, Dec. 3, 1765.

[36] Ibid., 764. Letter to Bishop Struzzieri (Father Thomas), Dec. 15, 1766.

[37] Cf. L. III, 571. Letter to Mrs. Marianna Girelli, Mar. 9, 1768.

Chapter XIX

[1] Cf. M. Viller, "La volonté de Dieu dans les lettres de saint Paul de la Croix," in *Revue d'ascétique et de mystique*, April-June 1951. This is one of the rare studies of St. Paul's spirituality, and we are deeply indebted to it.

[2] Cf. *Retreat Journal* of Paul of the Cross, passim.

[3] Cf. L. I, 538. Letter to Laura Gianotti, Mar. 19, 1734.

[4] Ibid.

[5] Cf. M. Viller, op. cit.

[6] Cf. L. III, 439. Letter to Father Peter of St. John, Oct. 24, 1764.

[7] Cf. L. II, 292. Letter to Mother Maria Crocifissa, Sept. 3, 1754.

[8] Cf. L. I, 530. Letter to Mrs. Marianna Alvarez, Jan. 15, 1735.

[9] Ibid., 646. Letter to Thomas Fossi, May 14, 1749.

[10] Cf. L. III, Nov. 16, 1764.

[11] Cf. L. II, 703. Letter to M. Forlani, June 7, 1748.

[12] Cf. "Diary . . . ," *Cross and Crown*, op. cit.

[13] Cf. L. I, 194. Letter to Agnes Grazi, Aug. 29, 1737.

[14] Ibid., 616–17. Letter to Thomas Fossi, July 6, 1752.

[15] Ibid. Sept. 23, 1747.

[16] Cf. Vacant, *Dictionnaire de Théologie Catholique*, art. by Father Pourrat, under "Tauler."

[17] Cf. S. 1, 358.

Chapter XX

[1] Cf. L. IV, 75. Letter to Joseph Strambi, Sept. 30, 1768
[2] Cf. S. 2, 741, 187.
[3] Cf. S. 1, 840, 81.
[4] Cf. L. III, 884. Letter to Anna Maria Calcagnani, May 23, 1769.
[5] Cf. *Storia*, lib. I, c. 37, p. 145.
[6] Cf. S. 1, 97, 61.
[7] Cf. L. III. Letter to Mrs. Anna Maria Calcagnani, July 9, 1769.
[8] Ibid., 710. Letter to Father John Baptist, Sept. 27, 1769.
[9] Ibid., 294. Letter to Brother Bartholomew, Aug. 8, 1769.
[10] Cf. Strambi, op. cit., Chap. 38, p. 201.
[11] Cf. L. III, 709. Letter to Father John Baptist of St. Vincent Ferrer, Sept. 27, 1769.
[12] Cf. POR, 1039, v.
[13] Cf. Strambi, op. cit., Chap. 38, p. 203.
[14] Cf. L. III, 713. Letter to Father John Baptist of St. Vincent Ferrer, Nov. 10, 1769.
[15] Ibid., 295. Letter to Brother Bartholomew, Dec. 13, 1769.

Chapter XXI

[1] Cf. S. 1, 2553, 36.
[2] Cf. L. II, 424. Letter to M.J. Francis Sancez, April 28, 1770.
[3] Cf. S. 2, 711–27.
[4] Cf. L. IV, 99. Letter to Mother Maria Crocifissa of Jesus, July 2, 1770.
[5] Cf. L. III, 832. Letter to Mrs. Anna Maria Calcagnani, Nov. 26, 1770.
[6] Cf. Strambi, op. cit. Chap. 40, p. 215.
[7] Cf. Father Louis, *Vie de la Servante de Dieu, Marie-Crucifiée*, p. 183.

Chapter XXII

[1] Cf. L. IV, 205. Letter to Clement XIV, 1773.
[2] Cf. brief of suppression, *Dominus ac Redemptor*.
[3] Cf. Strambi, op. cit., Chap. 42, p. 239.

Chapter XXIII

[1] Cf. S. 1, 232, 326.

2 Cf. PAR, 2299, v.
8 Ibid., 2373.
4 Ibid., 2269, v.

Chapter XXIV

1 Cf. S. 2, 520, 152.
2 Cf. AR, and *Boll.*, 1924, pp. 9–10.
3 Cf. S. 1, 770–71.
4 Cf. POR, 829, v.
5 Cf. S. 1, 967, 86.
6 Cf. S. 2, 987, 119.
7 Cf. S. 1, 961, 41.
8 Cf. Strambi, op. cit. Chap. 44, pp. 261–62.

Chapter XXV

1 Cf. L. IV. Letter to Giacomo Maria Massa, Mar. 1, 1775.
2 Cf. L. I. Dec. 29, 1720.

INDEX

279